Literature
═══ and ═══
Popular Culture
in
Eighteenth Century
England

Literature
=== and ===
Popular Culture
in
Eighteenth Century England

PAT ROGERS

Professor of English
University of Bristol

I need not repeat to you that Opera, masquerades, plays and taverns make
up so many points of the circle of which our joys in this great town are
chiefly composed.

A letter of 1734, quoted by Edward
Hughes, *North Country Life in the
Eighteenth Century* (1952) p. 386

THE HARVESTER PRESS • SUSSEX

BARNES & NOBLE BOOKS • NEW JERSEY

First published in Great Britain in 1985 by
THE HARVESTER PRESS LIMITED
Publisher: John Spiers
16 Ship Street, Brighton, Sussex
and in the USA by
BARNES & NOBLE BOOKS
81 Adams Drive, Totowa, New Jersey 07512

© Pat Rogers, 1985

British Library Cataloguing in Publication Data

Rogers, Pat
  Literature and popular culture in eighteenth-century England.
  1. English literature—18th century—History and criticism
  2. England—Civilization—18th century
  I. Title
  942.07   DA485
  ISBN 0-7108-0981-6

Library of Congress Cataloging in Publication Data
Rogers, Pat.
  Literature and popular culture in eighteenth century England.

  Includes index.
  1. English literature—18th century—History and criticism.
  2. Popular culture in literature. 3. Great Britain—Popular culture.
  4. Pope, Alexander, 1688-1744—Criticism and interpretation.
  5. Defoe, Daniel, 1661?-1731—Criticism and interpretation. I. Title.
  PR449.P66R64 1984   820'.9'005   84-14645
  ISBN 0-389-20511-7

Typeset in 11/12 point Baskerville by Witwell Limited, Liverpool.
Printed in Great Britain by Whitstable Litho Ltd., Whitstable, Kent

For Derek and Sally Beales

Some people consider fairs immoral altogether, and eschew such, with their servants and families: very likely they are right. But persons who think otherwise, and are of a lazy, or benevolent, or a sarcastic mood, may perhaps like to step in for half-an-hour, and look at the performances. There are scenes of all sorts: some dreadful combats, some grand and lofty horse-riding, some scenes of high life, and some of very middling indeed; some love-making for the sentimental, and some light comic business; the whole accompanied by appropriate scenery and brilliantly illuminated with the Author's own candles.

W.M. Thackeray, *Vanity Fair*

CONTENTS

PREFACE

Samuel Johnson, who once declared himself 'a great friend to publick amusements', was ready on another occasion to agree with his friend Sir Joshua Reynolds that 'the real character of a man [is] found out by his amusements'. Boswell supplies Johnson's famous supplementary remark: 'Yes, Sir; no man is a hypocrite in his pleasures.' There is now an extensive literature dealing with what is called the sociology of leisure, although the field cannot be said to have produced much work of high intellectual distinction. The aim of this book is to explore a phase of cultural history in which leisure was being organised and sold on a commercial basis in an entirely fresh way, and during which new boundaries were defined for élite and mass art forms.

There are two broad semantic elements overlapping in our customary usage of the word 'popular'. The first is 'intended for or suited to ordinary people' (*OED*, sense 4); and the second is 'favourite, acceptable, pleasing' (sense 6). This seems to me a valuable rather than a confusing ambiguity, and I have deliberately refrained from any attempt in this book to drive a wedge between the two uses. I apply the epithet, as we generally do, both to entertainments specifically designed for the common people, and to fashionable diversions such as Italian opera whose undoubted *cachet* was restricted to a small number of wealthy pleasure-seekers. This procedure seems to me wholly consistent with intellectual clarity, so long as we are not enlisting these eighteenth-century amusements as agents of social-class analysis. Such is not my purpose in this book.

The earliest portions of the text were written fifteen years ago, and three chapters appeared in a slightly different form between 1972 and 1975. Since the book was conceived, a number of important studies have appeared which bear on its argument. Most recently, Richard D. Altick has provided in his sumptuous work on *The Shows of London* (1978) a rich storehouse of material on popular recreations in the capital. I have incorporated findings from this work wherever possible, but my own intentions are different from those of Professor Altick in several crucial respects. His main emphasis lies in the early nineteenth century, where mine falls a hundred years earlier. He excludes the printed word, and concentrates on exhibitions and shows, defined 'more or less empirically'. This means the omission of many regular pay-at-the-door entertainments with which I am concerned, such as pantomimes or Haymarket masquerades. However, Professor Altick does cover public museums, a topic I have ignored. He tends to leave aside 'popular' entertainments in my second sense, and thus pays no heed to opera. Furthermore, as he tells us, 'spectacular official ceremonies such as the Lord Mayor's Show, royal marriages, state funerals, and celebrations of military victories have been entirely excluded' from *The Shows of London*. Such processional displays are central to Chapter 5 of this book, and indeed underlie many sections of the argument elsewhere.

More importantly, there is a fundamental difference in approach between Professor Altick and myself. He is interested in what might be termed the objective phenomena, as they illuminate the nature of public taste, the conflict of amusement and instruction, and ultimately the character of the 'popular mind' itself. My attention is directed towards the cultural circumstances in which the amusements had their being: the producers rather than the consumers stand at the centre of the picture. In particular, the book focusses on the reaction of the purveyors of 'high' art to the new leisure industry, and seeks to explore some of the interrelations of élite and mass culture. Beyond this, I have attempted to set the debate in its historical and political context—a task that is naturally easier when one is dealing with a limited period, rather than the span of some two hundred and fifty years charted in Professor Altick's book. Finally, I pursue the 'popular' outside its native element: from Smithfield to Drury Lane, from Penkethman to Colley Cibber, from waxwork coronations to Abbey ceremonial. Professor Altick, who has quite enough on his hands with the genuine popular article, restrains any impulse to follow this process of slippage.

I hope that the preceding two paragraphs will do something to explain the ways in which this book differs from *The Shows of London*—although total independence from such a seminal and informative study of the topic is a claim I neither could, nor would wish to maintain.

There is less by way of direct overlap with another important recent book, Ronald Paulson's study of *Popular and Polite Art in the Age of Hogarth and Fielding* (1979). Necessarily the paths of the two books collide occasionally, but our aims and approaches are distinct enough for me to hope that the present work will be found a complement rather than a competitor to Paulson.

P.R.

ACKNOWLEDGMENTS

Portions of the book have appeared in a different form as follows: Chapter 2 in *Papers on Language and Literature*, VIII (1972), 159-71; Chapter 3 in *Studies in English Literature 1500-1900*, XV (1975), 447-58; Chapter 4 in *Musical Quarterly*, LIX (1973), 15-30; Chapter 7, in *Books and their Readers in Eighteenth-Century England* ed. Isabel Rivers (Leicester, 1982), pp. 27-45. A few sentences in the Introduction and Epilogue have been adapted from material which has appeared in the *Times Literary Supplement*. I am grateful to the copyright-owners for permission to reprint these sections.

An earlier version of Chapter 1 was delivered as a paper to the University College of North Wales History Society. I have tried to make improvements in the light of the discussion on that occasion, and my thanks are due to Helen Miller for making possible such an agreeable evening.

ABBREVIATIONS

Altick	Richard D. Altick, *The Shows of London* (Cambridge, Mass., 1978).
Ashton	John Ashton, *Social Life in the Reign of Queen Anne* (London, new edn 1883).
Deutsch	Otto Erich Deutsch, *Handel: A Documentary Biography* (London, 1955).
DNB	*Dictionary of National Biography.*
Fiske	Roger Fiske, *English Theatre Music in the Eighteenth Century* (London, 1973).
Graphic Works	*Hogarth's Graphic Works*, ed. Ronald Paulson (New Haven, rev. edn 1970).
Journal to Stella	*The Journal to Stella*, ed. Harold Williams (Oxford, 1948).
London Stage	*The London Stage 1660–1800*, ed. G.W. Stone *et al.* (5 pts, Carbondale, Ill, 1960–8). References are to the part and *not* the volume number.
OED	*Oxford English Dictionary.*
Paulson	Ronald Paulson, *Hogarth: His Life, Art and Times* (New Haven, 1971).
Phillips	Hugh Phillips, *Mid-Georgian London* (London, 1964).
Pope, *Corr*	*The Correspondence of Alexander Pope*, ed. George Sherburn (Oxford, 1956).
Rosenfeld	Sybil Rosenfeld, *The Theatre of the London Fairs in the Eighteenth Century* (Cambridge, 1960).
Spectator	*The Spectator*, ed. Donald F. Bond (Oxford, 1965).
Stephens	F.G. Stephens, *Catalogue of Prints and Drawings in the British Museum*, Division I, *Political and Personal Satires* (London, 1870–3).

Swift, *Corr*   *The Correspondence of Jonathan Swift*, ed. Harold
                 Williams (Oxford, 1963–5).
Swift, *Poems*   *The Poems of Jonathan Swift*, ed. Harold
                 Williams (Oxford, rev. edn, 1958).
Swift, *Prose*   *The Prose Works of Jonathan Swift*, ed. Herbert
                 Davis *et al.* (Oxford, 1939–68).
TE   The Twickenham Edition of Pope's *Poetical
                 Works*, ed. John Butt *et al.* (London, 1938–67).
                 The Dunciad is quoted from Vol. V, ed. James
                 Sutherland (rev. edn, 1963).
Williams   Aubrey Williams, *Pope's Dunciad: A Study of its
                 Meaning* (London, 1955).

INTRODUCTION

Some few Days after *HARLEY* spies
The Doctor fasten'd by the Eyes,
At *Charing-Cross*, among the Rout,
Where painted Monsters are hung out.
> Swift, *Part of the Seventh Epistle of the First Book of Horace Imitated*,
> 11. 57–60.

Now the World being thus divided into People of Fashion, and People of no Fashion, a fierce Contention arose between them, nor would those of one Party, to avoid Suspicion, be seen publickly to speak to those of the other; tho' they often held a very good Correspondence in private. In this Contention, it is difficult to say which Party succeeded: for whilst the People of Fashion seized several Places to their own use, such as Courts, Assemblies, Operas, Balls, *&c.* the People of no Fashion, beside one Royal Place called his Majesty's Bear-Garden, have been in constant Possession of all Hops, Fairs, Revels, *&c.* Two Places have been agreed to be divided between them, namely the Church and the Play-House; where they segregate themselves from each other in a remarkable Manner: for as the People of Fashion exalt themselves at Church over the Heads of the People of no Fashion; so in the Play-House they abase themselves in the same degree under their feet.
> Fielding, *Joseph Andrews*, II, xiii.

High Life and Low Art

Every reader of eighteenth-century literature is familiar with passages describing the sights and sounds of city life—especially London life. Pamphlets, poems and even novels are organised around the itinerary of urban pleasure-haunts. No-one who came to the capital seems to have omitted this tour. For many others besides the young hedonist Boswell, 'coming up to London' meant acquainting oneself with these favourite

1

diversions. Here is Swift writing to Stella in 1710, a middle-aged man on his umpteenth visit to town:

> Lady Kerry, Mrs. Pratt, Mrs. Cadogan, and I, in one coach; Lady Kerry's son and his governor, and two gentlemen in another; maids and misses, and little master (Lord Shelburn's children) in a third, set out at ten o'clock this morning from lord Shelburn's house in Piccadilly to the Tower, and saw all the sights, lions, &c. then to Bedlam; then dined at the Chop-house behind the Exchange; then to Gresham College (but the keeper was not at home) and concluded the night at the Puppet-Shew, whence we came home safe at eight, and I left them.

A year or two later, a slightly less energetic evening out:

> I went afterwards to see a famous moving Picture, & I never saw anything so pretty. You see a Sea ten miles wide, a Town on tothr end, & Ships sailing in the Sea, & discharging their Canon. You see a great Sky with Moon & Stars &c. I'm a Fool.[1]

The last remark seems to indicate Swift's awareness that he was a ready target for every kind of popular entertainment. There was a credulous side in his nature, easily moved to wonderment: the interest in charlatans demonstrated by his 'Introduction' to *A Tale of a Tub* must have led him to join many a queue at Moorfields, Tyburn or Westminster Hall. Like Martin Scriblerus, he found his gaze irresistibly attracted by signs hung out to draw the public into a freak-show: man-tigers, or hermaphrodites, or Siamese twins.[2] Years later, he suggested to his friend Alderman Barber that Matthew Pilkington should arrive a few weeks early for his appointment as Lord Mayor's chaplain, 'to prepare him for his business, by seeing the Tower the Monument and Westminster Abby, and have done staring in the streets'.[3] In reality it was Swift himself who was prone to such idle jaunts when business ought to have taken priority.

But he was not alone. A few months after Swift's day out with the Shelburne family, Addison wrote in the fiftieth issue of *The Spectator*:

> When the four *Indian* kings were in this Country about a Twelve-month ago, I often mix'd with the Rabble and followed them a whole Day together, being wonderfully struck with the Sight of every thing that is new or uncommon.[4]

It will not do to hide behind the convenient devices of a persona: Addison is dramatising an enduring form of human curiosity, amply rewarded at this particular stage in history. The lifespan of the great Augustan satirists coincides with the period when sights and shows were promoted as never before. London had grown large enough to support a wider range of permanent places of recreation than previous centuries had known. As the outlets expanded, publicity techniques burgeoned, and a new class of person grew up, the purveyor or entrepreneur of entertainment. This was the beginning of what J.H. Plumb has called 'the commercialisation of leisure'.[5] Its effect on the performing arts was not confined to the popular end of the market, that is the shows catering for a largely uneducated audience. There were important developments running parallel in the more rarefied setting of Drury Lane and the Haymarket. Theatrical managers, for instance, were less commonly working actors; when they were, they owed their prominence as much to their skill as an impresario as to any skill as an executant. The royal patentee at the playhouse would no longer be some distant and amateurish aristocrat, but so to speak a working director. In an age of commercial consolidation, even the haunts of pleasure were put into the hands of a professional.

The places Swift visited with the Shelburnes were on everybody's list. Ned Ward's *London Spy* takes in a similar range of attractions: again we have the museum of scientific curiosities at Gresham College, the Royal Exchange, the madmen of Bedlam, the menagerie at the Tower. Ward moves on to other sights: taverns and coffee-houses, prisons and hospitals, the great fairs and the Lord Mayor's Show, theatre and gambling-den. He encounters quacks and mountebanks, beaux and bailiffs, quakers and street-sellers, toy-women and templars, jack-puddings and stock-jobbers. Along the way we are invited to witness a variety of activities: hemp-beating in Bridewell, a lottery, a music-house, a vaulting-school, fortune-telling in Whitechapel, law-courts, trading at Rag Fair, trainband exercises, and a great deal else. Ward is not satirising these activities, though a strong distaste shows through on occasions. He poses as a weary scholar, visiting the flesh-pots of a wonder-filled metropolis. As an 'utter stranger to the town', he perceives, responds, exclaims, but does not judge. It is a picture of the city as it appears to an outsider, trading on its own superficiality, even though Ward's intimacy with his material threatens the security of his pose.[6]

Once, such accounts were regularly quarried in works about eighteenth-century London. They can be traced in every Victorian and Edwardian book on the subject, even occasionally a little later. This was the heyday of what might be termed the Beau Brocade school of social historiography, when cliometricians were undreamt of, and archives were left to the antiquarian compiler or the pedantic annalist. In various ways the studies of Hanoverian London composed by Walter Besant, H.B. Wheatley and E. Beresford Chancellor illustrate this tendency; but it is in the work of Austin Dobson that the school finds its purest expression. Today Dobson's reputation does not stand very high, and—leaving aside his poetry—it is based chiefly on his essays and sketches, in particular *Eighteenth Century Vignettes*, rather than on his biographical and critical studies dealing with writers such as Fielding or Richardson.

One can readily understand the grounds for disparaging his work. The very title-pages of his books have had an offputting hint of the casual, the slight, the marginal: 'Vignettes', *Side-Walk Studies*, *A Bookman's Budget*. His essays originally appeared in journals of the Nineties: the *Cornhill Magazine*, the *National Review*, and other staider cousins of the *Yellow Book*. They retain an air of journalistic chatter, and they positively glory at times in their remoteness from 'the glitter and bustle of the more frequented promenades of letters'.[7] Even his full-length books display some of the weaknesses of the essayist: Dobson is always liable to wander off into topography, he hunts sources and analogues with something less than absolute discrimination, and he is fonder of quotation and paraphrase than of analysis. Lastly, he has a fatal predilection for the word 'old', which keeps turning up with talismanic force, as though it guaranteed some evocative quality. There is Old Kensington Palace, and Old Vauxhall Gardens, and An Old London Bookseller, and Old Whitehall, and much else along these lines. An unmistakable whiff of locutions such as '*dear* old ...' hangs over the page.

And yet there is more to be said in favour of Dobson. His volumes for the English Men of Letters series are not wholly obsolete even today: he manages to make sense of his subject's career, and he knows everything which was to be known at the end of the Victorian era. His qualities can be seen in the memoir (as he calls it) of Fanny Burney, written in 1903, which copes adroitly with that lopsided life. Outside the series, his study of Goldsmith (1888) is lucid and informative. More significant is his book on Hogarth, which appeared in various redactions between 1879 and 1907. The final edition amounts to a serious and indeed scholarly work, with a useful bibliography and a good attempt at a catalogue of the works: Hogarth specialists can still make surprising finds in this book, and come to the unexpected recognition that there *are* things not in Paulson. However, the most interesting area of Dobson's writing seems to me his essays, and these bear most directly on the theme I shall be pursuing in the following chapters. In an unbuttoned style modelled on Lamb rather than Hazlitt, they deal with a variety of eighteenth-century topics. No one today would find it easy to agree with an early reviewer that his collected essays present 'the most exact series of pictures of a certain past society which has ever been given to us';[8] but they do get close to the heart of some important issues in cultural history.

The trouble with Dobson, for a present-day reader, starts from the things which he chooses to write about. 'Titled Authors of the Eighteenth Century'; 'Lady Mary Coke'; 'At Leicester Fields'; 'A Garret in Gough Square'—are these not the fripperies of Hanoverian civilisation, surface froth concealing a less agreeable life beneath, tinkling echoes of a grimmer music of humanity? I do not think so. There is a danger here of confusing the sources and the methods of social history. Granted that we can no longer be content with a purely anecdotal approach, it does not follow that the subjects Dobson chose to handle are unworthy of attention. It seems to me on the contrary that his preferred topics—pleasure-grounds, artists' colonies, charitable provision, the fortunes of people like booksellers, actresses and engravers—these are extraordinary revelatory for any proper assessment of the eighteenth century. You can write superficially or flippantly about garrets, say: but the myth and reality of garrets in this period are far from trivial or tangential things. They forge a link between the literal or demographic (three- and four-storey houses did have an attic, commonly let out to persons above the servant class but possessed of a low income) and the archetypal or symbolic (*The Distressed Poet, The Life of Savage*).

What I would argue is this. In certain historical periods it may well be prudent to seek out traces of the submerged levels of society, not for sentimental or archaeological reasons, but because their values and aspirations have a powerful latent effect on the culture as a whole. This of course applies most obviously when a cohesive and self-aware proletariat attempts to mould or influence the thinking of the economically dominant classes. But it could apply also in a less developed social order, where for example a clerkly élite left public amusements to the masses and made little attempt to direct popular taste. Neither condition is remotely fulfilled in the Georgian era. It was a culture organised in large part around the needs of a prosperous and leisured minority, most of whom took their responsibility to be rich and idle with the utmost seriousness. That is to say, the growth of Hanoverian towns was dictated by the consumerism of a few as much as by the commericalism of the relatively many. The spread of London westwards and northwards, the infilling between suburbs and historic city, the development of great estates, all these were governed by what was fashionable, quite as much as by what was profitable to the speculator. Again, the pattern of land-use in a country town, and the architectural overlay which resulted, have a great deal to do with the kind of leisure provisions which the given community could support with decent style. Inns, assembly-rooms, coffee-houses, and bookshops (or their absence) determined the character of more eighteenth-century settlements than did manufacturing plants or warehouses. There were corn-mills in Thame as well as Aylesbury; dyers' shops in Melksham as well as Salisbury. The big difference lay in those things which the latter had and the former hadn't, and which made them more attractive to the gentry.[9]

If this analysis is correct, it follows that mere statistics will not reliably assess the cultural importance of different activities. The attendance figures at Rag Fair must have exceeded many times those at Ranelagh; at some historical junctures that would be a decisive factor, but in the eighteenth century the disparity counts for much less. It was, within limits, a deferential society; even if one could not emulate the pursuits of richer people, there was a widespread readiness to be impressed by them. London and provincial newspapers (a crucial innovation of the period, to which I shall return presently) give ample space to the opulence expended on the doings of the wealthy. At the level of intention, such conspicuous expenditure was probably dictated by the desire for solidarity with one's peer-group; but there must also have been an element of showing the lower orders one's credentials for class-dominance—perhaps, too, of drawing lines between oneself and the near-gentry.

To be able to spend enough money on a leisure activity, and to be seen to do so, was an act of social definition. Hence one reason, it may be, for the popularity of subscription ventures in the Hanoverian epoch. Aristocrats, as well as ladies and gentleman a little down the scale, would put down their names to support a ball, or a season of operas, or a translation of Homer, or a hospital for the insane, or a model prison, or a troupe of French players, or a circulating library, or a turnpike, or a funeral monument, or a midnight masquerade. The many were excluded; the few were able to recognise one another from the subscription list. In few societies have public-spirited causes satisfied so many private ambitions. Rarely have power and social éclat been so intimately bound up with the ability not to work, and to do other approved things instead.

All this, of course, went along with tendencies of a very discrepant kind. I do not deny that England was a busy and energetic place, taking important strides in agricultural and industrial development (nor that the upper crust had a hand in these things). It is equally true that there was an increasingly articulate and indeed vocal commercial class, making itself heard within and without doors at Westminster. Again, it is assuredly the case that there was a large majority of underprivileged men and women, playing a vital economic role but little rewarded in worldly terms. And no reader of Robert Malcolmson's book could doubt that they kept alive a wide range of popular recreations, generally of a traditional nature, at least until the full tide of industrialism made England predominantly an urban society. All I am contending is that it was the diversions of the gentry which set the tone; which fuelled building, landscaping and what we might call environmental design; which helped to mould the perceptions even of the least privileged strata of the population. Middle-class entertainments aped those of the rich, or vulgarised high forms of art, or produced genteel versions of lower-class fun. Popular recreations often took the form of galas organised by the gentry;[10] otherwise they tended to be localised and indeed resolutely provincial. They attracted little or no publicity in the new organs of information and opinion. They were more commonly participatory events rather than spectator-sports, another mark of their rusticity. They had a strong component of ritual: consequently, they did not need to be advertised (the natural calendar did that), they required no capital to mount and hence no conspicuous subscribers, and finally they gave minimal opportunities for social ostentation. In the eighteenth century this was as good as to say that they were peripheral to the dominant cultural impulses. Before the end of the eighteenth century there were comparatively few attempts by the authorities to suppress the popular pastimes of the common people. Until the work-discipline of the Industrial Revolution arrived, it was considered no bad thing for the poor to enjoy themselves in agreed ways.[11] It was safe for them to have a good time because, socially, it meant just that and nothing else. In the early Georgian period these was no symbolic or ideological meaning in the recreations of the people: only the pastimes of the well-to-do possessed recognisable cultural valency.

There are various implications here for the chapters which follow. In the first place, the recurrent pull of the material towards Dobson territory is not something that need be resisted. The chapters which take us to such enclaves of privilege as the Royal Academy of Music or Ranelagh are more than a diversion in the company of a frivolous minority. (We may recall how often the novel, from Charlotte Lennox right down to Thackeray, conducts us to the pleasure gardens.) But secondly, the matters which have come under discussion enable us to understand the Augustan critique of fashionable entertainments in a fuller perspective. Consider, for example, the disgust expressed in *The Dunciad* that low-grade farces and harlequinades should have penetrated to the heart of the legitimate theatre. There is undoubtedly a social cast to this line of thinking, just as there is with Hogarth's depiction of a motley crowd arriving at the masquerade, or the concern of some moralists that Vauxhall Gardens had unduly democratised social encounters. But the main thrust is aesthetic: Pope feels that the recreations which promote taste and sensitivity are being invaded by those which rely on cheap effects and tawdry 'glamour'. The satirists may or may not be right about this: it is hard for us to be sure, for none of us has witnessed a Lord Mayor's pageant as then performed, or a Smithfield droll, or one of John Rich's pantomimes. We therefore have nothing to set alongside Shakespeare and Otway and Congreve. From the surviving texts of such shows—Settle's *Fall of Troy*, or Thurmond's *Harlequin Dr Faustus*—one is certainly inclined to side with Pope and Hogarth. On the other hand the element of spectacle, so crucial to the appeal of these works, can never be reconstructed from a bare series of stage directions.

A third consideration is this. The Scriblerian party took the view that high life should be inimical to low art because gracious social living was itself a branch of élite culture, connecting at every point with the reading, *virtù* and classical ethos of a true gentleman. Part of their attack on Walpole derives from his failure to attach a sumptuous way of living at Houghton to any discernible code of values or traditional way of thought. (In fact, Walpole was a collector and connoisseur of painting: but that was continually suppressed in the socio-political case mounted by his opponents.) Today many readers find it difficult to imagine a genuine continuum existing between literary or philosophic values and the tone of high society. All that can be said here is that the Augustan idea of the gentleman, at its best, did place great emphasis on the kind of occupations with which an individual regaled his leisure hours. The life of Horatian retirement, so often set up as a model, involved both a measure of civilised study (no nonsense about pedantry or scholarship) and a corresponding amount of dignified ease. This is part of the recognition we arrived at earlier: the eighteenth-century distinctions of class, both social and cultural, relate most significantly to time spent outside one's narrow vocation.

Most MPs were men of the right sort, and to attend Parliament with reasonable assiduity was a gentlemanly enough pursuit. But election to the House did not in itself confer gentility, as upstarts quickly learnt. Merchants remained potential figures of fun, even (or especially) if they were very rich, like Sir Gilbert Heathcote—Pope's 'grave Sir Gilbert'. The dissenting interest remained largely separate, with few extra-parliamentary contacts as regards the majority of members. And the Commons was never more united than when it was able to assume a fit of probity, and sanctimoniously expel some grafting social climber, like Denis Bond. Somehow this fate escaped the most notorious rogues like Peter Walter, or the egregious Irishman Theobald Taafe, who (according to Horace Walpole)

> having betted Mrs Woffington five guineas on as many performances in one night, and demanding the money which he won, received the famous reply, *double* or *quits*.[12]

Such men generally ended up in Boulogne, as was then the custom for raddled adventurers. Walter was too cunning and too well protected, but he never achieved true equality with the great men he served, and his case conforms to the general rule. He remained an outsider despite all his money, his power and his ubiquity.[13] Augustan satire enacts contemporary social typecasting by consigning Walter to the ranks of the unacceptable. Ralph Allen, equally self-made, became a kind of insider because of his patronage of writers, architects and craftsmen. Satire reels away from such enlightened attitudes, and solemn panegyric is all that is left.

The Rise of the Impresario

I suggested earlier that the early eighteenth century saw the rise of a new leisure industry, managed by a fresh breed of professional entrepreneurs. These were the men who first seized the opportunities offered by greater affluence, better communications, wider outlets for publicity, and (for a crucial generation or so) relatively peaceful and stable conditions at the start of the Hanoverian era. I shall explore certain of these factors in more detail in the next section. These entrepreneurs worked to some extent in the larger provincial centres—spas like Bath and Tunbridge, cathedral cities and assize towns like Salisbury and Norwich, university towns. But their main sphere of influence was the metropolis, and it was they who catered for one of the basic desires of urban man—entertainment. They provided fun-palaces and gaming-houses, places to see sights and places to be seen, feasts for the stomach and feasts for the ear. They turned

Georgian London into an unprecedented gallery of delights. Almost every taste in recreation, from the most brutal to the most refined, was met by regular commercial enterprises functioning at set times.

The most conspicuous among the new cultural purveyors were a handful of men who came to maturity around the turn of the century, most of them born between Swift (1667) and Hogarth (1697). They include the operatic impresario John James Heidegger (*c.* 1665-1749);[14] the theatrical manager John Rich (*c.* 1692-1761); the bookseller Edmund Curll (*c.* 1683-1747); and the proprietor of Vauxhall Gardens, Jonathan Tyers (*c.* 1690-1767). On the fringe of this group stand persons straddling the roles of performer and entrepreneur: Handel himself (1685-1759); the poet laureate and Drury Lane Manager, Colley Cibber (1671-1757); the fairground conjuror Isaac Fawkes (d. 1731); and the mountebank of the Oratory, John Henley (1692-1756). An important representative of the breed not active in London is the arbiter of Bath fashions, Richard 'Beau' Nash (1674-1762). Most of these men turn up frequently in the literary and graphic satire of the time; one is liable to bump into nearly all of them in a single play by Fielding during the 1730s. They are usually portrayed in sardonic, if not hostile terms; despite their marked individuality, not to say eccentricity in some cases, they appear in satire as representative types, rather than fully individuated characters.

One noteworthy aspect of their contemporary image is the readiness with which they are equated with men of a rather different cast. Projectors in the field of popular entertainment, they find themselves more or less unfairly aligned with projectors in the economic or political field. Thus the 'regulator' of masquerades, Heidegger, goes with the 'regulator' of organised crime, Jonathan Wild (*c.* 1683-1725). Political connections are often enforced through allusion to the gamester Francis Charteris (1675-1732). The South Sea director Sir John Blunt (1667-1733), the company promoter William Wood (1671-1730), and the land-agent Peter Walter (*c.* 1664-1746) are similarly enlisted in derogatory comparisons.[15] Every one of the figures mentioned in this paragraph was linked at one time or another with Robert Walpole (1676-1745), and this is the ultimate bearing of the satire. I shall explore the political significance of this habit of association in the last part of the Introduction. Here I simply note the trick of double-implication: Peachum in *The Beggar's Opera* is both Wild and Walpole, whilst Fielding strikes at Walpole through Cibber in the character of Marplay in *The Author's Farce*, and through himself in the character of Pillage in *The Historical Register*.

All these men, apart from Nash, operated principally in London: although, like Walpole or Walter, they might maintain a place in the country. But scarcely any of them derived from London originally; they were drawn to the capital by its opportunities for profit and advancement. Handel and Heidegger were émigrés, the others mostly provincials. Charteris was a Scot with a base in Lancashire, Wild and Wood came from Staffordshire, Blunt from Kent, Curll apparently from the West Country, Henley from Leicestershire, whilst Walpole was a member of an old Norfolk family. Cibber, born in London, was the son of an immigrant from Schleswig. In their attraction to the metropolis, these men enact a powerful social dynamic; sooner than most, they respond to the pull of urbanism. In a sense they go where the market is to be found, though some of them spent less time in the market-place than in the graceful assembly-room or the playhouse.

It would be foolish to suggest that no kind of organised entertainment had existed previously. Elizabethan London, after all, had had its Bankside and Blackfriars theatres, its licensed companies, to go with the informal diversions of street and field. Nevertheless, it is clear that the Hanoverian city offered a far wider range of scheduled activities. Instead of a few strolling puppeteers, we have Robert Powell performing regular seasons at Southwark Fair.[16] In place of the occasional waxworks at Smithfield, we have Mrs Salmon in permanent residence in Fleet Street, just through Temple Bar. Mrs Salmon (*c.*1670–1760) promoted her concern through handbills and a prominent signboard. For sixpence a visitor could see all kinds of curious effigies, including the royal family and, later in the century, figures such as Dr Johnson and Wesley—it was a durable business. Often the tableaux would take up the themes of high art, and portray historical or allegorical subjects: the execution of Charles I and the temple of Flora alongside Mother Shipton's well. A rival concern was that of Mrs Goldsmith, whose effigies were set up in a crypt of Westminster Abbey. There was also Mrs Mills, whose advertisement was set up in a lozenge shape, and whose effigies could be seen 'from 9 in the Morn, till 9 at Night'. Such displays were said to be on display 'as well in *Christmas* and other Holidays, as at all other times'.[17] One begins to look for the claim, 'We never closed.' Entertainments obviously kept regular, and long, business hours. The widest range of non-legitimate shows could be seen at the great London fairs. In Settle's era the main promoter of spectacular shows was Mrs Mynns, who kept her booth over against the Hospital Gate, on the south-east side of the Smithfield fairground. Since Settle had the reputation of being 'the best contriver of machinery in England', his services were much in demand. But William Penkethman, senior, a straight actor on the side, was capable of responding with *The Siege of Barcelona or the Soldier's Fortune: With the Taking of Fort Mountjoy: containing the Pleasant and Comical Exploits of that Renown'd Hero Captain Blunderbuss and his Man Squib* (1706). The playbill continues: 'His adventures with the conjurer, and a surprising Scene of the Flying Machine, where he and his Man Squib are Enchanted; Also the diverting Humours of Corporal Scare-Devil.' There were topical references to the exploits of the Earl of Peterborough; what is more interesting today is the Smollett-like ring of the sub-plot. Conjurers and flying machines and grotesque dancers have spilled into the play from the adjoining booths, where rope-dancing, waxworks and 'outlandish monsters' were advertised with equal enthusiasm.[18]

Mrs Mynns may have been an impresario in a pretty small way, although she is said to have spent ten months and several pounds in preparing the greatest Smithfield show, *The Siege of Troy* (see Chapter 3 below). Even she represents a kind of professionalism.[19] Meanwhile, at the fair, the usual freak-shows went on. Walter Besant lists a number of attractions, including a camel; a girl without any bones; the dancing mare; the child born back-to-back with a live bear; the double girl; the man with one head and two bodies; the man whose body was only twenty-one inches high; the fairy (a hundred and fifty years of age); the hermaphrodite; the grimacing Spaniard; the German woman without hands or feet; the child with three legs; and the transparent child.[20] We know that Swift took an interest in the

Siamese twins exhibited in Cornhill in 1708:

> Here is a sight of two girls joined together at the back, which, in the
> newsmonger's phrase, causes a great many speculations; and raises
> abundance of questions in divinity, law and physic.[21]

These 'speculations' form the basis of the double mistress episode
in *The Memoirs of Martinus Scriblerus*, where Lindamira and
Indamora derive from the real-life Hungarian sisters. Other
monsters on show in London around 1711 furnish materials for
this section, in which the 'master of the show', Mr Randal, takes
a prominent part.[22] Similarly we find Pope making sport with
'the most reigning Curiosity in the town', a hermaphrodite,
around 1715; posing as a young gentleman about town he gives
an account of a visit to the 'monster' in a style of arch prurience.[23]
If the most sophisticated wits of the day were engrossed by such
sights, it is not surprising that the public at large flocked to the
booths, and the fairgrounds continued to put on freak-shows.

Other popular entertainments were bear-baiting and
pugilism. In 1717 a leopard twelve feet long was baited; a bull
and a bear were covered with lighted fireworks to enrage them,
as a minor improvement on the sport. The best-known bear
garden was that of Hockley in the Hole; here the proprietor,
Christopher Preston, fell into the enclosure among his own bears,
and was killed.[24] This was in 1709; few of the new entrepreneurs
were to die with quite such grisly appropriateness. Meanwhile,
prize fighting attained greater popularity than ever before. Most
prominent was James Figg (d. 1734), who was known as the
Master of Defence, and taught gentlemen the use of the sword
and quarter-staff. His 'academy' stood on the Oxford Road, near
the junction of modern Berwick Street and Oxford Street. But he
also performed at the 'Boarded House' in Marlyebone Fields and
in the Little Theatre in the Haymarket, scene of Fielding's
dramatic triumphs, and in the fairgrounds. Hogarth, indeed,
who depicted Figg more than once, is thought to have
represented him in the bald-headed rider at the right-hand
foreground of *Southwark Fair*. Figg certainly staged sword-
contests in a 'tiled booth' at the Fair. His 'Amphitheatre' or
'Great Room' rivalled the more fashionable salons of the West
End throughout the 1720s and early 1730s. His successor was

James Broughton (1705–89), whom Hogarth may also have drawn. Later still Daniel Mendoza (1764–1836) attained even more widespread celebrity, touring round the whole country.[25]

All these varied manifestations of the leisure facilities of London illustrate a growing public awareness of the pleasures available. Country cousins who had never before visited the capital quickly found their way to Mrs Salmon's exhibition or Figg's academy: so the pamphleteers and social commentators assure us, anyway. Grander entertainments obviously required larger amounts of capital to put on, and the entrepreneurs who took the largest risks acquired the greatest fame. Two of them who are rarely out of the prints are Heidegger and Rich, and it is therefore worth looking at each in a little more detail.

Heidegger was notable to the contemporary mind chiefly on account of his ugliness. Tracts of the time are full of references like this:

> Mr. *Heyd-g-r* had, at the slender Appearances at his *Balls* and *Opera*, so distorted his Countenance, that he was scarce known by his most intimate Friends and Acquaintance.

Or this:

> The very Thoughts of *Masquerades*, would have put [our grandmothers] into a Swoon; and the Sight of *Heydegger* would have terrified them, as much as one of their *Church-yard-Spirits*.[26]

We might find it odd that the worst which can be said of so ubiquitous a villain of the Augustan piece is that he is not blessed with a beautiful countenance. It was certainly a convenience for the satirists: Hogarth could introduce his physiognomy into a print and count on instant identification. Similarly Pope wrote in *The Dunciad* of

> a monster of a fowl
> Something betwixt a Heideggre and owl.
> (A I, 243–4)[27]

The mythic beast 'heideggre' suggests not just a monstrous being, but a sort of mutant; the harsh Saxon syllables would doubtless have struck contemporaries as funny, as did the Germanic accent of both Heidegger and Handel. There is a feeling lurking behind the words that the impresario has a Mephistophelean quality which will lure England to its ruin. Satire emphasises Heidegger's ugly face in order to bring out the perverseness of his popularity, or at least the popularity of the events he organises. He is at once ridiculous and fearsome, the ideal combination for a satiric target.

John Rich was the son of an attorney turned theatrical manager. The son attempted to make a career as a straight actor, but does not seem to have been up to it. He operated the Lincoln's Inn Fields playhouse planned by his father, except for a brief period, from 1714, and then opened a new house at Covent Garden in 1732. His achievements in high drama were fairly meagre, though it was of course Rich who put on the première of *The Beggar's Opera*. Nevertheless, he seems to have received an unduly bad press for a man who kept almost half of London's live theatre going for much of the early Hanoverian era. He was held to be illiterate, and that is not true. He was said to be mean to his company, and that is distinctly dubious.[28] Part of the animus must derive simply from the fact that Rich was so successful during many phases of his career. He was in business to make money if he could, and at least to survive if he could not. It does not behove a generation whose live theatrical entertainment is almost all subsidised, in one way or another, to condescend too easily.

Rich made a speciality out of what might be termed fringe theatrical entertainment. He was himself a grotesque dancer, whose best-known contribution to dramatic art was to dress as a dog and bark during his role as Harlequin in *The Rape of Proserpine* (1727). Harlequin was his most famous role, usually given under the stage-name Lun. Arthur Murphy, John Hill, even David Garrick himself, praised Rich's 'attitudes and movements' in this part, singling out his ability to turn himself into 'a wild Beast, a Bird, or a Serpent with a long Tail, and what not'.[29] It is a curious talent, but not inherently unworthy.

In a way what happened was that Rich transferred to the legitimate theatre a popular street entertainment. The great expert in vocal mimicry was Mr Clench of Barnet, who is mentioned in *Tatler* no. 51 as 'an artful Person' who could do 'several Feats of Activity with his Throat and Windpipe'. He was an inveterate advertiser, distributing endless handbills celebrating his skill in imitating the sound made by hounds, drunken men, old women, peals of bells and much else. He came to prominence in the early part of the century, but continued to feature regularly in advertising columns for a generation or more.[30] On his death in 1734 the *Gentleman's Magazine* gave his age as seventy. Clench perfectly embodied 'the art of sinking' as practised in contemporary fairgrounds (see the quotation from *Peri Bathous*, p. 78 below). It was Rich's dubious distinction to carry such performances into the West End theatre.

Rich took his first distinctive step when he put on *The Necromancer* in 1723. This was in rivalry to Drury Lane's smash-hit *Harlequin Dr Faustus* (indeed it appropriated that title for its own sub-title). In the years which followed, John Thurmond and Henry Carey supplied pantomime for the Theatre Royal, whilst Rich replied at Lincoln's Inn Fields with a series of elaborate shows, mixing *commedia dell' arte* with a kind of serious ballet based on mythological themes. Rich had a better setting for pantomime than his rivals, and his shows were more effectively staged. Only once was he caught out: in 1727 he had no response ready for Drury Lane's elaborate coronation pageant. 'Instead, he had to content himself with a pantomime farce, called *Harlequin Anna Bullen*, satirizing Drury Lane's expensive ... and very lucrative entertainment.' In 1761 he had learnt his lesson and put on a splendid coronation procession. It was spectacle of this sort which caused a writer in 1770 to dub Rich 'the God of Pantomimes, Jubilees and Installations'.[31]

When Rich died, his playhouse and patents fetched the huge sum of £60,000. Unquestionably he was one of the most creative figures in the eighteenth-century theatre; whether or not one likes his style of management, one has to acknowledge his capacity to give a large section of the public what it wanted. For Pope, he was the archetypal monster-breeding illusionist, an 'Angel of Dulness' who scattered 'Her magic charms o'er all unclassic ground':

> And proud his mistress' orders to perform,
> Rides in the whirlwind, and directs the storm.
>
> (A III, 259-60)[32]

Even gaming houses had their 'directors' and 'operators' at this period;[33] for Rich to be seen as *directing* ludicrous stage effects placed him even more firmly in the ranks of the dangerous new men, who pulled strings, threw levers, and collected the takings.

The Invention of Publicity

In few areas of mental life is the modern consciousness more remote from that of earlier generations than in its sustained exposure to the organs of mass publicity. Yet the early history of advertising is a surprisingly neglected subject. Studies of the commercial growth of Britain in the eighteenth century make passing references to this new element in economic life; whilst historians of the newspaper give it brief attention, usually in the context of revenue-sources and management. But the rise of advertising is a phenomenon of *cultural*, as well as economic and journalistic, history. The technique developed to attract an expanding range of consumers had considerable impact on writers of the early Hanoverian period. Apart from anything else, literary men could not miss the new arrival in their midst for the simple reason that books were among the first commodities to be extensively advertised in the press.[34] It also happened that one of the first time innovators in promotional activities was the publisher Edmund Curll.

It is well known that the lapse in 1695 of the Licensing Act (1662) permitted a rapid growth in the activities of the newspaper industry. As Laurence Hanson pointed out, the failure by Parliament to extend the Act's operation did not proceed from any utopian ideals of a free press. Measures to regulate the press several times came before both Houses in the next twenty years: when no official body had a restrictive bill to propose, Daniel Defoe could be relied upon to come up with a scheme of his own. The Copyright Act of 1702 left alone matters of regulating the periodical press, but the Stamp Act of 1712 was the first of a series of measures throughout the century which gave the government some powers (however difficult to apply) to control the flow of information. The licentiousnes of the press was an unruly animal to confine, and successive battles up to the time of Fox's Libel Act (1792) testified to the capacity of the trade to evade or countermand government restrictions.[35]

After its abortive life in the 1650s and 1660s, the English newspaper drifted on inconsequentially following the passage of the Licensing Act. It was not until 1695 that the *Post Boy* began its long and influential career. It was soon joined by the *Flying Post* and the *Post Man*. All three continued publication in the 1730s, and during its most important phase each appeared three times weekly—the interval which best suited the supply of news and the channels of distribution. A better known event is the foundation of the *Daily Courant* in 1702, the first true national daily paper. But the *Courant* always remained a conservative organ, unambitious editorially and sober in presentation to the point of dreariness. It seems at times to have seen itself as the rival of the official *Gazette*, the government newsletter and journal of record for such matters as bankruptcy commissions. Much livelier fare was provided by some of the new weekly papers, especially the organs which appeared every Saturday during the reign of George I: the *Journals* of Mist, Read and Applebee combed the remainder of the press for hot news, and developed their own styles and specialisms. Applebee is the most devoted chronicler of crime in the era of Jonathan Wild, Mist the most daring outlet for radical and dangerous politics. Papers such as the *British Journal* became notable for fullscale political essays in the early 1720s. Meanwhile the evening newspaper, which took some time to get off the ground, started to prosper with such durable titles as the *Whitehall Evening Post*, founded by Defoe in 1718 and running on for many decades. The age of Walpole brought with it further developments: the subsidised government press, the political weekly as humanist essay (*Craftsman*), the specialised gossip of literature and theatre in papers such as the *Grub-Street Journal*. Titles continued to multiply, and though many were short-lived the London newspaper industry steadily grew in scale and influence. As John Brewer has observed, there is 'overwhelming evidence for a burgeoning growth of the press' in the first three quarters of the eighteenth century. Not only total circulation, but the number of separate titles, showed the same rising tendency.[36]

Many London newspaper proprietors were also involved in the publication of books, or at least pamphlets. An important figure here is John Applebee, who employed Defoe on his *Weekly*

Post. Applebee was responsible for a steady flow of criminal lives, trial proceedings and the like. It was he who apparently encouraged Defoe to move into this branch of literary composition, and who published a whole series of works on Jack Sheppard and Jonathan Wild. According to Gerald Howson, 'Sheppard is an early example of what publicity can do. An "image", in the modern sense of the word, was created for him by Defoe.'[37] Wild was an even more popular subject for biographic or satiric treatment; he soon attained a life put out by the Diceys of Northampton, active both in the newspaper field and in chapbook production. There are further ramifications: Sheppard became the hero of a Drury Lane harlequinade, over which Colley Cibber presided. (Mist's *Journal* reports that the show met with a universal hiss, and soon expired.) To this John Rich responded with *The Prison-Breaker* at Lincoln's Inn Fields. The Prologue contains an interesting foretaste of *The Beggar's Opera*:

> Such was the Youth of whom our Muse doth sing,
> Who took for these Exploits a decent Swing;
> Yet by his Fall he this poor Comfort gains,
> The Muse revives him, spight of Ropes or Chains;
> Here in her Magick Empire, she Reprieves,
> Stabs, Poysons, Marries—Crowns or Halters gives.
> The Heroe whom this Night her Colours paint,
> Is but Low Life, and all her Drawings faint.
> Let him be therefore in your Censures spar'd;
> To execute him twice would be too hard.
> On the World's Stage he has his Doom receiv'd,
> Shew Mercy here, and let him be Repriev'd.

Applebee to Rich—the line is direct. 'Low Life' becomes the staple of a certain kind of fashionable entertainment, having already achieved prominence in newspapers and pamphlets. Instead of standing aloof from the material of the popular prints, West End dramaturgy takes its cue from this source. Grub Street has penetrated the West End: the same crowd spills through the streets from Bartholomew Fair to the Haymarket.

Thus far I have confined myself to the London end of the trade. But as well as the national circulation of these newspapers, there was of course a growing network of provincial papers. About 150 titles are known to have existed, however briefly, between 1700 and 1760. The *Norwich Post*, founded in the latter part of 1701, was the first in a distinguished line. A series of important journals sprang up in the English provinces: the *Norwich Mercury*, originally simply the *Weekly Mercury*, dates from 1714 and has long outlasted its rival. The *Northampton Mercury* began its life in 1720, the *Gloucester Journal* in 1722, the *Reading Mercury* in 1723. Bristol and Exeter were already catered for by ventures set up by the Farley family. Newcastle, Ipswich, Stamford and Nottingham were other towns early to achieve a well-established local paper. Oxford and Cambridge took rather longer, as did Liverpool, Birmingham and Sheffield. But by 1760 there were at least thirty-five titles, which according to one estimate constituted a fifth of the total volume of newspaper sales in England. In the third quarter of the century almost every town of any size possessed its own paper. Places as small as St Ives, Kendal, Middlewich and Ludlow attempted to support a journal, usually unsuccessfully, but the *Sherborne and Yeovil Mercury* managed to survive, in one guise or another, from 1737 to 1867.[38]

Scotland appears to have had more difficulty in keeping such ventures alive. Only Edinburgh, and from the 1740s Glasgow, sustained papers for any length of time. On the other hand Ireland, with its separate parliament, and generally easier communications, was able to sustain a much wider range of periodicals. The standard bibliography lists 172 titles of newspapers active between 1685 and 1750. Of these the great bulk were naturally concentrated in Dublin. Belfast, Cork, Limerick and Waterford are thinly represented; 157 derive from the capital. These include such major newspapers as the *Dublin Journal*, conducted by Swift's bookseller George Faulkner from the mid 1720s.[39] In Dublin, as in London and Edinburgh, it would have been hard to escape all awareness of the press at any stage in the Hanoverian era. It was an intensively competitive business, with mergers, collapses, plagiarism and piracy. As soon as one title died, another was born to replace it on the streets. Hawkers carried the papers to all but the remotest spots in the kingdom: Johnson and Boswell would have been safe from their importunities on Skye or Iona, but it is doubtful whether Pope, say, ever went to a single locality where the pedlars had not penetrated.[40]

The significance of the newspaper as a political instrument has recently been stressed by John Brewer, and many other writers have shown how the editorial content of periodical papers affected the way in which people constructed the world around them. (The rise in male literacy, especially, is a matter of contention among historians, but that the *habit* of readership increased few are disposed to deny). In this respect, the newspaper could be said to have been an agent of democracy by its very existence: seldom before had the same words been directed to such a disparate audience. News-stories reached Hogarth in London and Swift in Dublin in virtually identical forms, and within a few days. Moreover, the literate young mechanic in Derby and the squire's daughter in Wiltshire received the same message, as provincial papers were sedulous apes when it came to news coverage. A more homogeneous store of information was filtering through the country, reaching all kinds and conditions of person.

But there was another development alongside, and it is one much less widely appreciated. A significant portion of newspapers were given up to advertising matter. The authorities were not slow to realise this, and responded as is their custom to anything that looks popular—they put a tax on advertisements. In the Act of 1712, this was at the flat rate of one shilling per item: the charge to advertisers had been about twopence a line, but increased as a result of the levy to $2\frac{1}{2}d.$ or $3d.$ The rate of tax was stepped up to two shillings in 1757, and then to $2s$ $6d$ in 1780. An average length entry would cost the advertiser about two shillings in the early part of the century, and more like double that figure towards the end. It is probable, nevertheless, that the net receipts from this source were smaller than those from sales of the paper: newspaper proprietors had not yet become dependent on advertising income.[41]

As one would expect, the amount of advertising carried, and its nature, varied with the kind of journal. Some periodicals carried only book advertisements, some ventured as far as auctions and public notices. But the ordinary newspaper, whether in the capital or the provinces, took whatever it could get. This might include appeals for the return of lost property, strayed horses or runaway apprentices: what might be termed 'personal column' entries, such as disclaimers concerning stories which had appeared in the press: or a number of other private enquiries. However the most significant category of advertising was commercial in character. Books and quack medicines were the principal commodities involved,[42] but all kinds of services were advertised in the press. In London these were sometimes aimed at the luxury end of the market, with quite exotic products offered for sale. But more humdrum necessities of life, from candles to cutlery, are also to be found in these columns. It was this outlet for commercial exploitation which helped the provincial newspaper to gain such a relatively sure footing within the space of one or two generations.[43] Newspaper proprietors often ran a quite different business in tandem with their journal, and hawkers they employed would be as willing to sell corn-plasters to a passer-by as to unload the latest *Mercury*.

The existence of this new information outlet produced a marked effect in some spheres. For example, the London theatres had previously been confined almost exclusively to the 'Great Bills', printed in red and black, posted around the city. From 1702, the year in which the *Daily Courant* appeared, they started to use the new medium of publicity. The handbill was not abandoned, but came over time to play a less important part, especially where a comparatively sophisticated public was being sought. During Cibber's time at Drury Lane press advertising cost over £30 a season; whilst John Rich expended 4s. 6d. daily for notices inserted jointly in two newspapers (this was at the height of the pantomime craze in the 1720s). Playbills were more expensive to print, so that Rich was paying out £150 annually, quite apart from the wage of a full-time billsticker employed to post notices on tavern doors and city gates. Neither form of publicity was cheap, but the new impresario was happy to speculate in this direction so that he might accumulate at the box-office.[44]

Initially, there was no readymade technique for press advertising. It is not surprising consequently that, to begin with, 'the format of the Great Bills influenced that of the newspaper announcements' of theatrical performances.[45] But gradually advertisers learnt to cope with the limitations of eighteenth-century newspaper design. There was of course no display advertising as we know it. Announcements had to be couched in more or less continuous prose; but an occasional aid was available in the shape of a pointing finger or similar device. The format of newspaper advertising remained conservative throughout the century; a freer layout was used in tradesmen's cards, which were engraved for the most part rather than printed. Hogarth served his apprenticeship to a goldsmith's engraver, and actually made a shop-card for his master, as well as some for his own use.[46] Tradesmen's tokens were another form of publicity in wide use during this period. But such items of business stationery were only useful when first-hand contacts enabled them to be distributed to possible buyers. The great thing about newspaper advertising was that it enabled sellers to reach a predictable but unknown market, that is the whole range of people who bought papers or came upon them in the coffee-house. A completely new factor, with the growth of regular journalism, lay in the certainty that one could get one's message across to a broad public at specified intervals. This was vital for entertainments whose content changed frequently: above all, for the proprietors of a theatre or opera-house were quick turnover of repertoire was necessary to satisfy the fashion-conscious audience. Regular press announcements enabled managers to keep the town fully apprised of their programme, and made possible a more flexible organisation of the theatrical calendar.

The output of books was rather less seasonal than most things in Georgian England, but something of a lull did occur in midsummer. Nevertheless a steady flow of books and pamphlets appeared throughout the year. Pamphlets were commonly devoted to topical and indeed ephemeral issues; they answered a tract of the previous week, or even the previous day in extreme cases. Again it was vital to have instant publicity, before the issue dropped from public attention. There was still no established system of book reviewing in the press, so that publishers needed to make an impact as soon as a book came out. They might keep up a campaign for weeks or even months for an especially noteworthy book, where a long printing-run had been hazarded; but generally advertising was at its most intense at the time of publication (say, a week before the event, and a couple of weeks afterwards). Once this exposure had been arranged, the book would be left to take its chances or to find recommendation on a word-of-mouth basis. Catalogues of books in print appeared at the end of some published volumes, but this was a poor method of promoting works at the popular end of the market.

There are abundant echoes of these things in eighteenth-century literature. Addison wrote an early *Tatler* (no. 18) on the signs that used to festoon cities, and moved on later in the same number to the condition of newswriters with the prospect of peace. By no. 224 he had moved on to advertising itself, yet one further confirmation of the sureness of his instincts in detecting a new social trend. 'It is my Custom in a Dearth of News,' he has the *Tatler* remark, 'to entertain my self with those Collections of Advertisments that appear at End of all our publick Prints. These I consider as Accounts of News from the little World, in the same Manner that the foregoing Parts of the Paper are from the great.' He goes on to supply a parody notice for a 'spirit of lavender', and ends:

> It plainly appears, that a Collection of Advertisements is a Kind of Miscellany; the Writers of which, contrary to all Authors, except Men of Quality, give Money to the Booksellers who publish their Copies. The Genius of a Bookseller is cheifly shown in his Method of ranging and digesting these little Tracts. The last Paper I took up in my Hands, places them in the following Order:
>
> The true Spanish Blacking for Shoes, &c.
>
> The Beautifying Cream for the Face, &c.
>
> Pease and Plaisters, &c.
>
> Nectar and Ambrosia, &c.
>
> *** The Present State of England, &c.
>
> ‡‡‡ Annotations upon the Tatler, &c.
>
> A Commission of Bankrupt being awarded against B.L. Bookseller, &c.

Symbolically, this list joins together cosmetics, quack medicines, books and official notices (that the bankruptcy is awarded against the publisher Lintot is simply a private joke). This is no casual 'miscellany'; it incorporates the most heavily advertised items of the day.[47] One recalls that the *Spectator* carried a heavy load of book advertising, whilst one of its distribution agents was Charles Lillie, a perfumer often mentioned in the editorial columns. His speciality was 'simple essences distilled from herbs, but sold under glamorous Italian and oriental names'. He was an assiduous self-promoter, whose shop on the south side of the Strand attracted a fashionable clientele.[48]

Proprietary medicines and new books similarly conjoin in Pope's prose satires on Edmund Curll, especially *A Further Account of the most Deplorable Condition* (1716). (That pamphlet itself carries on its title-page a revealing imprint: 'Printed, and Sold by all the Publishers, Mercuries, and Hawkers, within the Bills of Mortality'—a parody of Grub Street production methods.) Repeated allusion is made by these squibs to Curll's promotion techniques; Pope has the bookseller speak of 'the second Collection of Poems, which I groundlessly called Mr. *Prior*'s, will sell for Nothing, and hath not yet paid the Charge of the Advertisements, which I was obliged to publish against him'. Curll also tells one of his understrappers that he has 'several *Taking Title Pages* that only wanted Treatises to be writ to them'.[49] The joke here rests on the practice of using the title-page as we today employ a dust-jacket: books were displayed in shop windows or on rails, with the title-page uppermost. Hence the elaborate trailers carried on the title-page of a book such as *Moll Flanders*.[50]

Every paragraph of these pamphlets displays the intimacy with which Pope knew the contents of Curll's advertising. This becomes even more important when we come to *The Dunciad*, where the notes and appendices could not have been compiled without reference to this source. The clash between Pope and Curll may be said to enact the classic encounter of literary man and commercial opportunist. *The Dunciad* dramatises Grub Street mores, and appropriately it makes telling use of the new publicity channels which Curll, above all, had exploited. There is reference after reference to show that Pope was a keen student of advertising columns: the poem displays 'dauntless Curll' competing in attention-seeking with fellow-booksellers. For this reason Curll belongs in the company of Cibber, Rich and Henley; like them, he has pioneered new modes of winning public notice.[51] The furore which greeted *The Dunciad* on its first appearance—with crowds of authors 'besieging' the shop, and booksellers and hawkers clamouring to get hold of copies—reflects this set of circumstances: but so does the text itself.

Another feature of the booksellers' contest in Book II is the award to Curll of a consolation prize:

> A shaggy Tapistry, worthy to be spread
> On Codrus' old, or Dunton's modern bed;
> Instructive work! whose wry-mouth'd portraiture
> Display'd the fates her confessors endure.
>
> (A II, 135-8)

The worsted carries effigies of Defoe, Tutchin, and others: it is to Grub Street what the shield of Achilles is to the world of Homeric heroes. Its barbaric heraldry suggests the crude but vigorous popular art of Hanoverian London: signs rattling above people as they went about their business, playbills, posters. We recall that Martinus Scriblerus had been mesmerised by 'a large square piece of Canvas' portraying the sights at a freak show: that Swift depicted himself as 'fasten'd by the Eyes' to the 'painted Monsters' at Charing Cross: and that Gay mentions in *Trivia* swinging signs, painted booths, and breathless hawkers. There is an obvious link here with the show-cloths in Hogarth's early works: *Masquerades and Operas* has a large cloth hanging out, near the centre of the picture, illustrating operatic affairs, whilst a harlequin who may represent John Rich points up to a poster for the current pantomime at Lincoln's Inn Fields. In *Southwark Fair* there are at least five show-cloths in addition to painted signs.

Swift, an inveterate loiterer who would hover on the fringe of any show or spectacle, gives abundant evidence of the enticements set before the public. One example occurs in his satire on Gilbert Burnet, and concerns the Bishop's decision to release an 'introduction' to the third volume of his *History of the Reformation*, some time in advance of the work proper. Swift sneers at this habit of 'producing a small Pamphlet to give Notice of a large Folio', and then works round to a characteristic analogy:

> I have seen the same Sort of Management at a Puppet Show. Some Puppets of little or no Consequence appeared several Times at the Window, to allure the Boys and Rabble: The Trumpeter sounded often, and the Door-keeper cried an hundred times, until he was Hoarse, that they were just going to begin; yet after all, we were forced some Times to wait an Hour before *Punch* himself in Person made his Entry.[52]

Notice that 'we' in the final sentence. Swift appears not to be dramatising for implicative effect so much as re-living his own impatient response to promotional tactics.

The emphasis placed on such publicity devices helps us to understand the drift of satire. A gullible audience is lured by hucksters and charlatans, expert in the new blandishments of a consumer society. Typically the satirists present to us the poster rather than the show itself, as though to say, 'You aren't missing anything.' More widely, one might describe this vein of satire as constituting a kind of poster art. The vivid colours of Hogarth's painting, the garish crowd-scenes of *The Dunciad*, the vaunting self-assertion of *A Tale of a Tub*: each in some way mimics the vulgar energy of the world it criticises. Frederick Antal has written that it is a measure of Hogarth's closeness to popular art that 'his works could so readily be transposed back into it',[53] for example in pantomimic versions of *The Harlot's Progress*. It might equally be said that the literary satires of Swift, Pope and Gay take on some of the demotic life of brash showmanship that exists within contemporary London. Gulliver's engraving regaled the eyes of everyone who passed the print-shop, whilst Macheath and Polly Peachum appeared on snuff-boxes and fans. It was Heidegger who brought the star system to opera, Rich who made freak-shows part of theatre, Curll who conducted literary debate within the pages of newspaper columns. But it was the satirists who captured these innovations, in their pristine rawness, their unembarrassed exhibitionism.

Showmen and Statesmen

In 1752 an anonymous satirist brought out a poem attacking John Hill, entitled *The Pasquinade*. It was one of many works modelled on *The Dunciad*, and here the imitation extends to the presence of a tutelary goddess named Pertness. The connection with Pope is made explicitly:

> Far hence the goddess spreads her kingdom wide,
> To Dulness, as in birth, in power allied.
> *She*, from her native Grub Street to Rag Fair,
> South to the Mint and west to Temple-Bar,

Included every garrison'd retreat—
Bedlam, Crane-Court, the Counters, and the Fleet;
Her sister boasted as extensive sway;
Fierce Broughton's bruizing sons her power obey;
St Giles's, George's, and the famous train
Of Bedford, Bow Street, and of Drury Lane.
Even the licens'd Park her chief resort,
And seize the privilege of great George's court.[54]

The syntactical muddle at the end weakens the satire; nevertheless, the idiom is recognisably Popian, with a watered-down version of the critique of fashionable Dulness. George II is still at the centre of the picture, having outlived Caroline, Walpole and Hervey, as well as Pope, Swift and Gay. The sights of London are still in evidence—Bedlam, the Park, the boxing booth. Modish entertaiment continues to be aligned with court patronage.

This critique goes back many years, but its high point occurs during the ascendancy of Walpole. The prime minister was repeatedly characterised as Punch, or as a *farceur*, or as a fiddler, or as a gang-boss, or a master of ceremonies. As I suggested earlier, this made it particularly handy for Opposition writers to enlist the promoters and publicists for the purpose of opprobious comparison. Walpole was accused of making politics into a business, a kind of crooked scheme to defraud the public, or alternatively a rigged lottery. This led to identification with Sir John Blunt, or Charteris, or William Wood. The Drapier is constantly gunning at the English government through the person of the contemptible tinker, Wood; and the same animus is apparent when Swift refers in a poem to Wood's '*Brazen Shield*'.[55] (*Brass* and *Screen* were nicknames for Walpole.) Again, the Opposition claimed that Walpole protected guilty men, and covered up malpractices: hence his identification with Wild. But the main thrust of the case emerged in satiric portrayals of Walpole as the great showman of state. Several examples of this habit will come under scrutiny in this book. Here I wish to suggest that there was a measure of accident about the satirists' cast of villains. Colley Cibber became laureate as well as theatrical manager, and thus qualified for the role of 'Lord-Chancellor of Plays' in *The Dunciad* (A III, 320). In many ways his son Theophilus, who gets a brief mention at A III, 131-4, would have been as appropriate a choice. Equally Beau Nash would have fitted the part admirably had his sphere of influence been situated in London, where the action clearly required it. Curll was too remote from the court to serve as arch-Dunce, though he did have his contacts with Walpole, as an informer.[56] But the men who straddle the world of fashion and the alleys of Smithfield, who unite high life and low art, meet the desiderata most closely. Thus the central role taken by the showmen who brought cheap spectacle to the royal theatres, and who let loose dancing dogs in aristocratic quarters of Westminster. The old, scattered 'sights' of the town had been given an official home, with court blessing.

The moment when court and spectacle mingled most intimately was during the coronation festivities. In the pages that follow I argue that this is a recurrent image in the buried fantasy life of *The Dunciad*. This contention involves the recognition of Elkanah Settle as a kind of *ur*-impresario, a pageant contriver for 'worthy' causes—civic, patriotic, protestant. He was the last of the City Poets, and the one who survived into an era when the verbal side of Lord Mayor's pageants died out, leaving only show and spectacle. There had been a time when it was just about possible to think of these municipal occasions as offering the basis for serious, or near-serious, art. Thomas Dekker's pageant of 1612, *Troia-Nova Triumphans*, illustrates this capacity; it was written in an era when masque was a live form, dressing ideology in convincing allegorical terms.[57] But by the end of the seventeenth century it was harder to sustain the Brutus myth, and harder to animate stock mythology. Pope constantly subverts these very things in *The Dunciad*, making the parallel between Troy and London a baneful prophecy, and turning the routine personifications into malignant monsters with horrid topical overtones ('*Wit* dreads Exile, Penalties and Pains').[58] Certainly Settle could not halt the decline of the pageants, and by the early eighteenth century the Lord Mayor's 'show' had become what it is today—a procession with sundry happenings *en route*.[59]

This processional element is deeply important within Augustan literature. It underlies Dryden's panegyrics, and appears only slightly transmuted in notable setpieces by Hogarth—*Masquerades and Operas*, most relevantly to this book, but also *The March to Finchley*, 'Chairing the Member' from the *Election* series, and elsewhere. Cibber at Drury Lane and Rich at Covent Garden presided over elaborate 'processions' at the time of a coronation. (Rich's other ideas in this line included a funeral procession for the heroine in *Romeo and Juliet*. When the great actress Mrs George Anne Bellamy told Rich that the large audiences had come along to see her perform, the manager disabused her: 'It is owing to the *procession*.')[60] The capacity of satirists to incorporate this popular mode of representation was often crucial to their success. They were able to reproduce that stately fatuity which processions can easily seem to embody. Above all, in *The Dunciad*, momentum is derived from the reader's sense of crowds in motion, eager to celebrate their Queen, now festive and now ugly, marching nowhere in particular with a sort of glazed intensity: 'a vast involuntary throng', a 'black blocade', stepping onwards to the sound of drums and trumpets:

There march'd the bard and blockhead, side by side. (B IV, 101)[61]

Such processions image a motley concourse of people, drawn on in the quest for novelty and sensation, just as—the satirist imply—the popular entertainments lure their audience.

It can be no accident that both Pope and Hogarth incorporated in their work a frontal treatment of the Lord Mayor's Day parade. *The Dunciad*, as I try to show in Chapter 5, makes both open and covert allusion to this branch of ceremonial, fixing on the special festivities of 1727 as an indication of the City's political loyalty. More widely the poem harks back to the allegorical vocabulary of the shows in its own diction. The dragons and monsters in Book III recall not just Rich's theatrical displays—as is usually supposed—but also the traditional features of Lord Mayor's processions. A contemporary pamphlet tells us that the two great giants, Corineus and Magog, needed restoration owing to the ravages of time. Around 1708, 'the dissolution of the two old, weak and feeble giants gave birth to the two present substantial and majestic giants ... Captain Richard Saunders, an eminent carver in King Street, Cheapside, was their father; who, after he had completely finished, clothed and armed these his two sons, they were immediately advanced to those lofty stations in

Guildhall, which they have peacefully enjoyed every since the year 1708'.[62] This crude pageantry lies behind much of the poem, as for instance the statement that Dulness

> Sees Gods with Daemons in strange league ingage,
> And earth, and heav'n, and hell her battles wage.
> (A I, 107–8)

Everyone alive in this era was familiar with the effigies carried in procession through the street, for which November was apparently the favourite month: Queen Elizabeth's birthday was somehow mixed up with Guy Fawkes saturnalia, and as we shall see the Lord Mayor's show of 1727 was viewed as a sequel or prolongation of the Coronation.[63]

Hogarth's reaponse is necessarily different: his Lord Mayor's show forms a triumphant culmination to the progress of the industrious apprentice (no. 12 in the sequence). It contrasts directly with the destination reserved for his idle brother, the gallows at Tyburn. 'Riches and honour', as the caption tells us, are held out by the Book of Proverbs as the reward of diligence. The scene, then, is for once unsatiric in its main bearings. However, the visual detail (crowds, effigies, posters and signs, hawkers and militia-men) includes many elements found in the ominous processionals of Augustan satire.

According to Robert W. Malcolmson, the urban-industrial population of the later eighteenth century found few ready-made diversions in the city:

> Much of the rural past had to be set aside, and most of the migrants discovered that the expanding urban centres had, as yet, only an extremely raw and restricted recreational culture to put in its place.[64]

This is not the sense one gets in London at least, during the early part of the century. Labourers were not among the subscribers to the Haymarket opera company; but we know that quite poor people from the less privileged quarters of London did patronise the West End theatre.[65] However, the immediate point is that a considerable expansion of organised entertainment was in progress by the second quarter of the century, linked to new means of publicity and involving larger capital outlay. Men like Swift, Pope and Hogarth,[66] who had enjoyed the older sights and spectacles, found this professionalisation of leisure a cause for satiric concern: it fitted in all too neatly with the 'projects' in politics and economics they so much distrusted:

> It is true, I have been concerned for several years past, upon account of the publick as well as of myself, to see how ill a taste for wit and sense prevails in the world, which politicks and South-sea, and party, and Opera's and Masquerades have introduced.

(Thus Swift to Pope in 1721.)[67] Defoe, meanwhile, working in the market-place, took on Grub Street frontally, rather than by means of parody. Much of the greatest literature of the age is thus implicated in popular culture, either by way of competition or by way of critical exploration. The subject-matter of high art incorporates newspaper advertisements, playbills, conjurers' turns, opera-house tiffs, street-carnivals. These and allied matters occupy my attention in the chapters which follow.

Notes

Epigraphs: Swift, *Poems*, I, 172; *Joseph Andrews and Shamela*, ed. Douglas Brooks (London, 1970), pp. 140-1.

1. *Journal to Stella*, I, 121-2; II, 647. For moving picture shows, *see also* Ashton, pp. 216-17; Altick, pp. 58-63.
2. *See The Memoirs of Martinus Scriblerus*, ed. Charles Kerby-Miller (New Haven, 1950; rptd New York, 1966), p. 143.
3. Swift, *Corr.* IV. 57.
4. *Spectator*, I, 211. For Swift's response to this paper, *see Journal to Stella*, I, 254-5: and Richmond P. Bond, *Queen Anne's American Kings* (Oxford 1952), pp. 85-6. The Indian Kings themselves made the usual round of visits—the Tower, Bedlam, Gresham College, etc: Bond, pp. 6-10. In their honour special shows were mounted, not just at the Haymarket, but also at Powell's puppet theatre and Hockley in the Hole (*see* p. 200 below).
5. *See* J.H. Plumb, *The Commercialisation of Leisure in Eighteenth-century England* (Reading, 1973).
6. Ned Ward, *The London Spy*, ed. A.L. Hayward (London, 1927), *passim*.
7. Austin Dobson, 'Prefatory Note' to *Side-Walk Studies* (London, 1924). The edition quoted is that of the World's Classics, and it is worth recalling that six of Dobson's books appeared in this estimable series.

8. Review of *Eighteenth Century Vignettes*, quoted on the end-paper of *A Paladin of Philanthropy* (London, 1899).
9. A good impression of a provincial town as the centre of culture and amusement is provided by the chapter on 'Diversions' in Edward Hughes, *North Country Life in the Eighteenth Century* (London, 1952), pp. 380–406.
10. Robert W. Malcolmson, *Popular Recreations in English Society* (Cambridge, 1973), pp. 56–71. Malcolmson observes that 'during the first half of the eighteenth century in particular, many gentlemen were not entirely disengaged from the culture of the people. They frequently occupied something of a half-way house between the robust, unpolished culture of provincial England and the cosmopolitan, sophisticated culture which was based in London. Most of the country-houses were not yet principally seasonal extensions of a polite and increasingly self-conscious urban culture, and many of their occupants remained relatively uncitified' (p. 68). There is some truth in this, certainly, although it applies to the lesser squirearchy rather than to the truly influential members of the governing class.
11. *See* Malcolmson, pp. 89–117. Another factor in the demise of such recreations, identified by Malcolmson, was the spread of evangelicism.
12. Quoted in *The History of Parliament: The Commons 1714–1754*, ed. Romney Sedgwick (London, 1970), II, 460.
13. *See* Howard Erskine-Hill, *The Social Milieu of Alexander Pope* (London, 1975) pp. 103–31.
14. Heidegger's age at his death was given as ninety, but little weight can be attached to this: old men were often allotted an exaggerated life-span, and this is particularly likely where they had been born abroad. The birth-date of both Curll and Rich is set too early in standard sources, including *DNB*. Nevertheless, the impresarios were a durable bunch: the men who are mentioned in this paragraph averaged something like seventy-six years. They carried with them the robust and earthy qualities of the seventeenth century, into a more self-consciously refined age. They had the stamina to survive when lesser men would have gone under. In their powers of endurance they recall not only Walpole, but also George II (1683–1760).
15. It is literally true that Blunt, Wood and Walter all had protectors and friends at court, whilst Charteris was known to be a 'runner' for Walpole. Even Wild seems to have been subsidised by the Treasury for a time at least: he certainly had mysterious connections with the 'quality'. But the Opposition attack on Walpole did not absolutely require such links: usually it was enough to suggest that Walpole and Wild *could* have followed the same trade, such were their gifts and characteristics. Incidentally, one of the creditors named in Wild's bankruptcy petition in 1711/12 is 'William Wood.' See Guildhall Library, Insolvent Debtors, f. 228.
16. *DNB*, s.v. Martin Powell—*London Stage* sometimes confuses the puppeteer with the actor George Powell (d. 1714); *Spectator*, I, 61; Ashton, pp. 215–16; Rosenfield, p. 100. Colley Cibber's daughter Charlotte Clarke operated a puppet-theatre in 1738 in the Tennis Court in James Street: previous attractions at this house had been Fawkes, Pinchbeck's musical clock, and a company of 'Lilliputians'—one of many transfers of Swift's masterpiece

to the area of popular entertainment. *See London Stage*, III, xxxiv.

17. Ashton, pp. 212–14; *Spectator*, I, 117; Altick, pp. 52–5 (the best account of eighteenth-century waxworks).

18. Rosenfeld, p. 18. Penkethman was himself an important transitional figure, a straight actor who came to specialise in fairground spectaculars; *see* Altick, pp. 58–60.

19. For the little known about Mrs Ann Mynns, *see* Rosenfeld, pp. 19–20. Her connection with Settle is noted in the *Lives of the Poets* (1753), falsely attributed to Theophilus Cibber. The latter *would* have been a good witness, since he often performed at the fairground.

20. Walter Besant, *London in the Eighteenth Century* (London, 1902; rptd 1925), p. 467. Besant's is another dated, anecdotal work which yet contains invaluable information with regard to such matters as gambling, a crucial activity in Hanoverian London too often passed over by modern historians as a frivolous or aberrant use of time. Altick, pp. 34–49, describes freak-shows in this period.

21. Swift, *Corr*, I, 82.

22. *Memoirs of Scriblerus*, pp. 143–53, 293–9. The raree-show is clearly identified as taking place at the pitch regularly used by a real-life showman, David Randall, in Channel Row, Westminster. For his press advertisements, *see Spectator*, I, 128–9.

23. Pope, *Corr*, I, 277–9.

24. Besant, p. 440; Ashton, p. 224.

25. For Mendoza, *see* J.H. Plumb, 'Sports of fortune', *The Listener*, 19 October 1978, pp. 497–8. On Figg, *see* Philips, pp. 226–7, 286, where he emerges as promoter as much as participant.

26. *Tricks of the Town: Eighteenth Century Diversions*, ed. Ralph Straus (London, 1927), pp. 172, 229.

27. *TE*, V, 91–2.

28. Paul Sawyer, 'John Rich's contribution to the eighteenth-century London stage,' *The Eighteenth-Century English Stage*, ed. K. Richards and P. Thomson (London, 1972), pp. 88–104, supplies the fullest and most up-to-date account of Rich's activities.

29. Sawyer, p. 91.

30. See Ashton, p. 212; *Spectator*, I, 102.

31. Sawyer, pp. 92–3. For the Drury Lane coronation pageant in 1727, see p. 131 below. There was a story that Rich had himself set up the false claim of a fire which disturbed the first night at Drury Lane, and his offer of a reward for discovery of the offender does not altogether allay suspicion. *See* R.H. Barker, *Mr Cibber of Drury Lane* (New York, 1939), p. 140.

32. *TE*, V, 179.

33. Besant, p. 458.

34. J.H. Plumb, 'The Culture Vultures', *The Listener*, 12 October 1978, pp. 470–1, notes the dominance of book advertisements in the provincial press, as an index of middle-class taste. It should be stressed that advertising did much to *create* taste as well as satisfy existing appetites; the new playhouses set up in provincial towns, which Plumb mentions, needed regular outlets for publicity. It was not just that the old 'barns, guildhalls, inns, even

"theatrical booths" ... were too unsophisticated, too barbaric, for those who had experienced the delights of the London theatre', as Plumb points out. The new theatres were *permanently*, rather than intermittently, devoted to dramatic productions. This specialism of function could only pay if the audience was kept continuously informed of the calendar of events.

35. Laurence Hanson, *Government and the Press 1695–1763* (Oxford, 1936; rptd 1967), pp. 7–33.

36. John Brewer, *Party Ideology and Popular Politics at the Accession of George III* (Cambridge, 1976), pp. 139–60: quotation from p. 142. Brewer's book is especially valuable in showing how politicians began to enlist the new techniques of publicity: he argues that John Wilkes was the first 'political entrepreneur ... [who] made a business of politics, especially of political journalism' (p. 198). I would add only that it was not Wilkes, but other leisure entrepreneurs like Curll who pioneered the use of handbills, planted newspaper stories, street theatre and other publicity devices.

37. Gerald Howson, *Thief-Taker General* (London, 1970), p. 225.

38. Data from G.A. Cranfield, *A Hand-List of English Provincial Newspapers and Periodicals 1700–1760*, Cambridge Bibliographical Society Monograph No. 2 (London, rev. edn, 1961). The standard account is Cranfield's book on *The Development of the Provincial Newspaper 1700–1760* (Oxford, 1962), a work of considerable relevance to all students of the period, which illuminates many of the issues discussed in this book. Many of the pioneers of the English provincial newspaper were men in the same mould as the great impresarios: in their smaller orbit such figures as Robert Raikes, Felix Farley, Andrew Brice and Henry Crossgrove exhibited the same qualities of commercial shrewdness, willingness to flout authority, and restless ambition. Cranfield, *Development of the Newspaper*, pp. 51–6, discusses the career of Robert Walker as foreshadowing the later 'press barons' in his appreciation of the new opportunities.

39. R.L. Munter, *A Hand-List of Irish Newspapers 1685–1750*, Cambridge Bibliographical Society Monograph No. 4 (London, 1960). Munter observes in his Introduction, 'a complete social history could be written from this one, largely ignored source', and argues that the early newspapers 'not only symbolized historical developments of great significance, but were themselves active forces in promoting this development' (p. xi). In no respect is this dual significance more apparent than in the advertising function of the press. For a good survey of the beginnings of press advertising in Ireland, see Munter's book, *The History of the Irish Newspaper* (Cambridge, 1967), pp. 55–62.

40. On distribution methods see Cranfield, *Development of the Newspaper*, pp. 190–205.

41. Cranfield, *Development of the Newspaper*, pp. 207–23, discusses advertising, and also on pp. 224–56 newspaper finances. Advertising rates in the provinces are quoted on pp. 226–7. They are not far out of line with London rates reported by D. Nichol Smith, 'The newspaper', *Johnson's England*, ed. A.S. Turberville (Oxford, 1933), II, 362–6. *See also Spectator*, I, lxix–lxx.

42. Significantly Cranfield is forced to exclude patent medicine advertisements from his main count, since the newspaper proprietor frequently has a direct interest or concession in these products, and would not be paid for insertions. *See Development of the newspaper* pp. 209, 233–4.

43. Cranfield points out that the use of *Advertiser* as part of a newspaper title became more frequent around 1740 (*Development of the Newspaper*, p. 227). This was somewhat in advance of London practice, where the tendency is most marked in the 1740s and 1750s. Obviously the title reflects a genuine fact about the paper's contents and its appeal.

44. *See London Stage*, II, lxxxix–xcv; and see esp. pp. xciii–xciv on puffs in newspaper editorial columns. It was part of the flair for publicity displayed by the entrepreneurs that they could get their activities talked about in any part of the paper. Thus Curll is the object of comment in Mist's paper, whilst Heidegger and Handel regularly turn up along with the star singers in the *London Journal* during the 1720s and 1730s. Mock playbills were sometimes used in satire: see the example quoted by Maynard Mack, *The Garden and the City* (Toronto, 1969), p. 129.

45. *London Stage*, II, xc.

46. Paulson, I, 43–54.

47. *Selections from the Tatler and the Spectator*, ed. Robert J. Allen (New York, 1957), pp. 43–7.

48. Phillips, p. 158; *see also* Richmond P. Bond, *The Tatler: the Makings of a Literary Journal* (Cambridge, Mass., 1971), pp. 175–6. For Lillie as a promoter of the new fashion for snuff, *see* Ashton, pp. 158–9. For other references, *see Spectator*, I, xxii–xxiv, 73–4; II, 46–7 (a mock-advertisement in the text); II, 507 (Lillie as agent for subscription concerts).

49. *The Prose Works of Alexander Pope*, ed. Norman Ault (Oxford, 1936; rptd 1968), pp. 263, 265, 273.

50. *See* below, pp. 187–90.

51. The quarrels of Pope and Curll are in serious need of an up-to-date scholarly treatment: meanwhile, the fullest information will be found in the notes to *The Dunciad* in *TE*, V, *passim*; and (not well documented) in Ralph Straus, *The Unspeakable Curll* (London, 1927), esp. pp. 49–64, 122–39, 154–87. Not only does Straus base his catalogue of Curll's productions (pp. 201–314) chiefly on Curll's own publicity: the main text of the book is heavily dependent on the same source. The narrative repeatedly quotes press advertisements by the two major combatants, along with side-notices by others caught up in the struggle. For one major episode in the contest, *see* 'The case of Pope vs. Curll,' *The Library*, xxvii (1972), 326–31. John Henley, who often figures in the text of Straus's book, was equally celebrated for his eccentric advertising: an early satire by Fielding makes special allusion to this fact. *See* Isobel Grundy, 'New verse by Henry Fielding', *PMLA*, LXXXVII (1972), 232. For Richard Savage's account of the furore attending publication of *The Dunciad*, see *TE*, V, xxii.

52. Swift, *Prose*, IV, 58.

53. Frederick Antal, *Hogarth and his Place in European Art* (London, 1962), p. 55.

54. Quoted by Thomas Wright, *Caricature History of the Georges* (London, n.d.), p. 227.

55. Swift, *Poems*, I, 340.

56. Straus, pp. 94–6. Orator Henley was a coadjutor in this episode. For another offer of 'help' concerning Bolingbroke's activities, *see* Curll to Walpole, 31 March 1730, Cholmondley (Houghton) Mss, Corr 1839, Cambridge University Library: and for information against 'that noted Hockley in the Hole-Squire', Eustace Budgell, *see* Curll to Walpole, n.d. [*c.* 1733], Cholmondley (Houghton) MSS, Corr 2086.

57. *See* F. W. Fairchild, *Lord Mayors' Pageants* (London, 1844), II, 7–32.

58. *Dunciad* B IV, 22 (*TE*, V, 342).

59. *See* Robert Witherington, *English Pageantry: An Historical Outline* (Cambridge, Mass., 1920), II, 65–6. A showman who performed equally at the Lord Mayor's procession, Tyburn executions, and the annual fairs was the eccentric 'Tiddy-doll', who is depicted by Hogarth in *Industry and Idleness*. *See* Phillips, p. 79.

60. Sawyer, p. 93. For the 'processional' device in panegyric, *see* James D. Garrison, *Dryden and the Tradition of Panegyric* (1975), p. 85. Panegyric is of course the legitimate sister of satire.

61. *TE*, V, 351. There were popular prints showing the progress of lavish processions through the city streets: for one example, *see* Phillips, pp. 166–76.

62. *The Gigantic History of the Famous Giants in Guildhall, London* (3rd edn, 1741), quoted by Christina Hole, *English Sports and Pastimes* (London, 1949), pp. 129–30.

63. For Swift's account of a Whig street-carnival in November 1711, *see* *Journal to Stella*, II, 415–16. For the relevance of Pope-burning ceremonies to *The Dunciad*, see *TE*, V, 183, and Pat Rogers, *Grub Street: Studies in a Sub-Culture* (London, 1972), pp. 112–13. The first critic explicitly to recognise the importance of civic pageants in the poem was Williams, pp. 29–41, although he does not see Pope's treatment of 'the whole clutter of the age's official symbols' as pointing in the direction indicated here.

64. Malcolmson, p. 117.

65. For one example, *see* Pat Rogers, *Henry Fielding: A Biography* (London, 1979), p. 211, concerning a poor girl from the East End of London who came to see a harlequinade by Rich and lost her scanty stock of money.

66. There is enough congruence in both the objects of attack and the satiric means to make this conjunction plausible; it is one which this book will, I hope, help to solidify. There are of course personal factors which precluded a direct Hogarth-Scriblerus connection. These included Hogarth's politics, and his link with the court painter Thornhill; his apparent willingness to satirise Pope at the start of his career, owing to the poet's association with Kent; and later his own friendship with John Rich. However, these minor differences in outlook are much less important than the profound sympathies present in the art of Hogarth and the Scriblerian group. I do not seek to show a concerted design, or simple 'influence': rather a shared response, a kind of fascinated outrage at the way things were going.

67. Swift, *Corr*, II, 368; *see also* Pat Rogers, 'Gulliver and the engineers', *MLR*, XXX (1975), 260–70. For a crowd scene linking theatricality with

projecting, see the print *The Great Mirror of Folly* in the Guildhall Library. This shows harlequins, card-sharpers, company promoters, a raree-show and other 'performers', framed by a proscenium arch. The setting is the Rue Quincampoix, but a year later it would have been Exchange Alley.

1

MASQUERADES AND OPERAS

Hogarth, Heidegger and others

Apr. 18 [1720] At the Lincolnsh.ᵣ Feast, Ship Tavern, Temple barr.
pres.ₜ Sir Is. Newton. Upon my mentioning to him the rehearsal of
the Opera to night (Rhodomisto) he said he never was at more than
one Opera. The first Act he heard with Pleasure, the 2d stretch'd his
patience, at the 3d he ran away.
2 June. Surprizeing scene in Change Alley. South Sea in the
morning above 900, in the evening 700 p cₜ, it has rose 100 p diem for
2 or 3 days. Professions and shops are forgot, all goe thither as to the
mines of Potosi. Nobility, Ladys, Brokers, & footmen all upon a level.
Great equipages setting up, the prices of things rose exorbitantly.
Such a renversement of the order of Nature as succeeding ages can
have no Idea of.
Sept. 23 1720. South Sea fallen from 1000 to 400. The world in the
utmost distraction—thousands of families ruin'd.
The Family Memoirs of the Reverend William Stukeley, M.A., ed. W. C.
Lukis (1882)

> Blest *H*[eide]*g*[ge]*r*, that could invent,
> A Scheme both Sexes to content!
> What longing Wife, what melting Maid,
> Who sighs not for a *Masquerade?*
> *Marriage A-la-Mode: An Humorous Tale* (1746)

In February 1724 William Hogarth achieved his first major
success with a print originally entitled *The Bad Taste of the Town*.
It has subsequently become better known as *Masquerades and
Operas*. There are two states of the engraving, which became
sufficiently popular to attract the attentions of pirates, and to set
off a running battle between Hogarth and plagiarists within the
trade. Valuable background to this print has been supplied by
Ronald Paulson, who shows the density of topical reference in its
crowded design.[1] My aim here is to explore this background from

40

a different angle, and to locate the satiric message within that wider context of debate concerning popular entertainment which is one of the themes of this book. I wish to suggest, too, some of the socio-political overtones of the print, which link it in certain respects with Hogarth's other early 'crowd scenes', *The South Sea Scheme* (1721) and *The Lottery* (1724).

The composition is organised around three principal elements. To the left is the Haymarket Opera-House, home not just of musical entertainments, but also of masquerades, conjuring-shows, and lottery-draws. In the background, centre, stands the gate of Burlington House, the sumptuous mansion in Piccadilly created for the arch-Palladian Earl. To the right is represented Lincoln's Inn Fields theatre, where John Rich had achieved huge success with his new pantomimes loosely tied to topical events. These three structures leave a triangular space, itself occupied by three groups of people. On the left is a queue of mixed character, led by a satyr and a fool into the Opera-House. On the right is a more turbulent mass of people thrusting their way into the pantomime. Between these groups passes a single figure, a woman hawker pushing a wheelbarrow full of books between the two crowds, with the cry 'Waste paper for shops!'. The books are identified as the works of Shakespeare, Dryden, Congreve and so on.[2] Near the apex of the triangle stands a detached group of three men: the central figure has been identified as Lord Burlington himself, flanked by his architect Colen Campbell and his postilion.[3]

The composition divides itself into two separate planes or eye-levels. All the persons I have just mentioned are found on the lower level, along with the entrance to the buildings. On the upper level are found three corresponding sections, each with its appropriate label and symbol. To the left, the first floor of the Opera-House contains a show-cloth representing opera, a sign advertising the conjuror Fawkes,[4] and the celebrated countenance of John James Heidegger, as the impresario gazes down from the upstairs window on the throng below. In the centre Burlington House gate is labelled proleptically 'Academy of Arts'; on the very top of the pediment is placed a statue of William Kent, supported by Michelangelo and Raphael. To the right, Lincoln's Inn Theatre displays a poster for the pantomime *Dr Faustus*, and a harlequin figure welcoming the crowd which presses urgently into the theatre.

The symbolism is quite transparent: in the words of Derek Jarrett, 'traditional English culture, in the shape of authors whose works were being carted off for waste paper, was about to be engulfed in a flood of fashionable foolishness'.[5] Paulson is right, too, when he emphasises the role of the new middle men in the entertainment industry: 'Three groups can be distinguished: the nobility; the rest of the people, lured by their patronage; and the impresarios like Heideggar who exploit the satyr and the fool in both of these classes.'[6] The targets are for the most part unmistakable. Heidegger is identifiable by a letter H beneath him, quite apart from his notorious physiognomy.[7] The harlequin may stand directly for John Rich, who performed grotesque dances in his own shows. William Kent is duly labelled, whilst large letters proclaim the metaphoric (if not literal) presence of the conjuror 'FAUX'. Among the principals only Burlington is not plainly identified: wise discretion which extended to the caption in the original print. The eight lines of verse refer only to 'monsters and masquerades' on the English stage, with no reference at all to architectural matters.[8] The common title 'Masquerades and Operas' applies literally only to the left-hand side of the design, but the verses refer particularly to the right-hand grouping.

Thus far, we have come on nothing either new or surprising. It would be possible to explore details of the composition further. For example, the isolation of the Burlington group at the back draws attention to their remote, élite status. Whereas the other groups, to left and right, are thickly packed together, buffeting one another in their anxiety to get inside, the Burlington trio stand in an elegantly leisured pose. Nobody is watching them, unless it is Kent (who benefits financially, as do Heidegger and Rich). The only other isolated figure is the woman with her barrow, ploughing a lonely furrow down the very middle of the print, and trundling her laborious way past unresponsive hordes. As contemporary observers pointed out, the door of Burlington gate is massively shut, whereas the theatrical entrances are doors are enticingly open.[9] In addition, there are guardsmen standing by the theatre queues: Paulson suggests their presence indicates royal approval. They may also hint at possible disorders, riots in the playhouse or misbehaviour at the masquerade.[10]

However, detailed explication along these lines is not my present concern. I wish to stress rather the symmetry of the conception, and the direct equivalence drawn between masquerades and pantomimes, operas and harlequinades. It is quite certain that the entertainment to be offered at the Opera-House is one of Heidegger's masquerades, although he was also connected with the opera. Above the door is written 'Masquerade', and this rather than the signs hanging above indicates this evening's attraction. The devil at the head of the procession is brandishing a note for £1000, which 'may refer either to the king's annual grant of that amount to the Royal Academy of Music, or to the Prince of Wales' donation of that amount in support of Heidegger's masquerades' (Paulson).[11] Probably it is both, but the latter predominates, for the mingled throng which form the queue are themselves in masquerade dress. Their costumes are those popular on such occasions: a bishop, a milkmaid, a clown, a Grand Turk, a chimney sweep and so on. Of course one suggestion is that all sorts and conditions of men and women are drawn to the Opera-House (just as there are peers and menials among the Lincoln's Inn Fields queue): but there is at the same time an implied comment on the habit of masquerade itself, in its reliance on deception.

I shall have more to say in due course about some of the particular allusions visible in Hogarth's composition. But the main issue before us is more general in character. What precisely was wrong with masquerades and operas, and why did the unpuritanical, spectacle-loving Hogarth link them together in this fashion, along with other popular entertainments of the day?[12]

I

The opposition to Italian opera is better known than are the attacks on masquerades, and I shall approach the matter from this angle. There was by 1724 a history of something like fifteen years' denunciation and ridicule. The first English opera, all sung, on the Italian model, was Thomas Clayton's *Arsinoe* (1705). With the opening in that year of the new theatre in the Haymarket, there was another outlet along with Drury Lane for the increasingly popular form. The opera house at first suffered from problems of acoustics, but in time these had been overcome. From 1710 Italian opera dominated the calendar at the Haymarket, and works such as Mancini's *L'Idaspe Fedele* and Handel's *Rinaldo* acquired considerable renown. The counterwave of opposition dates from the same period, with John Dennis among the first in the field in his *Essay on the Operas after the Italian Manner* (1706), lamenting the influence which 'the soft and effeminate Measures of the Italian Opera have upon the Minds and Manners of Men'. The moral precepts of spoken drama demand for their utterance 'a great many Consonants ... which cannot be pronounced without very frequently shutting the Mouth, which is diametrically oppos'd to the expressing of Musick'. This ingenious argument from phonetics reached the predictable conclusion that opera was 'below the Dignity' of the British Nation.[13] The element of xenophobia was echoed by Thomas Betterton, who deplored the ruination of serious drama while English men and women gave 'prodigal Subscriptions for Squeaking Italians and Capring Monsieurs'. He also thought it absurd that battle orders should be delivered in song, and soldiers 'melodiously kill'd with Sword, Pike or Musket'.[14]

It was however *Idaspe*, or *Hydaspes*, which prompted the most celebrated riposte. Addison had already offered some gentle satire of Rinaldo in *Spectator* No. 5 (6 March 1711); Steele weighed in ten days later (No. 14) and Addison kept up the attack in subsequent weeks (see nos. 29 and 31). In the latter paper he makes sport with the 'Projector' of the opera. The most considered attempt to devise a rationale for opposition came in no. 18 (21 March 1711), arguing for English-style drama as 'a much nobler Entertainment'. But the most amusing and noteworthy paper is no. 13 (15 March 1711), which makes superb fun of the lion which figured prominently in the cast of *Hydaspes*.[15] At the same juncture Steele attempted to organise recitals in York Buildings, regularly advertised in the *Spectator*, to serve as a showcase for a more sensible English medium, where the words would occupy a more central place and where there would be no 'squeaking Italian' like the castrato Nicolini. The project failed, in spite of Steele's plan to obtain the services of Pope to provide a musical interlude. As with Addison's English opera of 1707, *Rosamund*, the compositional talents of Thomas

Clayton proved unequal to the task. The search for a native form
to rival the Italian went on, with a leading figure the Buttonian
and poet-musician John Hughes. Hughes versified some of the
familiar objections ('Lull'd statesmen melt away their drowsy
cares/Of England's safety in Italian airs'). He supplied the
libretto for an English opera to music by Galliard, *Calypso and
Telemachus* (1712), but theatrical politics ensured its failure.[16]

In the next few years Italian opera lost some ground, even
without any effective English alternative. It was to remedy this
situation that the Royal Academy of Music was founded in 1719,
by about sixty prominent men. They were headed by the Lord
Chamberlain, the Duke of Newcastle, who subscribed £1000; the
minimum figure was £200, a sum guaranteed by peers,
politicians, courtiers, soldiers and diplomats. Even wealthy
merchants were permitted to join in: Dr Arbuthnot represented a
Scriblerian toehold in the operation. The proposed stock of
£10,000 was oversubscribed by more than fifty percent: opera,
always an expensive undertaking, was now entering the sphere of
high-risk capitalism. Newcastle became Governor and the Duke
of Manchester was elected Deputy Governor, to head a panel of
directors who inclined Arbuthnot. This was slightly ominous
phraseology in November 1719, less than a year before the great
Bubble burst. The King's grant of £1,000 per annum could be
differently viewed according to one's standpoint. Handel was
appointed 'Master of Music' and commissioned by Newcastle to
recruit a team of star singers. Heidegger became general
manager and Paolo Antonio Rolli librettist and artistic
consultant.[17]

The Academy seasons began in 1720, but not until the arrival
of the great castrato Senesino for the second season, in November
of that year, did the new venture make a real impact. Senesino
had signed his contract with Handel for no less than £2,000 (later
1400 guineas), an immense figure by the standards of the day.
The leading soprano supporting him received about half as
much. Senesino immediately captured London: Mrs Pendarves
wrote to her sister that he was 'beyond Nicolini both in person
and voice'. At the end of 1722 he was joined by the equally
famous *prima donna* Cuzzoni: newspapers reported the
impatience with which she had been awaited, and even gave the
size of the advance (£250) which Heidegger had been obliged to

pay in order to ensure her arrival.[18] Handel was writing one or two operas each season for the Academy, and despite continuing financial difficulties the Italian opera attained an almost flourishing condition at this juncture. The later part of the decade was to witness a decline, until the final dissolution in 1728. Throughout this period the opera remained news, particularly at the time of the celebrated fracas between Cuzzoni and her new rival Faustina, in June 1727:[19] but the high point of the Haymarket venture must be placed earlier—around the time Hogarth's print appeared.

By this date the chorus of opposition had grown louder. In February 1723 Gay wrote to Swift:

> As for the reigning Amusement of the town, tis entirely Musick. real fiddles, Bass Viols and Hautboys not poetical Harps, Lyres and reeds. Theres nobody allowed to say I sing but an Eunuch or an Italian Woman. Every body is grown now as great a judge of Musick as they were in your time of Poetry, and folks that could not distinguish one tune from another now daily dispute about the different Styles of Hendel, Bonocini and Attillio. People have now forgot Homer, and Virgil & Caesar, or at least they have lost their ranks, for in all polite conversation's Senesino is daily voted to be the greatest man that ever liv'd.[20]

There is perhaps more of a narrow littérateur about this complaint than of the broad humanist: but Gay was not alone in his feelings. Indeed, the success of *The Beggar's Opera* five years later was to show that many were tired of the highflown aristocratic airs Italian opera gave itself. As Roger Fiske remarks, the enthusiasm for this form had 'affected only a coterie of society people and intellectuals';[21] even among the latter group there was a substantial corps of dissidents. The satire in Gay's masterpiece no doubt reached a receptive public, for whom the novelty had worn off. Henry Carey voiced some widely shared sentiments in a poem he included in his 1729 collection—to which Handel, incidentally, subscribed:

> I hate this singing in an unknown tongue,
> It does our reason and our senses wrong;
> When words instruct, and music cheers the mind,
> Then is the art of service to mankind;

> But when a castrate wretch of monstrous size
> Squeaks out a treble, shrill as infant's cries,
> I curse the unintelligible ass,
> Who may, for ought I know, be singing mass.[22]

Similarly, in the second part of *The Fable of the Bees* (1729), through the person of 'Fulvia', Mandeville wrote drily of opera as a purely social ornament of gracious living:

> I never expected anything natural at an Opera; but as Persons of Distinction resort thither, and every body comes dressed, it is a sort of Employment, and I seldom miss a Night, because it is the Fashion to go: Besides, the Royal Favour of the Monarch, generally favouring them with their Presence, it is almost become our Duty to attend them, as much as it is to go to Court.[23]

Here we see George II's fondness for opera enlisted in anti-court, if not downright anti-establishment, satire. By the time Pope came to utilise opera in the *New Dunciad*, there was already a well established tradition of such innuendos.

The charges levelled against Italian opera are disparate and frequently unsupported. They range from outright prejudice to serious aesthetic concern; they spring from such things as jealousy of the power and prestige of London in national life, as well as the purest xenophobia. Fear of innovation allied itself to cultural isolationism; suspicion of court influence among disaffected Country politicians allied itself to Squire Western's brand of bluff John Bull sentiment.[24] That the leading purveyor of Italian opera in the 1720s, Handel, was one of the greatest of all composers did not usually figure centrally in the reckoning of critics. But these are extreme positions: some of the objections relate to deeper fears. They centre in particular on the role of *money* in operatic affairs. The point is difficult to establish with precision, because this line of criticism occurs in a dispersed manner, often submerged in allegory or poetic analogy, and rarely conveyed through open or explicit assertion. None the less, it is possible to make out a case which hangs together reasonably well, and it is one which connects with the critique of other entertainments fashionable in the 1720s.

One of the things which critics found most disturbing was the amount of money opera cost to stage.[25] Even in the early phase the outlay was considerable; in 1708, when no singer had a salary above £430 and the total salary bill for performers was only about £4,000, it still needed £177 nightly to mount the opera. Twenty performancs cost £4,000, exceeding receipts by more than £1,000. By 1725 it was estimated that costs had risen to £16,000 per annum, at a time when Lincoln's Inn Fields theatre got by on less than £11,000, despite the fact that it staged twice as many performances. This steep increase went on unchecked, and press comments in the mid 1730s point to a yearly outlay up to £22,000. Lord Hervey reports the most educated guess in 1734:

> By way of public spectacles this winter, there are no less than two Italian Operas, one French play house, and three English ones. Heidegger has computed the expense of these shows, and proves in black & white that the undertakers must receive seventy-six thousand odd hundred pounds to bear their charges, before they begin to become gainers.[26]

Most of the non-operatic companies (particularly at the Little Theatre in the Haymarket) could operate on a far lower budget, and if Heideggar's estimate is correct we must allocate at least £30,000 to the King's Theatre and Covent Garden—probably £40,000 or more.

Costs of every description had risen, for costumes, scenery, orchestral players and so on. But the most spectacular contribution to these inflated sums had been made by the rise in the singers' rewards. In 1720 Senesino commanded 2,000 guineas for a season, but even this was eclipsed in time. In 1722 Cuzzoni received £2,000 plus a benefit, in addition to other blandishments: her rival Faustina at least matched this figure on arrival in 1726, although she had been receiving only about £1,250 in Vienna. Even second-rank singers could increasingly demand salaries in the range between £500 and £1,000.

To meet these huge costs some regular subsidy was obviously needed. This was indeed the *raison d'être* of the Royal Academy of Music. The original subscription guaranteed something like £25,000, but this was either not enough or not sufficiently calculable in advance. A new scheme introduced in 1721 brought in a system of season tickets, sold at twenty guineas each: perhaps fifty such tickets were sold. The more regular source of income was a 'call' on the subscribers, normally for 5 per cent of their pledge: such calls were made about two or three times a year. In theory there might also be a distribution of profits, but only one dividend (7 per cent in 1723) is known to have been declared. In practice the Academy used the machinery of a joint stock company to subsidise opera, and the 'investors' must have known that they stood to lose more than they could gain in strictly financial terms.[27]

None of this monetary background escaped critics and satirists. The fact that the Academy was set up in 1719, and began its 'calls' just as the South Sea Company stepped up its own calls to subscribers, played into the hands of hostile commentators. As we have seen, the provision of a court of 'directors' under a royal governor directly mimicked the South Sea constitution. The existence of a market in season tickets prompted newspaper comments like this, from March 1723:

> The new Opera Tickets are very high, and like to continue so as long as Mrs Cotzani is so much admired. They are traded in at the other End of the Town, as much as Lottery Tickets are in Exchange-Alley.

The same newspaper wondered whether the Academy might even be 'engrafted on some of our Corporations in the City' if it could show a regular profit. Subscribers who defaulted were threatened by the directors with 'proper measures' to ensure full payment, and again the press took up the story.[28] Public awareness of the whole venture was focussed on its financial standing, as an exercise in risk-capitalism and a potential Bubble, rather than on its artistic qualities.

The rise of a star system, associated with the huge salaries paid to the leading singers, received frequent attention in the press. Another story of March 1723 reads as follows:

> On Tuesday last was perform'd the Opera of Otho, King of Germany, for the Benefit of Mrs. Cuzzoni; and a considerable Benefit it was to her indeed, for we hear that some of the Nobility gave her 50 Guineas a Ticket ... As we delight so much in Italian Songs, we are likely to have enough of them, for as soon as Cuzzoni's Time is out, we are to have another over; for we are well assured, *Faustina*, the fine Songstress at Venice, is invited, whose Voice, they say, exceeds that we have already here; and as the Encouragement is

so great, no doubt but she will visit us, and, like others, when she makes her Exit, may carry off Money enough to build some stateley Edifice in her own Country, and there perpetuate our Folly.[29]

In the event Faustina did not come for another three years: meanwhile, the suggestion that Cuzzoni had become the pet of the aristocracy constantly surfaced in newspaper coverage: 'She is already jumped into a handsome Chariot, and an Equipage accordingly. The Gentry seem to have so high a Taste of her fine parts, that she is likely to be a great Gainer by them.'[30] (A handsome equipage was the symbol of a fortunate Bubble speculator.) The sexual innuendo here is stronger than usual, but the basic theme of a corrupt and profligate gentry bowing down before the foreign stars is common to the 'opposition' case. A different newspaper printed a story that the Italian singers were to go over to France in the summer of 1723 and earn a 'gratuity' of 35,000 livres in return for twelve performances.[31]

Another mark of the superstar, along with colossal rewards, was a *prima donna* temperament. This came to a head in 1727, with the quarrel between Cuzzoni and Faustina; but the signs were apparent much earlier. The Royal Academy had given instructions to Handel in 1719 on how he was to handle negotiations with Senesino: he was 'to mencon pounds Sterling & not Guineas, & to make his Offer for two Years in case he finds him more reasonable, proportionable for two years, than One...'. Performers did not yet have agents, but they were clearly in a position to haggle. In 1720 the well-informed Rolli told a correspondent, 'Cuzzona has been engaged for this year; as for next year she refuses to come for less money than at Siena.' When she did come, as we have seen, she was able to get an advance of £250 from Heidegger, and there was press speculation on the terms she had extorted from an expectant body of opera-lovers. That her benefit nights were a part of the contract is often stressed in newspaper comment.[32]

Cuzzoni, too, though generally regarded as less attractive, had continued to be feted by her admirers. A newspaper report had stated that she was 'visited and entertained by our Nobility and Gentry', and received valuable presents from the same source.[33] It is possible therefore that the show-cloth in Hogarth's print does indeed depict the Earl of Peterborough in the act of offering her

£8,000—which she promptly spurns. This is the identification supplied in the *Graphic Works*, and has always been accepted. I do not think it has been remarked that Peterborough's object of passion was indeed an opera star, but one of English origin. This was Anastasia Robinson, a leading soprano for almost a decade. She had sung second woman in almost all Italian operas on the London stage since 1714, including the first performance of six works by Handel. In 1722 she had been secretly married to Peterborough and soon after she left the stage. The marriage was publicly acknowledged in 1724, and formalised in 1735. Now the secret was not officially out until the year of *Masquerades and Operas*, and perhaps not quite in time for Hogarth's purposes. However, it seems unlikely that the Earl would have been paying Cuzzoni sufficient court to justify such a portrayal in late 1723 or early 1724. There was plenty of gossip about these matters: both Swift (on 13 February 1724) and Lady Mary Wortley Montagu (in March of that year) refer in letters to Peterborough's acting as Anastasia's champion when she was insulted by Senesino.[34] Granted that Swift in distant Dublin could rapidly latch on to such episodes, it is surely probable that Hogarth, who was so much closer at hand, could do so. If the scene alludes to the Earl's courtship of Mrs Robinson, it loses point insofar as the one non-Italian in the Haymarket company is involved; but it gains in specificity and topicality.

Both Cuzzoni and Faustina were renowned for their vulnerability to diplomatic maladies: we often read of an illness suffered by one or other postponing a performance. Both women seem to have given some encouragement to the cliques organised on behalf of one of the other: in particular, Faustina does not appear to have put obstacles in the way of a catcalling campaign against Cuzzoni planned by the adherents of Faustina. Lord Hervey commented acidly both on the indecorous behaviour of the singers, and on their mercenary motives:

> I suppose you have heard already heard that both Cuzzoni and Faustina were so hissed and cat-called last Tuesday that the Opera was not finished that night: nor have the Directors dared to venture the representation of another since. They both threaten to go, but after a little bullying will infallibly stay. 1500 guineas are mediators whose interposition they'll never be able to resist . . . The Directors

have but to throw out these lures, as Hippomenes did the golden apples; and these Atalantas, like his, I'll engage will stay to gather them, though their minds are never so much set upon running.

Hervey went on to suggest that Senesino felt slighted by not having 'a share in these commotions' and determined to 'make himself a party concerned, whether they will or no'. He ended by deploring the taste of the English, who give 'these women ... £3000 a year to come there to have the pleasure of hissing them off [the stage] when they are there, and prefer their conversation in a barge to their voices in a theatre'.[35]

Here is the gravamen of a serious charge, against the audience as well as the performers. The star system is seen to have bred a race of temperamental and grasping invaders, who exploit the folly of a frivolous, gossip-mongering public. It is easy to see how this line of attack could be grafted on to a xenophobic criticism, or to quasi-aesthetic objections (the triumph of sound over sense). It could be buttressed by reference to the frequent playhouse disorders of the 1720s. But what gave this form of opposition its strongest support was the involvement of *money* at every turn: the need for a large amount of capital, which made it necessary to appeal to the market (a fickle and trend-conscious public, it is suggested); the independence of action which this allows to mere executants, as opposed to the original artistic creators; the encouragement provided to indulge in vulgar ostentation, what one modern commentator has called 'conspicuous waste';[36] and the general pull away from traditional cultural standards towards commercial considerations. Italian opera was in fact the arena where many aspects of what J.H. Plumb terms the 'commercialisation of leisure' first became apparent. Conservative observers saw many things to deplore—lavish spectacle, overpaid stars, widely publicised antics, foreign influence, and so on. All these charges could be tied more or less directly to the new power of money in the entertainment industry—as it could now, for the first time, be realistically styled.

By 1724 such grounds of opposition were already well established, though no literary or graphic work had set them out in a fully coherent way. Hogarth's print had no immediate successor, and the only work intervening between *Masquerades and Operas* and the *New Dunciad* which significantly advanced the

critique was James Miller's *Harlequin-Horace* (1731). This makes
the usual onslaughts upon foreign songsters, warbling flutes and
eunuchs; but it also politicises the issue:

> Since *South-Sea Schemes* have so inrich'd the Land,
> That Footmen 'gainst their *Lords* for *Boroughs* stand;
> Since *Masquerades* and *Operas* made their Entry,
> And *Heydegger* and *Handell* rule our Gentry . . .

Two years later, this component of the satire was extended in an
epigram printed in the *Craftsmen* as from the hand of Paolo Rolli:

> Quoth *W*[alpol]*e* to *H*[ande]*l*, shall We Two agree,
> And exise the whole Nation.
> > *H. si, Caro, si.*
> Of what Use are Sheep, if the *Shepherd* can't shear them?
> At the *Hay-Market* I, you at *Westminster*.
> > *W*. Hear him!
> Call'd to Order, their *Seconds* appear in their Place;
> One fam'd for his *Morals*, and one for his *Face*.
> In half they succeeded, in half They were crost:
> The EXISE was obtain'd, but poor DEBORAH lost.[37]

The parallel is established by Walpole's attempt to impose the
Excise, just as Handel unwisely put up admission prices for his
new opera *Deborah*—resulting in the work's failure. The epigram
mimics both parliamentary business and a recitative. Walpole's
second is presumably his brother Horace: Handel's without
doubt, is Heidegger. (*Face* could mean impudence, but puns here
on Heidegger's notoriously ill-favoured countenance). The main
thrust of the epigram is to align the two 'impresarios' of state and
opera-house as sharks out to fleece the gullible nation: the only
difference between them is that Walpole is the more successful.

In fact Walpole had not been one of the early addicts of opera.
However, he had taken the side of Faustina during the great
controversy of 1727, where the royal family had sided with
Cuzzoni. The Faustina party were led by the Countess of
Burlington, and here we have a direct clue to the meaning of
Masquerades and Operas. The Earl of Burlington had been a
founding subscriber to the Academy and had indeed guaranteed
a sum of £1000, a figure equalled only by the great dukes,

Newcastle and Chandos.[38] His patronage of opera is therefore a
fact which cements Hogarth's design. The 'Academy of Arts'
promised by the print will be a pressure-group for Palladian
ideals, and it will no doubt follow the pattern of the existing
Academy of Music in seeking royal patronage. That the Royal
Academy of Arts should actually have found its ultimate home in
Burlington House may disguise from us one topical feature, not
replicated when the Prince of Wales's grandson gave the new
society its charter in 1768. There was an existing 'academy' in
1724: one devoted not to the visual arts and to rather lofty
patronage, but one that functioned in order to promote Italian
opera on a commercial basis. The implication of *Masquerades and
Operas* is that Burlington's grand designs will go in the same way.
He will serve the narrow ends of a fashionable clique, foster the
growth of a meretricious foreign taste, and enlist unscrupulous
entrepreneurs like Heidegger to float the project.

II

So much for opera. But the left-hand side of the print is equally
concerned with masquerades: and here we enter slightly less
familiar areas of cultural history. Unlike opera, the masquerade
has no serious after-life following its span of popularity during the
eighteenth century; like the Venetian carnival which gave so
much prominence to this mode of entertainment, it shrivelled
during the nineteenth century.

   According to a pervasive, but not necessarily reliable,
tradition, the fashion for masquerades was introduced into
England by the French ambassador, the Duc D'Aumont, in the
latter part of Anne's reign. One celebrated occasion was the
masked ball at Somerset House on 17 August 1712; this had the
rare, if not unique, distinction of prompting a literary work
celebrating the masquerade. Susanna Centlivre's poem *The
Masquerade*, published a few days later, delights in the imaginary
representation of a 'spacious World' inhabited apparently by
persons of all races. All the participants 'quit their own, to take a
borrow'd Shape'—exactly the thing that moralists generally
found disturbing.[39] But D'Aumont did not arrive in England
until January 1713, and his own first ball seems to have taken

place in May of that year. However, nearly two years earlier the *Spectator* had deplored the fact that people adopted wish-fulfilling costumes, dressing 'in what they have a mind to be and not what they are fit for'. The whole aim of the 'libidinous Assembly', according to the *Spectator*, was its termination in 'Assignations and Intrigues'.[40] Some of this may be middle-class morality revolting against any expression of high spirits, or any conspicuous mode of high life: but there is a concealed cultural imperative, too—English men and women ought to be fostering 'rational' diversions instead, notably serious drama.[41]

Heidegger took over as manager of the Opera House in 1713. From this time on the Haymarket became the recognised home of masquerade, and increasing publicity confirms the popularity of this form of entertainment, within a narrow band (as it would seem to us) of the social register. In June 1717 we find Pope writing to Lady Mary Wortley Montagu:

> For the news of London, I'll sum it up short. We have Masquerades at the Theatre in the Haymarket of Mr. Heideker's institution; they are very frequent, yet the Adventures are not so numerous but that of my Lady Mohum still makes the chief figure ... The K[ing] and P[rince] continue Two Names: there is nothing like a Coalition, but at the Masquerade; however the Princess is a Dissenter from it, and has a very small party in so unmodish a Seperation.[42]

Around this date Gay wrote a ballad satirising Heidegger and all his works at the Haymarket. This includes a refrain which rebukes the impresario for being 'so wicked/To let in the Devil'—a favourite costume which is prominent in Hogarth's print, at the head of the queue entering the theatre. Hogarth is most unlikely to have known the poem, which was not published in its entirety until the 1970s: but his target was more or less identical with that of the Scriblerians, a matter of five or six years earlier.[43]

One of the fullest contemporary descriptions of a masquerade comes in Mist's *Weekly Journal* on 15 February 1718. At this date the balls were held in the Long Room, on the west side of the main auditorium of the King's Theatre. In style of gushing innocence, the writer describes the music, food, the opportunities for gambling and much else. He remarks:

By the vast variety of Dresses (many of them very rich), you would fancy it a Congress of the principal Persons of all Nations in the World, as Turks, Italians, Indians, Polanders, Venetians, &c. There is absolute Freedom of Speech, without the least offence given thereby; while all appear better bred than to offer anything profane, rude, or immodest, while Wit incessantly flashes in Repartees, Honour and good Humour and all Kinds of Pleasantry.

The English sobriety of the proceedings is stressed:

Nor does it add a little to the Beauty of the Entertainment, to see the Generality of Masqueraders behave themselves agreeable to their several Habits. The Number, when I was there on Tuesday, last week, was computed at 700, with several files of Musquetiers at Hand, for the preventing of any Disturbance which might happen by Quarrels, &c., so frequent, so frequent in Venice, Italy and other countries, on such entertainments.[44]

Defoe was writing for Mist at this moment, but it is hard to imagine him offering such indulgent comment on the taste of the town as this story represents.

On one celebrated occasion Heidegger missed his chance in a most uncharacteristic manner. This was in July 1717, when Handel's immortal *Water Music* received its first performance during the course of a trip by barge up the Thames to Chelsea and back. A report by the Prussian resident makes it clear that Heidegger could have stage-managed the event, instead of making difficulties which left the task in the hands of the courtier Baron Kielmansegg:

A few weeks ago the King expressed to Baron Kilmanseck His desire to have a concert on the river, by subscription, similar to the masquerades this winter which the King never failed to attend. The Baron accordingly applied to Heidecker,—a Swiss by origin, but the cleverest purveyor of entertainments to the Nobility. The latter replied that, much as he would wish to comply with His Majesty's desires, he must reserve subscriptions for the great events, namely the masquerades, each of which brings him in three or 400 guineas net. Observing His Majesty's chagrin at these difficulties, M. de Kilmanseck undertook to provide the concert on the river at his own expense.

Heidegger was to become less fastidious in later years. His obstinacy on this occasion prevented him from sharing in a major triumph of Hanoverian public relations. Newspaper accounts gave a rapturous description of what was clearly a 'great event' in a sense deeper than the masquerades could claim. Kielmansegg died a few months later, and thereafter court entertainments became increasingly dependent on the corps of outside entrepreneurs, headed by men like Handel, Cibber and Heidegger. Public subscription, rather than private munificence, was to support royal pastimes.[45]

Increasingly we encounter a chorus of hostility towards these Haymarket evenings, rather than the enthusiasm of Mist's correspondent. Heidegger comes in for a good deal of personal attack, and the masquerade is linked with any aspect of contemporary life that the given writer happens to find offensive. One of the most characteristic offerings of this sort is a pamphlet published in 1718, attributed to 'C.R. of C[orpus] C[hristi] C[ollege] Oxford' and dedicated to the great actress Mrs Oldfield. To define the scope of this work, it is enough to set out its full title: *The Danger of Masquerades and Raree-Shows, or the Complaints of the Stage, against Masquerades, Opera's, Assemblies, Balls, Puppet-shows, Bear-gardens, Cock-fights, Wrestling, Posture-masters, Cudgel-playing, Foot-ball, Rope-dancing, Merry-makings, and several other irrational Entertainments, as being the Ground and Occasion of the late Decay of Wit in the Island of Great Britain.* The miscellaneity of coverage inevitably weakens C.R.'s treatment of particular amusements, but his collocation does provide a kind of matrix for more lively criticism by the satirists. This is the first time I have encountered the coupling of 'masquerades and operas' in so many words. Most relevant to our immediate concerns is the author's effort to portray masquerade as a residuum into which all the other dreadful modes of entertainment finally drain: 'For as *Nits* by assembling together in corners do grow into Lice, so *Puppet-Shows, Raree-Shows, Balls, Assemblies,* and *Opera's* by a quick growth become a *Masquerade.*' The writer further suggests that wit and 'Traffick' (business) are incompatible, and that stockjobbing is a subject impenetrable by jesting. His main concern, however, is to contrast the wit of the legitimate stage with the '*dumb pageantry* of a *Masquerade*'—invoking the habitual primacy of the *word* in élite versions of culture at this date.[46]

The following year, 1719, saw an undistinguished comedy by Charles Johnson, *The Masquerade*, put on at Drury Lane. Then, in the Bubble year, came a number of satires presenting the social disruption engendered by South Sea as a 'world in masquerade'.[47] By this time there were masquerade ballads sung to well-known tunes,[48] and press comment remained frequent. For example, a report in Mist's paper on 6 August 1720 denied rumours that there were to be masquerades instituted at Belsize House in Hampstead, where 'there is a great resort of the Nobility and Gentry'. This time it would be plausible to connect Defoe with the item, for he wrote two censorious paragraphs on Belsize House in his *Tour* five years later. After alluding to the gaming and other unspecified 'diversions' which went on there, Defoe observed: 'Here was a great Room fitted up with abundance of Dexterity for their Balls, and had it gone on to a degree of Masquerading as I hear as actually begun, it would have bid fair to have had half the Town run to it.' With evident satisfaction Defoe reports the curtailment of these regrettable 'Liberties' by the intervention of authority.[49]

As we approach the date of Hogarth's print, the campaign against Heidegger grows more intense. Pamphlets and cautionary verses appeared at regular intervals. George Berkeley attacked the masquerades in his post-Bubble *Essay* towards preventing the 'ruin' of Great Britain (1721). Matters came to a head with the first mark of official displeasure: a presentment by the Middlesex Grand Jury on 12 February 1723 against six ridottos at the Haymarket, for which the impresario had invited subscribers. The presentment referred to illegal gaming as one of the undesirable features likely to be in evidence, and spoke darkly of 'other Impious and Illegal Practices ... which (if not timely suppressed) may promote Debauchery, Lewdness, and ill Conversation'. The result was that Heidegger had to cancel the three last ridottos of the season; but next year he was back with a new name for his entertainment—'balls'.[50] This provoked from Mist's paper a set of verses under the title of 'The Balls, a Tale,' inscribed to Heidegger.[51] By this time the manager was in deeper hot water, as Hogarth obviously knew.

On 6 January 1724 the Bishop of London, Edmund Gibson, preached before the Societies for the Reformation of Manners.

This influential prelate took the opportunity to stigmatise masquerades for the opportunities they offered to lascivious persons of both sexes. Disguise permitted a degree of freedom in speech and behaviour otherwise inhibited by shame. The court was acting disgracefully by permitting and even patronising these indecent affairs: the Bishop feared that the taste would spread to the whole nation, for this 'was usually the case of such diversions as were favoured and countenanced by persons of figure and standing, by whom they were generally carried ... into all parts of the kingdom'. As Paulson observes, many of Hogarth's enduring themes are shadowed forth in this attack.[52]

Masquerades and Operas came before the public in the following month, but the battle over masquerades went on regardless. In April James Roberts published another pamphlet on the subject, whilst an anonymous versifier produced *Heydegger's Letter to the Bishop of London*. The poem is signed with the impresario's name, as from the Haymarket on Easter Monday (which fell on 6 April). It suggests that the Bishop's sermon in St Mary-le-Bow had been over-severe:

> By which I find you seem afraid,
> That harmless Pastime, MASQUERADE,
> May spoil the *Reformation Trade*.

But the world itself is a mere ball, 'and Fashion favours the Deceit.' The underlying fear, it is suggested, lies in the thought that Cheapside dames will mix with the 'Courtly-Crowd.' Retribution was quick: the author of the supposed *Letter* was taken into the custody of the Secretary of State's messengers at the end of April; the printer and publisher had already suffered this fate.[53] It is uncertain exactly who was involved, apart from the bookseller named on the title-page, Nicholas Cox; and the ultimate fate of those arrested does not emerge. Nevertheless, it looks as if serious efforts were being made on the government's part to associate itself with Gibson's opposition and to deny the implicit accusation in *Masquerades and Operas* that Heidegger was a ministerial pet. This was difficult, in that the King continued to subsidise the Academy in its Haymarket operations, whilst royal support for Heidegger's coadjutor Handel was if anything growing. The politics of the pamphleteering battle do not directly concern us, but they indicate that Hogarth's own contribution can hardly have been innocent of partisan feeling. The building into which the crowd is flooding, after all, when we look at the left side of the print, is the King's Theatre. Understandably Hogarth did not dare to place the royal coat of arms above the doorway, but that is perhaps the logic of his design. Heidegger, gazing down like a monarch from his balcony, is the manager by appointment.

The later history of masquerade is a matter for separate treatment. Here I shall take account, selectively, of a few issues of direct relevance. The balls at the Haymarket went on despite all the criticism, and security precautions seem to have been stepped up to prevent disorders. A famous allusion to the mode comes in Fielding's early poem *The Masquerade* (1728), dedicated to Heidegger. Satire continued unabated throughout the 1730s: Fielding thrust against 'Count Ugly' in his plays, whilst James Bramston struck some familiar notes in *The Man of Taste* (1733):

> Thou Heidegger, the English Taste has found,
> And rulst the mob of quality with sound;
> In Lent if Masquerades displease the Town,
> Call them Ridottos, and they still go down.
> Go on, Prince Phiz, to please the British nation,
> Call thy next Masquerade a Convocation.

A political version of the social mix at the King's Theatre had already been offered by Edward Young in *The Love of Fame* (1727):

> Behold the Masquerade's fantastic scene!
> The *Legislature* joined with *Drury Lane*.

The 'fantastic scene' at the Haymarket, with the 'mob of quality' competing in self-display, had been most graphically portrayed in *Masquerades and Operas*, the source of so many later critiques of popular entertainment.[54]

The ease with which masquerades could be applied to general moral debate is something which can be illustrated from the work of a central figure in this book, Daniel Defoe. Late in life he set out in *The Complete English Tradesman* (1726) his vision of civic and social responsibility. Defining by negatives, at one point, he writes in these significant terms:

> Trade is not a Ball, where people appear in Masque, and act a part to make sport; where they strive to seem what they really are not, and to think themselves best drest when they are least known: but tis a plain visible scene of honest life, shown best in its native appearance, without disguise ...[55]

The opposite pole to sober virtue, the central component of a business ethic, is found in the world of a raffish aristocracy, here symbolised by the masqued balls popularised by Heidegger. The 'invisible', that is undecipherable or illegible, quality of life antithetical to the tradesman's plain-dealing existence, is what especially irks Defoe.

At the opposite extreme of the personality scale to Defoe stands James Boswell, who might be said to have attempted to turn life into a prolonged fancy-dress ball. In 1769 Boswell was to do his best to make the Stratford Jubilee into an occasion of Mediterranean festivity. But it would not work: the English climate, and the English *froideur*, triumphed as usual. The disgruntled Boswell set down his views in the *Public Advertiser* of 16 September 1769:

> I must observe that a Masquerade is an Entertainment, which does not seem to be much suited to the Genius of the British Nation. In warmer Countries, where the People have a great Flow of Spirits, and a Readiness at Repartee, a Masquerade is exceedingly agreeable: but the Reserve and Taciturnity which is observable among us, makes us appear awkward and embarrassed in feigned Characters.

So they should, the moralists would have said. Horace Walpole, interestingly enough, had found the masquerading habit more agreeable in Florence than in Britain: more deference was shown to those in disguise, and no advantage was taken of the opportunities offered to talk bawdy to a woman of quality. (See his letter to West of 27 February 1740.)

In time the main auditorium of the Opera House had come to be used for the masquerades, and however badly opera fared the sister diversion seems to have prospered. There is an account dating from around 1740 which emphasises the lavishness of the ridottos, still under Heidegger's direction.[56] The old man finally departed from the scene in 1749, but two years later Fielding still found it appropriate to show masquerades in a most unpleasant light, in Book Ten of *Amelia*. The author's mouthpiece, Dr Harrison, admits that they are not quite equal to brothels in debauchery, but argues that they are 'scenes of riot, disorder and intemperance, very improper to be frequented by a chaste and sober Christian matron'. The plot bears him out to some extent.[57] After Heidegger's death the central figure was to be Teresa Cornelys, another immigrant, who came to London in 1756. She gave balls and concerts in Soho Square, and their splendour is said to have rivalled those of Heidegger. She too suffered from the presentment of a Grand Jury: by this time middle-class morality had less opposition to face from a decorous court, and Mrs Cornelys ultimately fell into destitution. Another new home of masquerade was the Pantheon in Oxford Street; this was erected in 1771, but burnt down in 1792, only three years after the old King's Theatre had itself gone up in flames.

The case against masquerades is more coherent than that against opera, but it has ramifications of its own. We may disregard what might be called extrinsic factors: for example, the fact that unlawful gaming was often conducted, or thought to be conducted, under the cover of a masked ball. The basic charge centres around the adoption of disguise.[58] This was held to permit sexual freedom; to license every kind of indiscretion in behaviour; and to make promiscuous social contacts undesirably easy. One can readily see how the masquerade institutionalised a sort of unAugustan laxity in manners. The usual formalities of introduction, precedence, protocol, were in a sense bypassed: men and women at such an occasion could lay aside restraints that were inescapable elsewhere in Georgian England. Hence the fears of social instability. There are dramatised in the episode already touched on, where Mrs Atkinson goes to the Haymarket in Amelia's domino; by utilising the 'opportunity of speaking in a feigned [voice]', she is able to deceive Booth into mistaking her for his wife. Here sexual jealousy is implicated in the drama; a gentleman is unable to recognise his property (a wife), just as lords and ladies are liable to be duped into talking on equal terms with a social nonentity. Such freedom might perhaps be allowed in Venice, when a young man set out to learn the ways of a wicked world; but they were potentially dangerous in the midst of London society. Horace Walpole once wrote of a masquerade at Ranelagh, commanded by the King of Denmark, that it would be called by the bishops 'giving an earthquake'; this degree of moral outrage was not universally shared, but many people apart from the bishops felt that masquerades could be a subversive influence.

This sense of an habitual control lost—or relaxed, anyway, to an unpremeditated degree—lies behind the picture of a motley crowd queuing to get into the masquerade: a central feature in Hogarth's design. This was a peculiarly potent image in the years immediately after the Bubble, when memories were still fresh concerning the brief social convulsions of 1720. Allan Ramsay expressed these anxieties in one of several South Sea poems he composed, *The Rise and Fall of Stocks* (1721). A key passage runs as follows:

> The covetous Infatuation
> Was smittle out o'er a' the Nation,
> Clergy and Lawyers and Physicians,
> Mechanics, Merchants, and Musicians.
> Baith Sexes of a' Sorts and Sizes
> Drap'd ilk Design and jobb'd for Prices.
> Frae Noblemen to Livery Varlets,
> Frae topping Toasts to Hackney Harlots.
> Poetick Dealers were but scarce,
> Less browden still on Cash than Verse;
> Only one Bard to Coach did mount
> By singing Prose to Sir *John Blount*;
> But since his mighty Patron fell,
> He looks just like *Jock Blunt* himsel.[59]

This world of teeming confusion is richly energised in Hogarth's first great crowd scene, *The South Sea Scheme*; it finds different rendition in *Masquerades and Operas*, where the tumult is, so to speak, organised. Instead of a single milling throng, as in the earlier print, we have a channeled flood, flowing in opposite directions: the impression we get is of a willed, almost *contained* pressure. As before, the crowd is socially heterogeneous; but now it is governed by the lust for pleasure, not the lure of gold.

Entertainment-mania has replaced speculation-fever. The jobbers and bubble-merchants like Blunt have been replaced by the show-business hucksters and the self-appointed arbiters of taste.

III

Though visually placed at the edge of the design, Heidegger is truly central to the print's meaning. He is on the extreme left side, where the 'reading' of a print normally begins. He is the only openly identified figure in the entire picture: Burlington is identified by external clues, and Rich is indirectly portrayed through the harlequin figure. It is therefore crucial to remember that (in Paulson's words) Heidegger 'himself served as the link between masquerades and operas'.[60] His career sums up the life-history of an entrepreneur more neatly than of any other rival figure. Like Colley Cibber, he moved from the role of creator and executant to that of manager. Like Handel, he was an émigré who helped to bring an imported taste to the peak of popularity. Like John Rich, he specialised in lavish display and non-verbal arts of *performance*. Like Jonathan Tyers, he regularised an entertainment in such a way that the ultra-fashionable might consort with the humbler ranks in society. Like all these men—and others beside, Edmund Curll, Isaac Fawkes, Jonathan Wild even—he was a showman not afraid of publicity, whether good or bad. But more than any other individual, he represented the purest breed of impresario.

His grandfather had derived from Nuremburg, but had managed to get himself stranded in Zurich.[61] The family settled there and a son became a pastor. This was the father of John James, or Johann Jacob. The young man grew up to encounter the traditional unhappy love-affair; he then travelled through Germany as a valet, and disappears from view for several years. In 1707 we find him engaged in obscure negotiations with the English government on behalf of Swiss interests. Not long afterwards he had contrived to enlist in the Life Guards, which less surprisingly led to opportunities for contact with the upper ranks of English society. He became assistant manager at the Opera House, having probably brought himself to the attention of the proprietors by supplying libretti; he was certainly adapting texts for the opera by 1709. We have already observed his fortunes subsequent to his promotion to the post of manager in 1713. Two additional facts are worth emphasis. First, he was responsible for the sumptuous Coronation banquet in Westminster Hall in 1727, and was appointed Master of the Revels to the new King. Second, he received bounty from the secret service fund, along with Voltaire amongst others: the suggestion is that Walpole paid him to act as a spy, or at least to keep a tactful eye on fellow-countrymen living in England.[62]

It was the 'regulator of the Masquerade'[63] who most clearly symbolised in his own person the cultural tendencies explored in this book. In his revision of *The Author's Farce* (1734), Fielding brought in quick succession characters labelled 'Manager' and 'Director': later on, Count Ugly 'from the Opera House in the Haymarket' makes his appearance. The Count alludes to himself as '*Surintendant des plaisirs d'Angeleterre*', an explicit acknowledgment of his quasi-official role.[64] The satirists imply that Heidegger had been given a licence to corrupt the taste of the town, and worse than that to erode social distinction by hording persons of every quality into the same gimcrack entertainments. Why these diversions should have proved so popular to a wide range of people is not a matter into which the critics enquire. It is generally enough for them that the diversion is a novelty, and hence—we are meant to feel—bogus; that it has foreign roots, real or assumed; that it downgrades the word; and so on. Above all, the crime of these entertainments lies in the amount of money it takes to put them on. They call for elaborate staging, costly props, skilful production; they need to be loudly advertised if the promoters are to get back their outlay. They consequently need the services of managers more than artists. Augustan satirists can never accept that fact.

I have concentrated on the left-hand side of the composition. In different ways John Rich, with his fashionable harlequinades, and Burlington, the would-be impresario of taste, illustrate similar tendencies. The mid 1720s marked a high point in the craze for pantomimes, for Italian operas and masquerades, and for Palladian architecture. Hogarth brilliantly juxtaposed these things in a masterly design; the main blocks in the composition correspond with those in *The South Sea Scheme* and *The Lottery*,[65] but there is a subtler interplay between the parts in *Masquerades and Operas*. No other graphic work brings us into such intimte communion with the political and cultural issues of England in the aftermath of the great South Sea disaster. In its controlled handling of eddying movement, the print fixes for all time a certain directionless energy in that puzzled and pleasure-hungry epoch.

Notes

1. Paulson, I, 111–20. Close to some of the concerns of this chapter is a brilliantly suggestive recent essay by Terry Castle, 'Eros and Liberty in the English Masquerade', *ECS*, XVII (1983) 156–76.
2. This was one of the ideas taken over bodily by the young Henry Fielding, in a burlesque directed against Pope which he wrote *c.*1729. *See* Isobel M. Grundy, 'New Verse by Henry Fielding', *PMLA*, LXXXVII (1972), 213–45: '[Sooner shall] Wycherly Shakespear, Johnson Congreve's Scenes/Triumph o'er Nonsense, Shew and Harlequins.' For the accuracy with which Hogarth depicts Lincoln's Inn Playhouse, *see* Phillips, p. 192.
3. John Trusler, John Nichols, and John Ireland, *The Works of William Hogarth, with Descriptions and Explanations* (London, n.d.), p. 85.
4. For Fawkes, *see* Paulson, I, 115, and p. 75 below.
5. Derek Jarrett, *The Ingenious Mr Hogarth* (London, 1976), p. 51.
6. Paulson, I, 117–18.
7. His face is also clearly visible in Hogarth's *Masquerade Ticket* (1727). This has a lion and a unicorn as supporters above the clock, pointing to the patronage of George II: the clock shows wit at a low ebb (a 'score' of $7\frac{1}{2}$) and impudence thriving (scoring 30). On a shelf are ranged 'Provocatives', that is aphrodisiacs, or what are now termed sexual aids. 'Lecherometers' measure the lubricity of the crowd. On this print see Paulson, I, 173, and Frederick Antal, *Hogarth and his Place in European Art* (London, 1962), p. 74.
8. An indirect allusion may be present in the verses appended to the second state (see Paulson, I, 117).
9. *See* Paulson, I, 117. quoting *Pasquin*, 18 February 1724.
10. For the presence of a military guard in 1718, *see* p. 56 above: in 1725–26, *see* Deutsch, p. 81; in April 1724, *see* Phillips, p. 277.
11. Paulson, I, 117. Paulson is right to see the satyr as emphatically diabolic in appearance. *See* above, p. 55. The accompanying fool in motley has been read as a covert reference to the Prince of Wales (*see* Antal, p. 74), but there seems no way of enforcing this particular reading. The Prince has also been identified as one of the figures on the show-cloth, again with no direct evidence adduced (*see* Trusler, Nichols and Ireland, p. 85).
12. For Hogarth's interest in spectacle, *see* Jarrett, pp. 23–4.
13. *See* Fiske, p. 49.

14. Quoted by Madeleine Bingham, *Masks and Facades: Sir John Vanbrugh The Man in his Setting* (London, 1974), p. 114.
15. *Spectator*, I, 55-9.
16. *See* Fiske, pp. 53-6.
17. This paragraph is based on a number of sources, including Deutsch, pp. 89-93, and *London Stage*, II, lxi.
18. Deutsch, pp. 93-139, is the principal source.
19. *See* below, p. 113.
20. *The Letters of John Gay*, ed. C.F. Burgess (Oxford, 1966), p. 43.
21. Fiske, p. 66.
22. *The Poems of Henry Carey*, ed. F.T. Wood (London, n.d.), p. 99. Carey's poems include several dealing with operatic matters, with references to Heidegger, Handel, the *prime donne*, etc. For his own involvement in opera and pantomime, *see* Fiske, pp. 87-90, 127-35, 154-6.
23. *The Fable of the Bees*, ed. F.B. Kaye (Oxford, 1924), II, 37, *see also* II, 105. Attacks on the irrational nature of opera continue as late as Joseph Strutt's *Sports and Pastimes of the People of England* (London, 1801), VII, 218, which discounts such entertainments as 'contrived at once to please the eye, and delight the ear; and this double gratification ... was procured at the expense of reason and propriety'.
24. The 'effeminacy' of opera relates to a number of issues: among these are the presence of the castrati, the prominent role women had acquired (which together meant an eclipse of the lower voices), and the liquid sound of the Italian language. *See* Dennis's comment, quoted on p. 44 above.
25. Most of the facts in this paragraph are drawn from *London Stage*, II, lxviii-lxx. Note that the reference to Nicolini cited on p. lxx was a mistake for Senesino, as pointed out in Deutsch, p. 120.
26. *Lord Hervey and his Friends 1726-38*, ed. The Earl of Ilchester (London, 1950), p. 211.
27. *See London Stage*, II, lxxi-lxxvi, and Deutsch, *passim*.
28. Deutsch, pp. 150, 152. Satire on opera stock as what might be called a castrato version of South Sea is found in Steele's *The Theatre* on 8 and 12 March (cited by Deutsch, p. 101). Rolli wrote in October 1720, damning the South Sea directors, who had put the Academy at risk (Deutsch, p. 115).
29. Deutsch, p. 151.
30. Deutsch, p. 148.
31. Deutsch, p. 152.
32. Deutsch, pp. 97, 111, 138-9.
33. *London Journal*, 2 March 1723, quoted by Paulson, I, 114.
34. Swift, *Corr*, III, 6-7; *The Complete Letters of Lady Mary Wortley Montagu*, ed. Robert Halsband (Oxford, 1965-7), II, 37.
35. *Lord Hervey and his Friends*, pp. 18-19, one version of events, partly deriving from Carey, has Faustina demanding £2,500 in advance in order to come to London: *see* Deutsch, p. 195. Hervey's figure may be exaggerated, but not by very much.
36. George E. Dorris, *Paoli Rolli and the Italian Circle in London 1715-44* (The Hague, 1967), pp. 36-7.

37. Quoted by Deutsch, p. 313. As Deutsch points out (p. 309), Walpole was not himself Handel's protector; but the King had remained loyal to Handel, and the composer thus could be depicted as a pensioner of the court.

38. Deutsch, p. 91. Burlington's patronage of Handel and Bononcini is well documented in studies of both men.

39. John Wilson Bowyer, *The Celebrated Mrs Centlivre* (Durham, N.C., 1952), pp. 150-2. A rumour spread that the Pretender himself attended the masquerades incognito, so as to meet with English adherents; but this is almost certainly myth. For D'Aumont's masquerades, *see Guardian* no, 154 (7 September 1711), and the notes by J.C. Stephens: *The Guardian* (Lexington, Kentucky, 1982), pp. 501-4, 734.

40. *Spectator*, I, 36-8. The masquerades in question were probably those held at the Lambeth Wells, Spring Gardens. For advertisements in the journal for such entertainments, *see Spectator*, nos. 53 and 239.

41. Paul Henry Lang has commented on the inability of a highly developed theatrical culture, such as England possessed, to accept the primacy of music over words, wit, and verbal ingenuity: *see George Frideric Handel* (New York, 1966), pp. 147-73.

42. Pope, *Corr*, I, 407. For a reference in *Polite Conversation, see* Swift, *Prose*, IV, 116.

43. *See* P.J. Crofts, *Autograph Poetry in the English Language* (London, 1973), I, 64-7, for a version in Gay's holograph: for a short fragment *see* David Nokes, 'Pope and Heidegger: A forgotten Fragment', *RES*, XXIII (1972), 308-13.

44. Quoted by Deutsch, p. 80. In the same month appeared Mrs Centlivre's *A Bold Stroke for a Wife*, in which the old beau, assured that this 'branch of pleasure . . . naturalized by the ingenious Mr Heidegger' will 'become part of the constitution', duly subscribes a hundred guineas. *See* the edition by Thalia Stathas (London, 1969), pp. 24-5.

45. Deutsch, p. 77. For the King's attraction towards masquerades which reminded him of the Hanoverian carnival, *see* Ragnhild Hatton, *George I: Elector and King* (London, 1978), p. 124. But on one occasion, the King was forced to apologise to the Archbishop of Canterbury when Colonel Charles Churchill appeared in the guise of a bishop (Hatton, p. 292).

46. *The Danger of Masquerades and Raree-Shows* (London, 1718; rptd New York, 1974), pp. 10-11. The publisher, W. Boreham, was also associated with Defoe at this date.

47. *See* Stephens, II, 459.

48. Claude M. Simpson, *The British Broadside Ballad and its Music* (New Brunswick, 1966), p. 464.

49. Daniel Defoe, *A Tour through the Whole Island of Great Britain* (London 1927; rptd 1968), I, 384-5. For the story of the Belsize House assembly, *see* my edition of the *Tour* (Harmondsworth, 1971), p. 703.

50. Deutsch, p. 149. Some years later Heidegger was again presented as the 'principal promoter of vice and immorality'—observe the first noun. Another word, baneful in the era, which was often used of Heidegger was 'project', 'projector', and derivatives.

51. *Mist's Weekly Journal*, 8 February 1724. We are told in the *London Journal* on 11 February that at the last ridotto a prize had been won by a daughter of the Archbishop of Canterbury (William Wake).
52. *See* Paulson, I, 116. Gibson was one of those to accept the story that d'Aumont had introduced the fashion to England.
53. *British Journal*, 2 May 1724. *See also* Deutsch, p. 156, where the pamphlet is attributed to John Macky, Charles Povey and Cox. The printer, Samuel Aris, was also arrested: *see* PRO, SP 44/80, which also suggests that Thomas Power, not Povey, was the author involved.
54. *Marriage A-la-Mode: An Humorous Tale* (1746) is a Hudibrastic poem in six cantos, loosely based on Hogarth's cycle. The opera-lover predictably follows 'Sounds devoid of Sense', whilst the manager himself is apostrophised: 'Blest *H-g-r*, that could invent, / A Scheme both Sexes to content! / What longing Wife, what melting Maid, / Who sighs not for a Masquerade?' (p. 32). Even in 1746 'scheme' was likely to carry some of the odious overtones it had acquired in South Sea days.
55. *The Complete English Tradesman* (London, 2nd rev. edn, 1727), I, 117. Masquerade dress is used in a similar moral context in *Roxana*. *See* David Blewett, '*Roxana* and the Masquerades,' *MLR*, LXV (1970), 449–502.
56. Phillips, p. 277. Phillips comments on the popularity of witches' hats in fancy dress occasions—there is one in the middle of Hogarth's theatre queue.
57. *Amelia* (London, 1966), II, 165–88. There is a brief reference to Heidegger as 'the great *Arbiter Deliciarum*, the great High-Priest of Pleasure' in *Tom Jones*, Book XIII: *see* the edition by Martin C. Battestin (Oxford, 1974), II, 712. Battestin assembles other references by Fielding (II, 708–9). Masquerades figure in other novels by Richardson, Smollett, Fanny Burney *et al*.
58. From time to time one comes on newspaper reports of a person arrested in masquerade costume, and suspected of using this as a cover for crime. *See* for instance Mist's *Weekly Journal*, 23 January 1725. Profane costumes excited condemnation: so did cross-dressing between the sexes.
59. *The Works of Allan Ramsay*, ed. Burns Martin, J.W. Oliver (Edinburgh, 1953), I, 177–8. Thirty years later, a parting salvo to Heidegger, probably written by William Kenrick, depicted a similar world:

> Fools, dukes, rakes, cardinals, fops, Indian queens,
> Belles in tye-wigs, and lords in harlequins,
> Troops of right honourable porters come,
> And garter'd small coal-merchants crowd the room;
> Valets stuck o'er with coronets appear,
> Lacquey's of state, and footmen with a star;
> Sailors of quality with judges mix,
> And chimney-sweepers drive their coach and six:
> Statesmen, so used at Court the mask to wear,
> Now condescend again to use it here;
> Idiots turn conjurers, and courtiers clowns,
> And sultans drop their handkerchiefs to nuns.

Quoted by Thomas Wright, *Caricature History of the Georges* (London, n.d.), p. 68. Hogarth's crowd awaiting entry to the Haymarket displays the same fantastic and jumbled quality.

60. Paulson, I, 113.
61. There is no satisfactory life of Heidegger. One of the fullest of the early accounts is found in the *London Magazine*, XLVIII (1779), 452-3; but none can be regarded as very reliable. The impresario's age at his death is given as ninety, but this was a conventional estimate for seemingly aged persons, and should not be taken literally. *See* p. 34.
62. *See* Cambridge University Library, Houghton (Cholmondley) MSS, 53/20, 23: *An Account of all Moneys Paid out of His Majesty's Exchequer 1721-45* (London, 1769), p. 8. Another beneficiary listed in the latter source is the notorious Peter Walter.
63. John Nichols, *Biographical Anecdotes of William Hogarth* (London, 1785), p. 128.
64. *The Author's Farce*, ed. Charles B. Woods (London, 1966), pp. 94-100.
65. Paulson points out (I, 113) that lotteries were drawn on the Haymarket stage: this was a regular occurrence, and the print called *The Lottery* can be assumed to depict this precise scene. It should be stressed that *Masquerades and Operas* unmistakably depicts the Haymarket theatre: compare the view of the east frontage in Phillips, p. 90. Finally, it is interesting to recall that John Gay was a Commissioner for the official government lottery, which was drawn in the Guildhall.

2

SHAPES AND POSTURES

Swift, Walpole and the Rope-Dancers

> But these are merry Times, and the Church Magick out-does
> all the Conjurings of the Antients, as much as Madam
> *Violante* out-does a common Stage-Tumbler . . .
>
> Daniel Defoe, *A System of Magick* (1726)

I

The sections of *Gulliver's Travels* embodying direct political allegory have not been well served in recent criticism. Such notice as they generally get is confined to the hunt for particular identifications. In this chapter I wish to take one well-known snatch of political satire, not in order to suggest a new identification (indeed I shall bring evidence to support the orthodox view, in this regard) but rather to indicate the ways in which such a passage may be seen to minister to the most inward workings of the satire as a whole. I shall try to show that the topical allegory goes in consonance with the entire moral dialectic of the book. My argument is that the terms in which the allegory is couched connect the satire at this point with the sustained technique of Scriblerian farce, and with a running critique of 'sights and shows' mounted by Swift and his friends.

The passage occurs in the first paragraph of chapter 3 in 'A Voyage to Lilliput', where the narrator describes his gradual acceptance by the Lilliputians. 'The Emperor had a mind one Day to entertain me with several of the Country Shows; wherein they exceed all Nations I have known, both for Dexterity and Magnificence. I was diverted with none so much as that of the Rope-Dancers, performed upon a slender white Thread, extended about two Foot, and twelve Inches from the Ground. Upon which, I shall desire Liberty, with the Reader's Pleasure,

71

to enlarge a little.' And Gulliver proceeds, as everyone will recall, to give an account of the rope-dancing contests among 'Candidates for great Employment' in the state. He reports, too, that 'Flimnap, the Treasurer, is allowed to cut a Caper on the strait Rope, at least an Inch higher than any other Lord in the whole Empire. I have seen him do the Summerset several times together, upon a Trencher fixed on the Rope, which is no thicker than a common Packthread in England.' Gulliver goes on to express his opinion that Reldresal, 'principal Secretary for private Affairs', runs Flimnap most closely in this art. Finally, the narrator mentions the risks attendant on the activity, including on occasion fatal accidents. Even Flimnap, he tells us, 'would have infallibly broke his Neck' a year or two earlier, but for providential assistance supplied by a discarded cushion.[1]

There has been a good deal of agreement, both as to the overall meaning of this section and as to particular allusions. Flimnap is taken on all sides to represent Robert Walpole. Less confidence has been displayed with regard to Reldresal. Marlborough (d. 1722) is one candidate. G. R. Dennis suggested the name of James Stanhope (who was dead by 1721), and a more plausible ascription is that of A. E. Case, who substituted Walpole's brother-in-law Charles Townshend, secretary of state for the Northern Department at the time *Gulliver* appeared.[2] Such uncertainty is only an isolated case however. Most commentators have read the passage as a straight attack on the politics of intrigue and see the episode of the cushion as an allusion to the help Walpole is thought to have received from the Duchess of Kendal in 1721. The unconscious reasoning seems to be that, since the passage points unambiguously at Walpole, and since Swift's dislike of the latter is well known, there can be no need to go any further into the matter.

And point at Walpole the passage does. Even if one were to discount the fact that he held the office of First Lord of the Treasury, there is enough evidence in book 1 as a whole (mainly in the sections irrelevant to this present study) to clinch the attribution. Yet the special applicability of the passage I have quoted has been described only in the vaguest of terms. Sir Charles Firth provides about the fullest explanation: the rope-dancing for him 'symbolises Robert Walpole's dexterity in parliamentary tactics and political intrigues'. More commonly editors offer a more cautious gloss—for instance, Louis Landa asserts briefly that 'his [Walpole's] political dexterity is here satirised'.[3] Quite so: but the manner in which the ridicule operates ought to be considered in much greater detail.

The first signal to be heeded occurs in the introductory phrase. Gulliver's expression, 'Country Shows', works in much the same way as Pope's invocation to 'The Smithfield Muses' in the second line of *The Dunciad*. The word *shows* is loaded with associations of low pantomimic entertainment. It connotes the whole range of undignified and unedifying theatricality which figures so conspicuously in the retinue of Queen Dulness. Harlequinades, raree-shows, peep-shows, punch-drama, waxworks, perhaps even masquerades—these are the modes of display which the word calls up. And, along with rope-dancing, these were precisely the 'dramatic' performances for which Bartholomew Fair was renowned. In the words of Pope's note (*Dunciad* A. 1.2): '*Smithfield* is the place where Bartholomew Fair was kept, whose Shews, Machines, and Dramatical Entertainments, formerly agreeable only to the Taste of the Rabble, were, by the Hero of this Poem and others of equal Genius, brought to the Theatres of Covent Garden, Lincolns-inn-Fields, and the Hay-market, to be the reigning Pleasures of the Court and Town.'[4] The side-shows of the fair, in other words, served as an accurate emblem of what Thomas Edwards calls the 'entropy' of Dulness.[5] The fair was a teeming, noisy, noxious place: it had once been closed for a year, owing to its contribution to the spreading of the plague (that crucial image of the Augustan satirists).[6] As Jonson's play reminds us, it was notorious for pickpockets and whores. There were 'Straits and Bermudas' in West Smithfield, as well as off St Martin's Lane.[7] In King Street stood 'the Cloisters', where Moll Flanders wandered during the course of the fair and where she met an opportune dupe. Incidentally, it was through the narrow alleys of the district—Bartholomew Close and Little Britain—that both Moll and Colonel Jack made their escape after robberies.[8] Again, the Poet tells us in Fielding's *Author's Farce*, 'My Lord Mayor has shortened the time of Bartholomew Fair in Smithfield'—and as a recent editor notes, this event took place in 1717 on account of 'the Great Vice and Profaness, occasion'd there by Stage-Plays'.[9]

A few years later James Ralph, the friend and colleague of

Fielding, was to write of Smithfield in his *Critical Review*: 'A scene of filth and nastiness, one of the most nauseous places in the whole town.' He suggested the erection of an obelisk or pyramid in the middle of the market.[10] This was at the best of times—Cloth Fair contained sheep pens (inhabited) all the year round. But it was particularly true at the time of the fair, when adjoining streets such as Hosier Lane and Giltspur Street were crowded with booths.[11] The fair, indeed, showed a marked propensity to expand, both in time and space. This was another characteristic of Dulness, whose empire may be seen growing throughout *The Dunciad*. As Bredan O Hehir has suggested, there may be an implication in Swift's *City Shower* that Smithfield is still infested by the fair (though its official term has lapsed), occasioning the descent of yet more 'Filth of all Hues and Odours' toward that universal artery of squalor, the Fleet Ditch.[12] This was, then, an appropriate scene to symbolise both the sordid and the theatrical elements of contemporary life. I wish, however, to suggest a more particular relevance. This arises from the precise nature of the theatrical 'shows' which Smithfield laid on every year, as these have been described by a number of students and as contemporary sources reveal them to us.

Swift makes few explicit references to the fair, but one of these is significant. In the Partridge papers, there are a couple of passing allusions: Bickerstaff predicts that 'much Mischief will be done ... by the fall of a Booth'.[13] The irony perhaps lies in the fact that Swift believes (and expects his readers likewise to believe) that the least mischievous event which could occur, involving a booth, would be for it to collapse and prevent any further performances. There is a much richer implication in the other reference. It comes at the end of *Examiner* no. 39 (40 in the original issue). 'A DOG loves to turn round often; yet after certain *Revolutions*, he lies down to *Rest*: But Heads, under the Dominion of the *Moon*, are for perpetual *Changes*, and perpetual *Revolutions*: Besides, the *Whigs* owe all their Wealth to *Wars* and *Revolutions*; like the Girl at *Bartholomew*-Fair, who gets a Penny by turning round a hundred Times, with Swords in her hands.'[14] As Irvin Ehrenpreis says, 'the remote but striking parallelism turns out to be figuratively absurd, yet explosive with hostile innuendo'.[15] This was no distant similitude in one sense, however— it was not dredged from any far recess of Swift's imagination. Such displays were commonplace at Smithfield. Thomas Dale, for example, who kept the Turk's Head music booth, advertised 'as an extra attraction a young woman who performed prodigies of dexterity with fourteen wine glasses, turning all the time "above a Hundred Times as fast as a Windmill".'[16] Even Flimnap might envy such 'prodigies of dexterity.'

As is well known, dancing on the slack or tightrope became a favourite spectacle at this period. The most celebrated exponents were perhaps Signor and Signora Violante. Either one or the other of this pair is seen in the background of Hogarth's 'Southwark Fair' (1733); but a more conspicuous figure in this print is that of Cadman (or Kidman), mentioned by Horace Walpole for his exploits suspended from St Martin's steeple. One display of this kind took place in June 1727, just too late to influence the writing of *Gulliver*, but not too late to augment its satiric point. That Cadman subsequently fell while trying to cross the Severn at Shrewsbury adds further proleptic resonance to Gulliver's account of the rope-dancing.[17] But there was at least one well-known practitioner of the real-life art who had already suffered this fate. This was Mrs Finley, a regular performer at the fair along with her husband, also an acrobat.[18] She was generally known as 'Lady Mary', an epithet which incidentally helps to fill out Pope's reference to 'Duchess and Lady Mary's'.[19]

It is another booth depicted in 'Southwark Fair' which provides the major clue. This is the stall kept by the conjuror Isaac Fawkes, or 'Faux' as he appears in Hogarth's 'Masquerades and Operas' (1724). Comparatively little is known of this showman's career, although James Caulfield did include him among his 'Remarkable Persons'. Fawkes was principally a conjuror, but this profession then merged with that of contortionist—and both were equally grist for the satirists' mill. He died in May 1731,[20] reputedly worth ten thousand pounds, but for more than a decade previous he had been among the most celebrated stallholders at the fair. A fan picture depicting the scene in 1721, though probably executed long after, shows him conspicuously flanking peepshows and rope-dancing displays.[21] There are two additional factors which make Fawkes of special interest in the present context.

The first relates to Walpole and provides a fuller rationale for the rope-dancing episode than Swiftian scholars have so far brought forward. There is a story, not well authenticated but nevertheless potent and tenacious, which links the Lord Treasurer with Fawkes. According to this tradition, Walpole had a special fondness for the conjuror's act and regularly visited his booth. (Fawkes operated in London all the year round and not just at the time of the great annual fairs). A figure in court dress displayed on Fawkes's stall is supposed, indeed, to represent Walpole. Whether this story is true does not particularly matter. That it undoubtedly was current would be enough to give added bite to Swift's picture of Flimnap cavorting on the rope. Certainly Robert Walpole was commonly portrayed in satire of the 1730s as a puppetmaster or theatrical stallholder.[22]

A further piece of evidence serves to confirm this thrust of satire. In 1731 the frontispiece to each of the seven volumes of the *Craftsman* was published in a print called *Robin's Reign* (British Library print no. 1822). It occasioned widespread interest, and an associated pamphlet caused the publisher, William Rayner, to be indicted by the Grand Jury of Middlesex. The second plate in the series depicts Fawkes as offering diabolic assistance to Walpole, his 'Patron'. The implication is that he uses the black arts of conjuring to exercise his nefarious power, just like the 'Harlequin of State', Fawkes.[23]

Secondly, it is noteworthy that Fawkes increasingly branched out from the specialist skill of conjuror to that of grand showman at large.[24] Even during his own lifetime, his entertainment came to include waxworks, harlequinades, and much else. It was his partner Edward Pinchbeck who chiefly effected this change, especially after Fawkes senior had died and been succeeded in his business by his son. Pinchbeck described himself professionally in terms which play right into Swift's hands. He was known as the 'mechanist'. That is, he manipulated various contrivances such as a kind of prototype cinematograph. One description of the show which the partners put on seems hardly to require satiric reworking at all: 'Feats of posturing were exhibited between Fawkes' conjuring tricks and the exhibition of Pinchbeck's ingenious mechanism.' Not to stray beyond *Gulliver*—for the whole of Swift's oeuvre is instantly laid open by this sentence—one can hardly fail to note that book 1, especially, is dominated by 'feats of posturing'. The next 'Tryal of Dexterity', immediately succeeding the rope-dancing, involves '*leaping* and *creeping*' with the maximum possible agility. (This is a 'ceremony' recalling the levée scene in book 4 of *The Dunciad*.) The whole Lilliputian regime, one might say, rests on the exercise of posturing: court ceremony is made up of elaborate physical contortions, the strict protocol and graceful pointlessness of which clash with the intrinsic turpitude of the obsequious placeman taking part. The object of Swift's attack, as everyone agrees, is the system which permits the self-seeking politician to play courtier and gain his ends. The means of this attack is largely straight parody of existing entertainments. That Walpole perhaps patronised one of the leading showmen is, from Swift's point of view, convenient but contingent. The main point is that agility connotes elasticity of conscience.

After the death of Fawkes, as remarked, Pinchbeck carried on with the former's son. Frost, in his book on *The Old Showmen, and the London Fairs*, quotes publicity material put out by the new partnership.[25] Again, very little gloss is required. One advertisement mentions five attractions to be witnessed at the booth. The first is 'the surprising Tumbler . . . who shows several astonishing things by the Art of Tumbling; the like never seen before since the memory of man'. The agility with which Flimnap does the somersault now begins to appear even more suspect. Secondly, the audience is to be regaled by the 'incomparable dexterity' of Pinchbeck himself, again performing feats whose novelty is stressed. One of his tricks involves a machine for perpetual motion. Swift, of course, aligned the *perpetuum mobile* with squaring the circle, discovering the philosopher's stone, and other chimerical quests for the absolute. Thirdly, the advertisement mentions a nine-year-old boy described as 'the famous little posture-maker', a description which fits Flimnap (or indeed the Emperor) with perfect accuracy. This boy 'shows several astounding postures by activity of the body, different from any other posture-maker in Europe'. But not, one is tempted to add, from any in Lilliput—thanks to Swift's kind offices. It comes as no surprise to find that the same child danced on the slack rope. The fourth item on the programme is Pinchbeck's musical clock, no doubt the model favoured in Laputa; and the fifth is the 'Venetian machine', apparently a sort of cyclorama. At other times the partners announced marionette displays, wax models of historical characters à la Mrs Jarley, Indian tricks, trees springing out of flowerpots, and a gnomic happening said to involve a 'man in a maze'. Many of these belong to Gulliver's third voyage. The visit to Glubbdubdrib, in particular, is little more than a conducted tour of Smithfield shows. The Governor, when he dismisses his attendants 'with a Turn of his Finger, at which to my great Astonishment they vanished in an Instant, like Visions in a Dream', behaves less like Prospero than like Pinchbeck.[26]

II

The material I have presented in summary form could be greatly extended. It is unnecessary to rehearse the importance of the 'mechanist' concept in Swift, notably in the *Mechanical Operation*. John Bullitt has written particularly well on 'The Comedy of Mechanism'.[27] Rather, I wish to raise an issue of broader significance. This involves the entire aesthetic of Scriblerian comedy and relates to what might be called the farce of the grotesque.

One of the main principles of Scriblerian humour, in fact, is an awareness of the satiric power of physical misadventure. A clear example occurs in *Peri Bathous*. Chapter 5 of that helpful treatise on how to achieve anticlimax without really trying is headed 'Of the true Genius for the Profound, and by what it is constituted.' According to one especially relevant section, 'nothing seem'd more plain to our great authors, than that world had long been weary of *natural things*. How much the contrary are form'd to please, is evident from the universal applause daily given to the admirable entertainments of Harlequins and Magicians on our stage. When an audience beholds a coach turn'd into a wheelbarrow, a conjuror into an old woman, or a man's head where his heels should be; how are they struck with transport and delight?' The art of sinking is confessedly an art of the grotesque. Bodily contortions or ungainly postures are its proper motif: the figure of the diver is a favourable one, since it couples the idea of searching the profound with that of physical inversion. ('Is there not an Art of Diving as well as of Flying?' asks Martinus Scriblerus.[28] Indeed yes, as the aquatic sports in the *Dunciad* were shortly to make clear.) Additionally, 'diver' was a contemporary cant word for pickpocket, as Colonel Jack reminds us. It is not a very long step from this kind of indignity to the painful embarrassment undergone by all humanity in the earlier Scriblerian squib, *Annus Mirabilis* (1722), probably by Arbuthnot. Here a universal sex change poses a number of what might be called problems of adjustment. Equally the foolish participants in *Three Hours after Marriage* (1717) find themselves cumbered with a variety of ungainly disguises, ranging from an alligator to an Egyptian mummy.

In Swift's own work the same use of inelegance, as a satiric comment, appears on more than one occasion. But a single example should suffice. It comes from 'On Poetry: A Rapsody' (1733).

> ... When you rashly think
> No Rhymer can like *Welsted* sink.
> His Merits ballanc'd you shall find,
> The Laureat leaves him far behind.
> *Concannen*, more aspiring Bard
> Climbs downwards, deeper by a Yard:
> Smart JEMMY MOOR with Vigor drops,
> The Rest pursue as thick as Hops:
> With Heads to Points the Gulph they enter,
> Linkt perpendicular to the Centre:
> And as their Heels elated rise,
> Their Heads attempt the nether Skies.

The same poem contains a passage satirising what John Oldmixon (himself a Dunce) had called the 'Smithfield-Bards'.

> Some famed for Numbers soft and smooth,
> By Lovers spoke in *Punch's* Booth.
> And some as justly Fame extols
> For lofty Lines in *Smithfield* Drols.

Elsewhere Swift had referred to 'Balls, and Masquerades, and Shows', with the same sneering insistence on the last word. One recalls, too, that in *A Tale of a Tub*, Lord Peter was 'The Original Author of *Puppets* and *Raree-Shows*'.[29] Bullitt has illuminated the use Swift makes of the notion of puppetry; but a broader mode of rhetorical attack is evident here. Swift invokes several species of theatrical display—what they have in common is a quality of senseless or balletic spectacle. (This is the 'Magnificence' of the Lilliputian shows.) Most of these references concern writers. But Duncenia, as the 'Rapsody' styles the commonwealth of folly, numbered politicians as well as poets among its inhabitants. Ministers of state are seen as performers in the puny harlequinade of parliamentary flummery.[30] Politics is imaged as a gaudy *théâtre des machines*.

The word *dexterity*, used by Swift of the candidates for office, is itself significant. The expression was loaded with associations of chicanery, deceit, sleight of hand. (These were utilised by Swift's superior, Archbishop King, in a letter of 1721.) Indeed, the moral overtones correspond closely to those one might call up today by speaking of 'ambidexterity'.[31] The clearest example of this semantic process is to be found, perhaps, in a work usually attributed to Defoe. In *The True and Genuine Account of the Life and Actions of the late Jonathan Wild* (1725) occurs the notion of dexterity exploited with consistently damaging force. The writer speaks of Wild's 'dexterous way of managing', in reference to his thief-catching and informing activities. Shortly afterwards Defoe writes: 'he [Wild] managed with such dexterity, that he always obtained public applause as a mighty forward man to detect the villainies of those people [rogues whom Wild had sacrificed], to bring offenders to justice'. If this is not clear enough, the writer spells out the precise connotations of the term a page or two later: 'The said Skull Dean, Mrs. Wild's first husband, was a very dexterous fellow in his calling, and particularly expert in breaking into houses.' Finally, after the lapse of a few more paragraphs: 'If the correspondence he [Wild] kept was large, if the number of his instruments was very great, his dexterity in managing them was indeed wonderful.'[32] It should be stressed that *The True and Genuine Account* is not written with the same sustained irony as Fielding's subsequent 'life'. At times the author does adopt a flippant tone, but he does not shirk the word *murder* in describing Wild's operations.

Passages such as the rope-dancing episode, with their emphasis on low theatrical display, strike simultaneously at the prime minister and at his royal master. When *Gulliver* was published, George I still occupied the throne; and his record as a patron of the arts was (from the Scriblerian viewpoint, anyway) an indifferent one. Originally the King had conferred his favours principally on the Italian opera, itself a dubious object as the Swift circle saw matters (see Chapter 4). But there is evidence, described in detail by Louis D. Mitchell, which indicates that he turned increasingly towards Lincoln's Inn Fields and the harlequinade. On the basis of his examination of command performaces, Mitchell concludes:

> Although he commanded seven fine plays at Hampton Court—with an interpreter at his side all the while—he leaned decidely toward Italian opera and relatively low-brow farce at King's. His commands over the course of his reign ... indicate a shift in taste from opera ... [evidenced by] more frequent appearances at pantomime performances. For example, in the season of 1726-1727 alone this first of the Hanoverians commanded a total of thirty-three such producions ... He was encouraged by his politically minded ministers at court, and at Drury Lane, thereby lending support, both financially and personally, as the London stage developed from the dearth of help during the reign of Queen Anne to an increasingly influential artistic enterprise.[33]

What kind of enterprise, Swift would ask? Essentially, in his estimation, the recipients of court patronage were the purveyors of fringe theatre—the shadow and not the substance of dramatic art.

The picture of the Lilliputian games, then, combines a number of ideas all conveying the sense of unprincipled tergiversation. Some of these connotations, of course, survive in present-day language. We can still speak of moral acrobatics and of a political tightrope act, and the phrase 'brinkmanship' perhaps calls up a similar visual image. A historian of the reign of Anne, writing in 1967, refers to Robert Harley as 'performing an extraordinarily skilful political balancing-act'.[34] But other parts of this cluster of associations are less apparent to the modern reader. And unless he is alive to the suggestions of both folly and turpitude which are evoked by the rope-dancing episode, he will miss much of the satiric impact that the passage carried with it. This would be a pity in itself; and it would further encourage the mistaken assumption that the areas of direct political satire in *Gulliver's Travels* are inert and relatively lacking in resonance. It is of great interest, moreover, that the comedy depends on allusions to various aspects of contemporary London which Swift had observed during his own sojourn in the capital.[35] It it true, as recent commentators have taught us to recognise, that Augustan satire draws much of its vivacity from the direct landline it maintains with older traditions—with Lucian and Juvenal, with Rabelais and Erasmus, with Scarron and Cervantes. But not all the fictions of satire derive from that source.[36] They relate as well to the actualities of eighteenth-century life. With the rope-dancers, as so often with the Scriblerian group, the iron necessities of art are wrought from the evanescent contingencies of topical circumstance.

Notes

1. Swift, *Prose*, XI, 38-9. For another use of the metaphor of walking on a high wire, in a political context, *see Prose*, II, 75.
2. Miriam K. Starkman, ed., *Gulliver's Travels and Other Writings* (New York, 1962), p. 54; Dennis, in his edition of the work for *The Prose Works of Jonathan Swift*, ed. T. Scott (London, 1897-1908), VIII:39 n.; Case, *Four Essays on Gulliver's Travels* (Princeton, N.J., 1945),pp. 77ff. A further candidate might be the other secretary of state, the duke of Newcastle, more of an intriguer than Townshend. For an interesting discussion of the political satire in book 1, *see* W.A. Speck, *Swift* (London, 1969), pp. 105-14, and for a general review of the topic, see Irvin Ehrenpreis, *The Personality of Jonathan Swift* (Cambridge, Mass, 1958), pp. 85-91. Two earlier discussions of the rope-dancing episode are those of Nicholas Joost, 'Gulliver and the *Free-Thinker*', MLN LV (1950): 197-9, arguing that a possible source may be Ambrose Philips's periodical, *The Free-Thinker*, no. 144 (7 August 1719); and Edward W. Rosenheim, Jr., 'A 'source' for the rope-dancing in *Gulliver's Travels*,' *Philological Quarterly* XXXI (1952) 208-11, pointing out an analogy in Swift's own *Remarks on . . . The Rights of the Christian Church*.
3. *Firth, Essays Historical and Literary* (Oxford, 1938), p. 221; Landa, in his edition of the book (London, 1965), p. 244. Cf. Robert Hunting, *Jonathan Swift* (New York, 1967), pp. 99-100, 120.
4. *TE*, V, 59-60.
5. Edwards, *This Dark Estate* (Berkeley and Los Angeles, 1963), esp. pp. 127 ff.
6. *See* for example R.J Mitchell and M.D.R. Leys, *A History of London Life* (Harmondsworth, 1964), p. 137.
7. *Bartholomew Fair*, ed. E. Partridge (London, 1964), p. 65. On Smithfield's general reputation, *see also* my *Grub Street* (London, 1972), pp. 37-8.

8. Daniel Defoe, *Moll Flanders*, ed. G.A. Aitken (London, 1965), pp. 166, 192-4, 206; idem, *Colonel Jack*, ed. S.H. Monk (London, 1965) pp. 13, 43.

9. *The Author's Farce*, ed. C.B. Woods (London, 1967), p. 49 and n.

10. *A Critical View of the Publick Buildings ... in ... London and Westminster* (London, 1734), p. 15.

11. Thomas Frost, *The Old Showmen, and the London Fairs* (London, 1874), p. 300.

12. O Hehir, 'Meaning of Swift's Description of a City Shower', *ELH*, XXVII (1960): 204-5. O Hehir stresses, too, the profligacy associated with the Fair and attempts to suppress it. Still more appositely, he points out that a droll by the arch-Dunce Settle was performed at Smithfield in 1707. *See also* the *Grub-street Journal*, 26 August 1731.

13. Swift, *Prose*, II, 148, 206.

14. Swift, *Prose*, III, 147.

15. *Swift. The Man, his Works and the Age*, 3 vols. (London, 1963-)II: 413-14.

16. Quoted by Mitchell and Leys, p. 138. Another contemporary advertisement refers to 'Dancing on the Ropes, after the French and Italian fashion'. (Ashton, p. 189). One can imagine the Scriblerian response to this blandishment.

17. On the Hogarth print, Violante and Fawkes, *see Graphic Works*, 1: 157; H.B. Wheatley, *Hogarth's London* (London, 1909), pp. 424-33; Frost, *Showmen* pp. 110ff; Rosenfeld, pp. 14-18.

18. Frost, *The Lives of the Conjurors* (London, 1876), pp. 73-8; Rosenfeld, pp. 109-10; Ashton, pp. 190, 197: J.P. Malcolm, *Anecdotes of the Manners and Customs of London, during the Eighteenth Century* (London, 1810), II, 122. Malcolm quotes a newspaper on Lady Mary's 'perform[ing] such curious steps on the dancing rope'.

19. On this phrase, see Aubrey Williams's article in *Review of English Studies* IV (1953): 359-61.

20. *Graphic Works*, 1: 157; Wheatley, p. 430; Rosenfeld, p. 37.

21. Rosenfeld, p. 26. Henry Morley, *Memoirs of Bartholomew Fair* (London, 1859), p. 396, reproduces a section of the print showing a sign which blazons forth Fawkes's 'Dexterity of Hand'. Incidentally, the generic term Swift uses of these capers—'Diversions'—was applied to fairground shows in contemporary advertisements. As for Flimnap's preeminence, consider this paragraph in the *London Journal* for 5 January 1723: 'Mr Fawks, the famous Artist, goes on performing his Legerdemain Exploits with vast Success and Applause, being admired by every one that sees him, as out-doing all the Undertakers in that Way'. *Undertaker* could mean political jobber. In terms of a satiric proportion sum, Fawkes is to Flimnap as Flimnap is to Walpole.

22. Morley, p. 398; E.B. Chancellor, *The Pleasure Haunts of London* (London, 1925), p. 329. See also Sheridan W. Baker, 'Political Allusion in Fielding's *Author's Farce ...*,' *PMLA* LXXVII (1962): 223-4. Maynard Mack, *The Garden and the City* (Toronto, 1969), p. 129, quotes a mock playbill of 1735, advertising 'Robin's great theatrical booth'. According to OED, s.v. 'Budget' (4), the first use of the word *budget* (meaning pedlar's bag) in connection with politics was in the title of [William Pulteney?], *The Budget*

Open'd (London, 1733), p. 8, where Walpole's manipulations of the excise scheme are seen in terms of the tricks of a conjuror or mountebank. There is also mention of the 'Art of Political Legerdemain.' Walpole is termed 'our State Emperick'—quackery was always associated with the Fair. *See* Alan S.C. Ross *Etymology* (London, 1958), p. 142. *The Craftsman* on 22 August 1730 accused Walpole of encouraging not eminent writers but rather 'those sublime Productions, *Hurlothrumbo* and *Tom Thumb*'. This was low enough on the theatrical scale, as Swift and Pope saw it.

23. For a description of the print, *see* Stephens, II, 604. It is reproduced in Herbert M. Atherton, *Political Prints in the Age of Hogarth* (Oxford, 1974), Plate 9; *see also* pp. 69–70.

24. The account of Fawkes and Pinchbeck is taken mainly from Frost, *Showmen*, pp. 110–23; Frost, *Conjurors*, pp. 115–18; Morley, p. 399; George Speaight, *The History of the English Puppet Theatre* (London, 1955), p. 105 ff. According to Speaight (p. 106), the phrase 'dexterity of hand' is commonly found of the puppet masters. One might add that the word was applied to Rich's skill in his antics as Harlequin: *see Pasquin* for 4 February 1724, quoted in *London Stage*, II, clxxv.

    Attention has recently been focussed on Fawkes by Paulson, I, 115, and Altick, pp. 60, 62. Throughout the 1720s his names appears in the press, and almost always his 'dexterity' is emphasised. His show also included a 'posture-master' and a musical clock. Examples are cited by Paulson, I, 115, 519n; and John Nichols, *Biographical Anecdotes of William Hogarth* (London, 1785), p. 133. Many other examples could be culled from journals such as the *Daily Post* and Mist's *Weekly Journal*, around 1723 in particular—when *Gulliver* was in the process of composition. In 1725 Fawkes agreed with 'the famous *Powell of the Bath*,' who had 'the finest machines in England', to mount a joint show in the Haymarket.

    For Edward Pinchbeck (son of Christopher the elder, and brother of Christopher the younger), in his role as puppet-show proprietor, see *London Stage*, II, xxxv–xxxvi; Altick, pp. 60–3. The father was a clockmaker and the brother an inventor and patentee. 'Pinchbeck' as the name of a cheap alloy used in gimcrack jewellery derives from the father (*OED*).

25. The terms in which such performers were advertised can be gauged from the following advertisement in the *Norwich Gazette* on 7 January 1727, though it comes slightly too late to enter directly into calculations: 'the famous and original Posture-Maker of the World, who turns his Body into all Manner of deformed Shapes and Postures'. Quoted by G.A. Cranfield, *The Development of the Provincial Newspaper 1700–60* (Oxford, 1962), p. 217. An earlier 'turn' of a Lilliputian cast had been the dwarf, 29 inches high, without hands or feet, who operated ',machines of his own contrivance and work', played on musical instruments (like Gulliver in Brobdingnag), and had had performed 'before three Emperors'. See *Daily Journal*, 8 May 1724.

26. Swift, *Prose* XI: 178. Of this broad subject, there is an excellent survey by Aline Mackenzie Taylor, 'Sights and monsters and Gulliver's Voyage to Brobdingnag', *Tulane Studies in English* VII (1957): 29–82; Mrs Taylor makes but one glancing allusion to Lilliput (p. 63). *See also* Altick, pp. 35, 43.

27. *Jonathan Swift and the Anatomy of Satire* (Cambridge, Mass, 1953), pp. 132ff. It may be worthwhile, however, to add this passage from a sermon by Ralph Cudworth, which Swift would almost certainly have known. 'They that are acted only by an outward Law, are but like Meuropasts; or those little Puppets that skip nimbly up and down, and seem to be full of quick and sprightly motion, whereas they are all the while moved artificially by certain Wires and Strings from without, and not by any Principle of Motion, from themselves within: or else, like Clocks and Watches, that go pretty regularly for a while, but are moved by Weights and Plummets, or some other Artificiall Springs, that must be ever now and then wound up, or else they cease' (*A Sermon preached before the Honourable the House of Commons* [Cambridge, 1647], pp. 74–5).

    For Swift, Flimnap and his rivals similarly lack the 'self-moving Principle' accorded by the 'Law of the Spirit', and the appropriate emblem is that of a puppet. Cf. Pope's image for Hervey in the 'Sporus' passage. Mrs Taylor, pp. 61–2, cites the case of the famous puppet master Powell, for whom see below, p. 94.

28. *The Art of Sinking in Poetry*, ed. E.L. Steeves (New York, 1950), p. 15. It is relevant that 'the Ups-and-Downs' were a popular fairground machine, a sort of vertical carousel.

29. Swift, *Poems*, II, 654, 650, 631. Swift's use of the puppet image in his *Preface to the Bishop of Sarum's Introduction* is quoted by Speaight. *See also* the lines 'In pity to the emptying Town', *Poems*, I, 122–3. This describes the 'corrupted Tast' for May Fair entertainments, with dancing dogs and 'Puppets mov'd by wire'—'So are the Joys which Nature yields/Inverted in May Fair.' And see *A Tale of a Tub* in Swift, *Prose*, I, 67.

30. It is noteworthy that the line between puppet show/Smithfield 'entertainment' on the one hand, and legitimate drama on the other, was becoming increasingly blurred. William Penkethman made a career in both, for instance. On this issue, *see* Rosenfeld, *passim*, and Altick, pp. 58–9.

31. The King of Brobdingnag enlists these associations when deploring the 'Dexterity' of the British nobility in gaming: Swift, *Prose*, XI, 131. Some years earlier, Swift had alluded to the incursion of new City figures as the coming of 'new dextrous Men into Business and Credit' (*Prose*, III, 6.) He applies the terms, unflatteringly, to the Lord Lieutenants of Ireland in the *Drapier's Letters* (*Prose*, X, 60). For an allied critique of politicians as conjurors and exponents of legerdemain, see 'The Origins of Swift's Poem on "Sid Hamet"', *MP*, LXXIX (1982), 304–8.

32. Defoe, 'The life and actions of Jonathan Wild' in *Romances and Narratives*, ed. G.A. Aitken (London, 1895), 16: 246, 253, 258, 260. For 'dexterity' applied to the art of the pickpocket, see also *Colonel Jack*, pp. 16, 44, 185, and *Memoirs of a Cavalier* (London, 1926), p. 9. The word is used of Wild and his associates in several contemporary texts quoted by Gerald Howson, *Thief-Taker General* (London, 1970), pp. 77, 81, 144, 157, 167: *see also* William Lee, *Daniel Defoe: His Life and Recently Discovered Writings* (London, 1889), III, 334–38, for its application to Jack Sheppard. For the quotation from King, see L.-A. Landa, *Swift and the Church of Ireland* (Oxford, 1954), p. 172. Foreign visitors appear to have been particularly

impressed by what went on at the Fair. De Saussure speaks of the 'tricks of equilibrium' performed by rope-dancers; whilse Sorbière uses the precise half-dead metaphor I am considering: 'dextrous cut-purses and pickpockets' are aligned with rope-dancers as principal ingredients of the Fair. Cf. Dorothy Marshall, *Dr. Johnson's London* (New York, 1968), p. 157; Morley, p. 337. Morley's section on 'Bartholomew jugglers', notorious as imposters, is highly pertinent (pp. 25–33); see also pp. 339–62.

33. Louis D. Mitchell, 'Command performances during the Reign of George I', *Eighteenth-Century Studies*, VII (1974), 343–9: quotation from pp. 346–7.
34. Geoffrey Holmes, *British Politics in the Age of Anne* (London, 1967), p. 379.
35. Firsthand testimony that Swift knew Duck Lane and Little Britain, which led out of Smithfield market, is found in *Prose*, XII, 264: see also Swift, *Corr*, V, 118. Another lexical side-effect was that 'Smithfield bargain' came to mean a sharp deal: see *Journal to Stella*, I, 214, and Swift, *Corr*, III, 253.

3

BOOTHS AND THEATRES

Pope, Settle and the Fall of Troy

In Lud's old walls, tho' long I rul'd renown'd,
Far, as loud Bow's stupendous bells resound;
Tho' my own Aldermen conferr'd my bays,
To me committing their eternal praise,
Their full-fed Heroes, their pacific May'rs,
Their annual trophies, and their monthly wars,
Tho' long my Party built on me their hopes,
For writing pamphlets, and for burning Popes ...
Dunciad, A III, 275–82

Thy dragons Magistrates and Peers shall taste,
And from each show rise duller than the last:
Till rais'd from Booths to Theatre, to Court,
Her seat imperial, Dulness shall transport.
Dunciad, A III, 299–302

Of the aesthetic value which attaches to Pope's characteristic indirection in *The Dunciad*, there can be little doubt today.[1] But the density of allusion remains an obstacle even in the more enlightened—or at least favourable—climate which the poem now inhabits. The dominant approach in recent years has involved the relegation of biographic considerations in favour of an ethical/metaphysical/cultural reading of Dulness. In the process we sometimes lose sight of what a recent critic has called 'the daring contemporaneity' of Pope's satire.[2] And such a mistake has a double effect: it skews the poem in the direction of one incomplete aspect of its artistic working, and at the same time it diminishes the impact of that very aspect of the poem. Biographic allusion comes to the aid of every level of meaning in *The Dunciad*, abets every mode of satire which Pope turns to account. To illustrate this point, I shall take the role of Elkanah Settle in the poem.

I

Settle is a particularly interesting figure because he represents in his own person the literary consequences of a profound cultural shift. He was a municipally subsidised 'poet' whose function was to supply material for a traditional pageant: the last of a line stretching back to the high Renaissance, operating in an age which had lost the art of reading public allegory in an unselfconscious way. Furthermore he was a hackney author in very direct terms: that is, he composed set verses to order on special occsions, such as a birthday or a funeral. The poetry provided by Settle differed very little, no matter what was the source of the commission: only the names were changed in the text. The sumptuous binding in which the verses would be enclosed mattered more than their flabby content.

Whichever version of *The Dunciad* we consider, it is apparent that Settle occupies a key position. Only the King Dunce himself and Queen Dulness contribute more to the entire action. He is the 'great Father' (A.III.34) eclipsed among the Dunces only by his 'greater Son.' Through his agency, principally, the poem is anchored in the tradition of *Mac Flecknoe*.[3] His vision of the new empire of Dulness in Book III takes up over three hundred lines, out of 358 (A text) and 340 (B text). In this sequence the arch-Dunce is reduced to the vicarious indignity of a looker-on (if not a voyeur): he is permitted only one spluttering question, more worthy of Mr. Badman or the unnamed interlocutor of formal satire than the titular hero of an epic. Moreover, it should be recalled that in the original form Settle's vision extends up to the last three lines of the poem—thereby incorporating its most famous setpiece. In the revised *Dunciad* the prophecy of universal Dulness is uttered by an impersonal narrative voice: previously, this climactic speech had been spoken with the tongue of a recognisable human (only too human) individual—ghostly as he may be. The great epiphanal moment of *The Dunciad* was vouchsafed to Settle.

Strange, then, that the commentators should have so little to say of his role, or of his suitability for that role. Pope tells us quite a lot in his notes, but not the whole truth—and, as ever, scholarship has been least vigilant where Pope has seemed to do the editorial work himself. By some odd freak Settle has been omitted from the biographical appendix to the Twickenham volume;[4] and Elwin and Courthope furnish little more. Aubrey Williams has some pertinent and sharply put observations on Settle in the context of his own stimulating account of the work: 'In the person of Settle . . . the epic and civic metaphors again are fused: he was the last City Poet to have charge of the annual mayoral festivities, and in Book III of *The Dunciad* he plays the role of Anchises: he is represented as the father of Pope's fictive Aeneas, Theobald. On Settle's death one empire ("Troy", or the City) of Dulness is "destroyed", but then his poetical heir undertakes . . . to establish another and larger empire of the same general character as the old'.[5] All this is well said, but Pope has told us a good deal of it. The interesting point concerns the issues which the poet, with characteristic deviousness, has *not* openly broached.

The episodes in Settle's career which give fresh impetus to the satire have long been on record, and it is surprising that their relevance should have been overlooked. The result is that an important strand in the dialectic has been missed, and a good joke wasted on the desert air (as it now seems) of Pope's contemporaries. My aim is to recover this satiric ground by relating the fictive circumstances of 'Settle' as they emerge through the poem to the actual life-history of his avatar in this world. I shall confine myself for the most part to the original text. As it happens, little alteration is made to Settle's role before the end of Book III.

Settle first enters the poem, if we disregard the argument to Book I, at line 88—and early manuscript reference at line 6, 'And when a Settle falls a Tibbald reigns', having been dropped.[6] When he does appear, the idea of falling is still present: night is doing just that, and so is the quality of pageantry at the Lord Mayor's Show in its declining years: 'Now Night descending, the proud scene was o'er,/But liv'd, in Settle's numbers, one day more' (A.I,87). This is naturally enough by way of excuse for Pope to launch into a deftly contrived account of Settle's career. The note mentions Settle's work as City Poet, the last of the line; his opposition to Dryden; and his party pamphleteering. 'For the latter part of his History' we are referred to a subsequent note; and Pope is not one to break that sort of promise. The threat, proleptic and fastidious, confirms the impression of the detailed *curriculum vitae*. Settle is a marked man, as Jacob, Eusden, Tate, or Philips (all of whom have already made their entrance) are not.

Shortly afterwards we are told how Queen Dulness, gazing at Theobald, 'Sees Gods with Daemons in strange league ingage,/And earth, and heav'n, and hell her battles wage' (A.I,107). The note explains: 'This alludes to the extravagancies of the Farce of that author; in which he alone could properly be represented as successor to *Settle*, who had written *Pope Joan, St. George for England*, and other pieces for *Bartlemew-Fair*.' There are other respects, as we shall see in a moment, why Settle might be named with especial propriety in conjunction with this couplet. However, for the present we may confine ourselves to these observations: (1) Settle's *Female Prelate: Being the History of the Life and Death of Pope Joan* first saw light as a blank verse tragedy, when it was performed at Drury Lane. Its anti-papist bias is perhaps too obvious to underline; but it is more significant that its motifs include 'the use of ghosts . . . peculiar disguises and devices . . . the employment of fire to betray the guilt of the intriguing villains', as well as a papal procession and a 'rabble' of Romans.[7] This piece antedates by some forty years the droll proper which is *St. George*. The timelag illustrates the comprehensive scope of Pope's malicious interest in Settle, whose dramatic fortunes encapsulate the movement of Dulness, *in reverse*: 'rais'd from Booths to Theatre' (A.III.301). (2) Theobald had actually collaborated with Settle, as the former's biographer R.F. Jones points out: 'In 1718 he [Theobald] furnished the songs and a little of the poetry to Elkanah Settle's *The Lady's Triumph*, as well as the masque of *Decius and Paulina*, which occurs in the last act of Settle's production.'[8] The two men were thus the more appropriately linked in the fictive alliance of *The Dunciad*. (3) However, Theobald was not himself, strictly, a Bartholomew Fair dramatist. He produced harlequinades and pantomimes but not drolls as such. It was Settle above all who had been a votary of the Smithfield Muses (A.I.2), as the most famous of all droll-contrivers. It was no doubt for this reason that Pope introduced his name into the note. When Colley Cibber took over the leading part, there was no need for such an understudy—his own ballad opera reached the Fair in 1729, his son was acting there from 1725, and his daughter from 1732.[9] Consequently the note disappears in this form, and with it mention of Settle. It could be argued that this was one way in which the versatile Cibber possessed greater heroic potential than Theobald, as far as Pope's contorted epic ambitions went.

Later in Book I there occurs the most interesting passage from our present standpoint. Theobald, having assembled his pyre of unread literary works, soliloquises on the subject of his own career:

> Me, Emptiness and Dulness could inspire,
> And were my Elasticity and Fire.
> Had heav'n decreed such works a longer date,
> Heav'n had decreed to spare the Grubstreet-state.
> But see great Settle to the dust descend,
> And all thy cause and empire at an end!
> Cou'd Troy be sav'd by any single hand,
> His gray-goose-weapon must have made her stand ...
>
> (A.I.181)

Pope's own note identifies the Virgilian parodies: the Twickenham edition supplements these by references to the translations of Dryden and Christopher Pitt. Aubrey Williams draws out the thematic meaning: 'with the death of Settle (our poetic Hector here), Pope's mythic "Troy" is doomed'.[10] Yes, and there is a propriety beyond the simple equation of Troy and Grub Street, which supports much of the poem. The pathos of Settle, attempting singlehanded to stem the tide of battle with his feeble weapon (a pen is a feeble weapon at best, but Settle's, we understand, is a feeble pen anyway)—this pathos derives not just from an allusion to Virgil, but also from the dramatist's own life-history. The next line of the passage in the *Aeneid* supplies one clue.

Anchises, in Book II of that poem, gives vent to an exclamation whose opening section is quoted by Pope:

> Me si caelicolae voluissent ducere vitam,
> has mihi servassent sedes. satis una superque
> vidimus excidia et captae superavimus urbi.

(Loeb version: 'For me, had the lords of heaven willed that I should lengthen life's thread, they would have spared this my home. Enough and more is it that I have seen one destruction, and survived one capture of this city.')[11] The reference is to the destruction of Troy by Hercules. However, Settle himself had already witnessed, indeed shared in, one such razing of the city. In May 1701 Settle had produced at Drury Lane his 'opera' *The Virgin Prophetess, or the Fate of Troy*. This itself was garnished with enough elaborate machinery to have been instanced by Emmett L. Avery as evidence of a growing emphasis on spectacle.[12] Elephants, twenty-foot chariots, and elaborate 'prospects' fill the stage. But this is as nothing beside the Smithfield version, performed at Bartholemew Fair in 1707 as *The Siege of Troy* and many times subsequently.[13] This piece has been called 'perhaps the most remarkable of the Bartholomew-Fair dramas which have found their way into print' as well as 'the most famous and most elaborate of all drolls'.[14] Pope could not have failed to be aware of this celebrated show, the high point of all Smithfield dramaturgy. *The Siege of Troy* was even reprinted in the very year that saw the appearance of *The Dunciad*, this time described as 'a *Tragi-Comedy*'.

Apart from anything else, his close friend John Gay had witnessed a performance of the droll in 1726, and had thought it worth providing the Countess of Burlington (herself an ally of Pope) with a detailed description:

> I write this Letter on Sunday night while I imagine you to be at the Opera. How poorly are we oblig'd to entertain ourselves! for [William] Kent and I thought ourselves very happy on Friday night with Bartholomew Fair and the Siege of Troy. I think the Poet corrected Virgil with great judgment in the Poetical justice which he observ'd; for Paris was kill'd upon the spot by Menelaus, and Helen burnt in the flames of the town before the Audience. The Trojan Horse was large [as] life and extreamly well painted; the sight of which struck Kent with such astonishment, that he prevaild with me to go with him next day to compare it with the celebrated paintings at Greenwich ... For my own part, I was in concern that the show-man did Sir James Cornhill (as he call'd him) so much injustice for he pointed out to us four Cardinals near King William, which he called the four Cardinals of Virtue ... This is a proof that a fine puppet-show may be spoild and depreciated by an ignorant interpreter.[15]

There is much of *The Dunciad* in little here—and Gay goes on to make further play with the 'cardinal virtues', standard props of baroque iconography parodied in the tableau of Queen Dulness. We have a fairground poet 'correcting' Virgil; Bartholomew Fair adopting the mannerisms of high art; and astonishing spectacle replacing thoughtful use of stage illusion. Gay reports ironically that Kent was inclined 'to give the preference to Bartholomew Fair' over the Greenwich paintings: a confirmation of present-day taste, which elevated vacuous entertainment over serious drama.

One final line of evidence confirms Pope's awareness of Settle's show. In March 1715 he had been attacked by the young Whig men about town, George Duckett and Thomas Burnet, in a pamphlet called *Homerides*. In the preface to this satire occurs 'An Epilogue', for Mr Punch to speak. Curll reprinted this in 1728 in his *Key to the Dunciad*, maliciously underlining the thrust, which lay in the suggestion that Pope would use his friendship with the puppet-master Robert Powell to mount a production of *The Siege of Troy* for his [Pope's] benefit. The show would be used to puff the Homer subscription. In the epilogue itself, Duckett and Burnet connect Homer's 'Tale of Troy', as now translated by Pope, with the crude puppet version of the story. We know that Pope did not forget such insults easily, and that he reserved a satiric niche for both Burnet and Duckett. Whilst paying off old scores, however, he characteristically trapped the energy of a hostile pamphlet in *The Dunciad*'s own field of force.[16]

The droll is in three acts. According to Settle's biographer, F.C. Brown, 'the serious portions of the original [opera] have all been shortened, while the scenes of buffoonery, in which the drunken mob appears, have been considerably lengthened to please the Bartholomew-Fair audience'.[17] King Mob is indeed strongly in evidence in *The Siege of Troy*. But more remarkable than the divergences are the elements carried through from one version to the other. These include, most pertinently, a transformation scene in which a view of Heaven is instantly converted, by a wave of Cassandra's wand, into a scene of Hell, with 'a Dance of Furies arising from under the Stage'. This occurs in the second act of the droll: in the third, we witness the city of Troy, elaborately mounted on the stage, as it is taken and set on fire by the Greeks. We see the flames 'breaking forth through all the windows, and the whole Battlements blazing with one continued Range of Fire'. Shrieks and cries rend the air.

Throughout, the stage directions read like instructions for a dramatisation of *The Dunciad*.[18] It is easy to understand Henry Morley's judgment, pat as it may appear: 'Though Settle was one of the worst poets, he was one of the best planners of spectacles and pomps.'[19]

The relevance of this scenic display to Theobald's soliloquy should be plain enough. It is a somewhat harsh joke that Settle should be cast as the forlorn defender of Troy, since it was he who had devised its perdition in the best-known contemporary version of the story. To men and women of Pope's time, it was this lurid droll, and not the inventions of mythological painters, which presented the liveliest imaginative picture of Troy 'tottering to her fall'—the phrase is adapted from Dryden. Subliminally, the effect is to insinuate Settle's *complicity* in the fall. In other words, the Grub Street hacks who complain most bitterly of their loss of empire are themselves responsible for their ruin. Settle's death is at once a species of auto-da-fé (the heretic punished by the Grub Street tribunal) and a ritual self-sacrifice, necessary for the rebuilding of the empire of Dulness. *Urbs antiqua ruit*: Settle, fire-raiser, victim and would-be prevention officer all at once, dies with his city.

So much is, I think, straightforward. Certain other implications of Settle's career deserve fuller attention. (1) It happens that the opera of 1701 appeared a year later entitled *Cassandra: or, The Virgin Prophetess*. The soothsayer does indeed figure prominently in the action; and it is unlikely to be accidental that Settle should be cast in the role of prophet in *The Dunciad*, Book III—or that his vision should be (objectively considered) so dire in its portents. (2) The droll was especially popular for a number of years. It seems to have reached a fifth edition by 1718, an unusual bibliographical permanence for such a show. Around 1715 and 1716, it was performed at Southwark Fair by Mrs Mynn's well-known company. In Hogarth's famous *Southwark Fair* (1733), the droll is still holding the boards.[20] One can hardly doubt that it would be entirely familiar to Pope: even disregarding the fact, mentioned by Sutherland, that Settle was 'probably one of the first authors that Pope read', here was the Smithfield muse in full flight.[21] (3) *The Siege of Troy* was taken over by the puppet theatres by 1712. In that year, the most famous of the puppet-masters, Martin Powell, put on the show as *The False*

Triumph. Even supposing that Powell's version owed little to the Settle production, which is a large assumption, it is noteworthy that Powell hit on this theme. As George Speaight's handlist makes clear, there were very few puppet plays on subjects drawn from classical mythology, in proportion to other sources. Besides, Powell was known for his tendency to exploit contemporary and indeed topical themse. In 1726, Powell's son again performed *The False Triumph, or the Destruction of Troy*, although this time the piece was listed as operatic burlesque.[22] (4) Further emphasis is laid on the Troy legend in the succeeding portion of *The Dunciad*. Theobald, of course, lights the 'structure' of books; 'rowling smokes' surround the object of sacrifice (A.I.205). We hear of a 'quick flash' and of devouring flames: it is the exact counterpart of the stage-direction for Settle's droll. Finally comes: 'Then gush'd the tears, as from the Trojan's eyes/When the last blaze sent Ilion to the skies' (A.1.211), complete with a pedantic note by Scriblerus on the misnamed 'Trojan' horse. This is indeed the poetry of allusion; but it alludes not only to the second book of the *Aeneid*—it calls to mind equally a famous episode in Settle's dramatic biography.

II

With these issues before us, we can now turn to Book III of Pope's poem. The visionary Settle is but a ghost in the infernal regions; yet his monologue is studded with references to a career in Dulness that was too too solid in the contemporary remembrance. He is introduced with precise description of his physical bulk, his Charterhouse livery and general appearance of habitual dilapidation. Then begins his Pisgah sight of the new empire, a conducted tour of Augustan culture and society as seen from the Mount of Vision. 'Old scenes of glory, times long cast behind,/Shall first [be] recalled' (A.III.55) is the opening threat: together, the past and future will 'fire' Theobald's brain. As is appropriate, the past scenes of glory invoked are allusively linked to that Smithfield tradition in which Theobald metaphorically, Settle (and later Cibber) historically, shared.

The ghost of Settle now reveals to Theobald the course of Dulness: the progress is one of raging fire—'One bright blaze turns learning into air ... There [in the South] rival flames with equal glory rise' (A.III.70). The image of folly ravaging the civilised world draws an added satiric point from its applicability to the speaker's own (as it were) cultural history. The apocalyptic tone of this book, moreover, corresponds to the prevailing dramatic note in Settle's theatrical works, a kind of charged exoticism. A common ingredient in his plays is a cosmic tableau: the allegorical machinery in *The World in the Moon* (1697) suggests nothing so much as a ceiling by Thornhill: 'Twelve golden Chariots are seen riding in the Clouds, filled with Twelve Children, representing the Twelve Celestial Signs. The Third Arch entirely rolling away, leaves the full prospect terminating with a large landscape of Woods, Waters, Towns, etc.'[24] Settle sees the encroachment of barbarism on Rome in strikingly similar terms: 'See the Cirque falls! th' unpillar'd Temple nods!/ Streets pav'd with Heroes, Tyber choak'd with Gods!' (A.III.99). A host of minute references, whilst inconclusive in themselves, support this implied parallelism. At the line 'He, whose long Wall the wand'ring Tartar bounds' (A.III.68), readers of Pope's day might have recalled *The Conquest of China, By the Tartars*, a play of 1673/4 (published 1676). Settle's marked fondness for settings either Persian (*Cambyses*), Moorish (*The Emperor of Morocco*) or Indian (*The Ambitious Slave*) might be attributed to a general legacy of heroic drama. But it fits in well with the sweeping geography of Settle's prophecy. That Settle's literary satire on John Dunton, *The Athenian Comedy* (1693), should include a poetry professor called Obadiah Grub is surely a contingent fact, but none the less a felicitous accident in the context of this poem.

The crucial passage occurs well into the book, where Settle breaks off his narrative to show Theobald 'a sable Sorc'rer':

> All sudden, Gorgons hiss, and Dragons glare,
> And ten-horn'd fiends and Giants rush to war.
> Hell rises, Heaven descends, and dance on Earth,
> Gods, imps, and monsters, music, rage, and mirth,
> A fire, a jig, a battle, and a ball,
> Till one wide conflagration swallows all.
>
> (A.III.231)

There follows the famous picture of the 'new world', where

forests dance and rivers upward rise. Pope in his note mentions
Theobald's *Rape of Proserpine*, and there can be no doubt that
such later pantomimes put out by John Rich were in the poet's
mind. Yet it is important to note that the spectacular cosmic
dance recalls the dramatic practice of Settle also. In *The Siege of
Troy*, as we have seen, there is a transformation from Heaven to
Hell; the droll includes a fire, a battle, dancing, and gods, not to
mention 'music, rage, and mirth'. The primary allusion is
directed towards the contemporary harlequinades at Lincoln's
Inn Fields. All the same, no poem ushered in by invocation of the
Smithfield muses could subdue the accumulated references to
Bartholomew Fair shows at this point. And Settle, we need not
emphasise, was the acknowledged master of the fairground droll.

Such reference is, admittedly, distracting if we pay it too much
heed during the description of Rich and the battle of the theatres
(A.III.249–68). However, Settle returned to the forefront with
his self-pitying catalogue of insult and injury. He speaks
unmistakably in his own person, mentioning his party writing,
his work as City poet, his anti-papist spectacles and the rest. The
verse would seem explicit to the point of verging on the prosaic.
Yet Pope underlines the gravamen with a note full of malicious
accuracy ('He had managed the Ceremony of a famous Pope-
burning on *Nov.* 17, 1680')[25] Then the poetry erupts into a bitter
exclamation:

> Yet lo! in me what authors have to brag on!
> Reduc'd at last to hiss in my own dragon.
> Avert it, heav'n! that thou or Cibber e'er
> Should wag two serpent tails in Smithfield fair.
>
> (A.III.287)

The innuendo here, if it is not too direct to merit that word, has
been better understood, largely because Pope provides the
essential information: 'After the Revolution he kept a Booth at
Bartlemew-fair, where in his Droll call'd *St. George for England*, he
acted in his old age in a Dragon of green leather of his own
invention.' Settle's biographer was not able to date this droll
exactly, but it was performed around 1720. By 1725 this show too
had reached the puppet theatre, and Swift's 'Mad Mullinix and
Timothy' (1728) alludes to the play in this form: '*St George* himself

he [Punch] plays the wag on,/ And mounts astride upon the *Dragon*.'[26] 'Thus *Tim*', the poem continues, 'Philosophers suppose,/ *The World consists of Puppet-shows.*' The trope is a recurring one in Swift, especially. Settle's presence further enriches the theatrical metaphor, since his works had proved so remarkably accommodating as far as translation into puppetry was concerned.

There is a stray fact here which may have been active at some remote level of Pope's imagination. On 8 September 1727, a showman was playing the puppet version of *St. George* at Burwell, not far from Cambridge. The business in this show included a dragon who 'seemed to spout real fire out of his mouth, with a noise like thunder and lightning'. During the performance, a fire only too literal in nature broke out in the barn which was the venue. Eighty people were killed in the blaze.[27] This episode remains a live recollection in local annals; and it is not beyond the bounds of possibility (though I put it no higher) that Pope, who was then at work on his poem, may have noted the incident. The conflagrations, thunder and lightning of Book III are as applicable as the direct allusion to Settle's droll on St George.

Settle reaches a climax in his rhetoric with these lines:

> Grubstreet! thy fall should men and Gods conspire,
> Thy stage shall stand, ensure it but from Fire.
> Another Aeschylus appears! prepare
> For new Abortions, all ye pregnant Fair!
> In flames, like Semeles, be brought to bed,
> While opening Hell spouts wild-fire at your head.

(A.III.309)

The clutter of exclamation marks answers to the nervous excitement of the rhythms. Well might the ghostly Settle feel involved in this prediction. His real-life embodiment had compassed many a theatrical denouement of this order. One level of the wit plays on the familiar eighteenth-century fact that playhouses were notoriously combustible things. Another, more inward, suggestion rests on the earlier identification of Grub Street with Troy. The pageant of a gaping Hell, shooting forth flames, suits the context for reasons other than those superficially apparent. Such scenes were endemic to the fair-ground droll;

and the actual speaker at this point was the leading practitioner of that debased literary kind.

Almost immediately there succeeds, in the first version, the famous apotheosis of Dulness. In the new *Dunciad*, apart from the transposition of this section (and its alienation from Settle's person), comparatively few changes of any moment are made. There is little occasion for an Anchises in Book IV, where the Queen and Cibber are able to envisage quite enough imminent folly by themselves. However, it is worth remarking that Cibber was himself a Smithfield dramatist by adoption. His son performed there, and his daughter actually ran a puppet theatre for a short while.[28] In this respect, though he had unlike Theobald no direct link with Settle, he was appropriately leagued with the older dramatist in the satiric pageant Pope has contrived.

If one structural prop for the work is the theatrical levee, as George Sherburn argued,[29] a recurrent metaphor is the dramatic show. In particular, the visionary scenes of Book III belong to a world of allegorical pantomime deriving from the booths of popular tradition. The choice of Settle as seer and narrator has several advantages, not least the linkage of Grub Street with Smithfield which his career itself lived out. In addition, Settle firmly sets the King Dunce in his true apostolic succession; the very fact that Settle had so often incurred the scorn of the wits suited Pope's purposes. But beyond this there is a special aptness. Elkanah Settle, more than any man, cements the imaginative relation proposed between the *Aeneid* and the sordid byplay of the Dunces—a wider mental distance for Pope to bridge than two centuries of scholarly comment may allow us to see.[30] The central document here is the famous droll which Settle made out of his mildly successful opera. The burning of Troy was, according to legend, necessary to the foundation of Rome. This was a teleology which Virgil's masterpiece had memorably enshrined. To hint at a similar trajectory in the progress of Dulness, Pope needed a Grub Street figure who had treated the legendary theme. He found one in the dramatist by whose hand the fall of Troy had been acted out at Smithfield.

Notes

1. The principal sources to which reference is made are as follows: F.C. Brown, *Elkanah Settle: His Life and Works* (Chicago, 1910); Henry Morley, *Memoirs of Bartholomew Fair* (London, n.d.[c.1874]); Rosenfeld; George Speaight, *The History of the English Puppet Theatre* (London, 1955); and Williams. The *Dunciad* quotations and line numbers refer to the Twickenham edition, vol. V (London, 3rd ed., 1963), edited by James Sutherland (*TE*).
2. Manuel Schonhorn, 'The audacious contemporaneity of Pope's *Epistle to Augustus*', *SEL* VIII (1968), 431–44.
3. *See* Sutherland's remarks in *TE*, V, xxxviii–xxxix, as well as V, xlv, on the 'historical setting of dullness'.
4. *TE*, V, 454.
5. Williams, p. 40. Settle was also a suitable case for satiric treatment because he had been at least twice in the Fleet Prison (Guildhall Library, Insolvent Debtors files). Like other dunces, he knew at first hand this great 'Haunt of the Muses' (A.II.396).
6. *See TE*, V, 61.
7. Brown, p. 90.
8. R.F. Jones, *Lewis Theobald* (New York, 1919), p. 26.
9. Rosenfeld, pp. 29, 32, 38.
10. Williams, p. 19; *see also* pp. 20–2.
11. *Virgil: Aeneid I-VI*, ed. H.R. Fairclough (London, 1946), p. 337.
12. *The London Stage*, II, cix; for performance *see* I, II and Allardyce Nicoll, *A History of Early Eighteenth-Century Drama 1700-1750* (Cambridge, 1925), pp. 233–4. For the text, see Abel Roper's publication of *The Virgin Prophetess* (London, 1701).
13. Brown, pp. 35, 105 and n.; Morley, pp. 284–91 (much of the text reproduced); Rosenfeld, pp. 161–5.
14. Brown, p. 105; Rosenfeld, p. 19.
15. *The Letters of John Gay*, ed. C.F. Burgess (Oxford, 1966), pp. 53–4. Pope was in regular touch with Gay at this juncture, and it is conceivable that the story of this 'improvement' on Virgil gave Pope some part of his inspiration for *The Dunciad*.
16. *See Homerides: or, a Letter to Mr. Pope* (London, 1715), p. 7: *A Compleat Key to the Dunciad* (London, 1728), pp. 20–2; J.V. Guerinot, *Pamphlet Attacks on Alexander Pope 1711-1744* (London, 1969), pp. 20–4.
17. Brown, p. 105.
18. *See The Siege of Troy, a Dramatick Performance* [1707?], pp. 5–23; *The Virgin Prophetess*, p. 27; Morley, pp. 290–1, and Rosenfeld, p. 164, on the changing 'vista'. The words 'vista' and 'prospect' are both significant for any consideration of Book III of *The Dunciad*. Note also the reference to 'prodigies' in *The Siege of Troy*, p. 5.
19. Morley, p. 292.
20. Brown, p. 35.
21. *TE*, V, 183.
22. Speaight, pp. 330, 332. Speaight lists the 1726 performance under 'Ballad

Operas' (etc.); but I can find no reference in the checklist of such works provided by E.M. Gagey, *Ballad Opera* (New York, 1937), pp. 237–43. Powell was a famous man in his day, as references by Swift, Defoe, and others indicate; his repertoire would in all probability have been familiar to Pope. Certainly after the publication of *Robert Powell* in 1712, few of the Harley circle could have been unaware of this successful showman.

24. Brown, p. 101. On the elaborate sets for this play, *see* R.H. Barker, *Mr. Cibber of Drury Lane* (New York, 1939), pp. 55–56. Barker aptly quotes the *Post Boy* for June 15, 1697: and cites the stage-directions, which call for a 'full prospect terminating with a large landscape of woods, waters, towns', land so on. Cf. *Dunciad*, A.III.241–2.

25. For the pageant of 1680, *see* Brown, pp. 62–3. The affinities with the procession of the Dunces are marked.

26. Swift, *Poems*, III, 777. A reference in 'Strephon and Chloe' (1731), line 292, may suggest that Swift was familiar with *The Siege of Troy* (p. 527: *see* Speaight, p. 330.) Speaight records no St George puppetry prior to 1725, a date strongly indicative of Settle's influence. For Swift's use of puppet-shows and other fairground diversions, *see* pp. 79–80 above. St George and the Dragon was a favourite subject in Lord Mayors' pageants: *see* p. 97 above.

27. Speaight, p. 152: cf. C.J.W. Messent, *Suffolk and Cambridgeshire* (Harmondsworth, 1949), p. 138.

28. Speaight, pp. 102–8.

29. Sherburn, '*The Dunciad*, Book IV,' *Texas Studies in Literature and Language*, XXXIV (1944). 174–90.

30. It is worth adding that amongst Settle's earliest works, since lost, is a poem entitled *An Elegy on the late Fire and Ruins of London* (1667): Brown, p. 12. For a ritual Pope-burning, a Jesuit in the shape of a devil, and the like, *see The Coronation of Queen Elizabeth* (1680). This was performed at Bartholomew Fair in the year named: Rosenfeld, pp. 159–60; Morley, pp. 197–217. Finally, it is interesting that Gay's farce *The What d'ye call it*, in which Pope may have had some small part, was performed at Southwark Fair in September 1716, along with *The Siege of Troy. See* Rosenfeld, p. 78.

4

NOISE AND NONSENSE

The Critique of Opera in *The Dunciad*

> To please this vitious Taste, what Arts were try'd?
> Our *Beaus* have scolded, and our *Belles* have cry'd,
> And famous *Op'ras* reign'd their Day,—and dy'd:
> Tho' crowded Theatres your Numbers grac'd,
> To soothe the tastless Fews, you were displac'd ...
> Amusements less polite the Town will charm,
> We want some Crowd—and Sounds—to keep us warm;
> In place of promis'd Heaps of glitt'ring Gold,
> The good *Academy* got nought—but Cold.
>
> *An Epistel to Mr Handel* (1724)

> *Operas* and *Masquerades*, and all the politers elegancies of a wanton
> age, are much less to be regarded for their expence (great as it is) than
> for the Tendency which they have to deprave our manners. MUSICK
> has something so peculiar in it, that it exerts a willing Tyranny over
> the Soul into whatever shape the melody directs.
>
> *The Craftsman*, 13 March 1727

According to Pope's early biographer, 'William Ayre', the poet
was 'always a Discourager of *Italian* Operas, always a Promoter
of *English* Sense'.[1] Nowadays the view deriving from John
Mainwaring that Pope was totally insensitive to music is
dismissed as without any real foundation. Nevertheless, we still
have no full explanation for Pope's alliance with the anti-opera
party over a long period of time. To understand his attitudes
requires some exploration of political and cultural affairs as well
as strictly musical matters. In any case, we are handicapped
because regrettably little attention has been given to the sections
concerned with opera in *The Dunciad*. Despite a large number of
explicit references in the first version of the poem, Pope still
thought it necessary to introduce the 'harlot form' of Opera as a
character in Book IV of the greater *Dunciad*. I wish here to

consider the relevance of this theme, both at the level of particular allusion and at that of broad imaginative effect. I shall argue that Pope's awareness of the contemporary operatic scene was greater than has generally been realised. Further, that Italian opera serves throughout as a metaphor of sound without sense—in other words, it is a living image of Dulness. This is not just because some of the grotesque and *outré* choreographic effects in the poem have analogues in opera of the day. George Sherburn in a famous essay has related the loose-knit form of Book IV to the levee scene, as developed by Fielding in his comedy of the 1730s. My view is that the last book is really more like one of Heidegger's masquerades (Reuben Brower calls it 'a kind of fancy-dress ball of all the best people').[2] But prior even to that, it is a variant of the 'Sessions' form, as Pope himself tells us (though no one seems to have heeded this). An important link here is an attack on Heidegger and some popular operatic figures, *The Session of Musicians* (1724). Here we find a surprising overlap in content and phrasing with the 'operatic' parts of *The Dunciad*. Pope, indeed, defines Dulness in symbolic terms which to a large extent derive from the opera house.

It is often asserted, following Burney, that Pope had little knowledge of music. A contrast is often drawn with Dr. Arbuthnot, who 'seems to have been as musical as his friends Pope and Swift were unmusical ...'[3] Swift's reputation for having no ear may have something to do with the story of his putting obstacles in Handel's way in 1742, but it is probably a just one for all that. However, the case is different with Pope. He may have lacked technical knowledge, but there is evidence of a warm response to the work of Bononcini amongst others. More directly to the point, it is clear that (like other men and women of the age) he was deeply impressed by theatrical spectacle—a point which has been well made in respect of Hogarth.[4] It is not far-fetched to see in the baroque elaborations of *The Dunciad*, its crowd scenes, its sudden transformations and its foreshortened epic action a quality which might be called operatic. The structure of Book IV, particularly, with its carefully mounted set pieces (the Grand Tour, say; the dispute of the two botanists) is built around this pattern. Much of the writing is couched in the form of stage directions ('When lo! a Spectre rose', B.IV,139) or choreographic instructions:

> There march'd the bard and blockhead, side by side ...
> Courtiers and Patriots in two ranks divide,
> Thro' both he pass'd, and bow'd from side to side:
> But as in graceful act, with awful eye
> Compos'd he stood, bold Benson thrust him by:
> On two unequal crutches propt he came ...
>
> (B.IV,101, 107–11)

This is apart from explicit reference to aural phenomena: 'the heavy Canon roll' (B.IV,247), 'the voice was drown'd / By the French horn' (B.IV,277), and so on.[5] The whole book consists of a theatrical show, interspersed with solos, recitative, and a kind of inane arioso (B.IV,541–42). The only substantial innovation is that the peerage, instead of patronising such entertainments, have become members of the *dramatis personae*.

I

The climate of opposition to opera in the early eighteenth century has not been thoroughly investigated. Usually, commentators restrict themselves to a citation of familiar passages, such as the satire on *Rinaldo* by Addison in the *Spectator*, No. 5, which appeared on 6 March, 1711. (See p. 44 above.) A great deal of water had flowed under the bridge when Pope published his revised *Dunciad*, with the mincing character of Opera, in 1742. There were important changes in the financing and administration of opera; and (partly consequential on those) significant developments in the musical and theatrical content. Pope was in a favoured position to observe both areas of change. His presentation of opera as a decadent and frivolous art form, then, cannot be put down simply to a general antipathy to an Italianate import among intellectuals at large. Doubtless there was such an attitude abroad; but it had evolved into a far more elaborate case than Addison, say, had advanced. Moreover, Pope extracted only what he needed from the anti-opera 'platform'. He selected and augmented detail to suit his immediate needs—that is, he viewed the follies of opera under the aspect of Dulness. Other critics stressed the improprieties and immoralities of the form; Pope was more aware of the uneducative side of opera.[6]

Among the changes which had taken place in this period the emergence of John Jacob Heidegger as the leading impresario was a crucial fact. In 1711 Heidegger was known merely as an assistant manager at the Haymarket Theatre and as an aspirant librettist of little promise. By early 1713 he was in charge of administration for the new cooperative company at the theatre. In the 1720s and 1730s he was the main figure in the presentation of opera in London, sometimes as a colleague and sometimes as a rival to Handel. He also achieved prominence from about 1720 by reason of his assemblies, variously known as masquerades, 'ridotto's', or simply balls.[7] As we have seen, he figures prominently in Hogarth's *Masquerades and Operas*, published in January 1724. Heidegger makes only a fleeting entrance into *The Dunciad*, and it has been asserted by a distinguished authority that his notorious ugliness was 'the main reason for his being brought into [the poem]'.[8] That may have been the chief motive for mentioning Heidegger directly, leaving aside his conveniently grotesque surname:

> The Goddess then o'er his anointed head.
> With mystic words, the sacred Opium shed.
> And lo! her bird, (a monster of a fowl,
> Something betwixt a Heideggre and owl,)
> Perch'd on his crown ...

>   (B.I,287-91)

However, his activities as impresario had been primarily responsible for the course opera had taken in England; and he is present by implication in most of what Pope says of the form.

Emmett L. Avery has aligned Heidegger with Handel as one of 'the principal entrepreneurs in operatic enterprises'.[9] The first noun is significant; and it could be set against Heidegger's own use of the terms 'Undertaking', 'undertake', and so on.[10] Now the word *undertaker* had some baneful overtones to the contemporary mind, perhaps the Tory mind in particular. It suggested graft and sharp operating: it was applied to such men as the army contractor Sir Henry Furnese, a butt of the Scriblerian group more than once.[11] This could be put another way. Heidegger was one more of those pushing managerial figures whom Pope so deeply distrusted. There was the King Dunce himself, Colley

Cibber, a poetaster made royal laureate and patentee:

> See, see, our own true Phoebus wears the bays!
> Our Midas sits Lord Chancellor of Plays!
>
> (B.III,323–4)

But there were many similar cases—Beau Nash, the vulgarian who made himself *arbiter elegantiarum* at fashionable Bath;[12] William Benson, the dilletante architect who supplanted Wren as Surveyor-General; and Robert Walpole himself, the great 'manager' in politics. Opposition critics in the 1730s often portrayed Walpole as a showman or fairground huckster.[13] All these men have in common a lack of talent and real moral engagement (as the satirists viewed it); they are not creators but operators.

It was under Heidegger's direction that opera had moved into the star system. This not only made for exorbitant salaries and the cult of dubious personalities.[14] It led to quite explicit artistic limitations, especially a sort of dramatic short-cutting. As Giuseppe Riva outlined the desiderata in 1725:

> If your friend wishes to send some [librettos], he must know that in England they want few recitatives, but thirty arias and one duet at least, distributed over the three acts. The subject-matter must be straightforward, tender, heroic, Roman, Greek, or even Persian, and never Gothic or Longobard. For this year and for the two following there must be two equal parts in the operas for Cuzzoni and Faustina; Senesino is the chief male character, and his part must be heroic; the other three male parts must proceed by degrees with three arias each, one in each Act. The duet should be at the end of the second Act, and between the two ladies. If the subject has in it three ladies it can serve because there is a third singer here[15]

Note that these constraints derive not from the composer (though they have definite musical consequences) but from the performers. I shall return presently to the handle which was offered to Pope by the presence of two rivals as prima donna. But the existence of a star castrato had its own riders:

> Firstly, the lower male voices were virtually restricted to minor parts, because the chief 'male' characters were always castrati.

Secondly, even women found it difficult at times to gain a principal role unless they were extremely gifted. The three most famous 'cantatrices' (i.e. virtuoso women singers) were the sopranos Francesca Cuzzoni ... and Faustina Bodoni ... The third cantatrice was Vittoria Tesi ... who excelled as a contralto of great power, so much so, in fact, that she became renowned in masculine roles, an unnatural state of affairs that many less-gifted women singers were forced into by the supremacy of the castrati. Thirdly, the ordinary opera-goer was perfectly prepared to accept the spectacle of a castrato ... looking magnificently masculine as, say, Hercules draped in a leopard skin, but singing in a soprano voice. Lastly, most composers and librettists, apart from being more concerned with the placing of arias according to the [current] conventions ... than with wedding music to drama,. ... were obliged to alter, replace, or add to what they had originally written if a 'star' singer so required.[16]

Pope may not have been alive to every baneful feature of this situation, such as the restriction in tone-colour produced by the sparing use of tenor and bass voices. ('The whole vocal structure of opera seria,' it has been said, 'and consequently the instrumental texture as well, was based on a predominance of high voices.')[17] But he certainly shared the widespread view that opera implied unnatural sexual antics.[18] This chimed in with the traditional British attitude towards the Italian nation, and also with the hostility towards masquerades (also promoted by Heidegger), where a measure of transvestism was sometimes indulged.

It could also be said that Heidegger presided over the conversion of art into a joint-stock venture. As manager of the Royal Academy of Music, a corporation set up in 1719, he stood in much the same relation to the company's subsequent crash as did the cashier Knight (satirised in *The Dunciad* B.IV,561) to the South Sea venture.[19] Like Swift, Pope had a sceptical eye for institutions headed by the Lord Chamberlain, a Deputy Governor and a board of directors; one in receipt, moreover, of a royal subsidy and financed by subscription. It is true that Handel, whom Pope admired, was employed by the Academy; that his friend Anastasia Robinson took part in its early seasons; and that his patrons Bathurst, Burlington, and Lansdowne (not to mention his close ally Dr Arbuthnot) were among the original subscribers. True also, that Pope made his fortune through a subscription venture. Nonetheless, he seems to have shared some of the Tory prejudice against this method of raising money, especially after the madness of 1720. The animus is clearer in Swift, who disliked almost all credit and mortgage arrangements, and who constantly deplores the modern tendency to levy debts upon posterity to meet present needs. But Pope, too, saw in contemporary financial developments a risk of corruption. The *Epistle to Bathurst*, with its ironic vision of 'Blest paper-credit' (69), makes a cognate point (121–24):

> Ask you why Phryne the whole Auction buys?
> Phryne foresees a general Excise.
> Why she and Sappho raise that monstrous sum?
> Alas! they fear a man will cost a plum.

Of course there is a difference between a shaky joint-stock enterprise such as the York Buildings Company and an inadequately funded musical venture. But there was also a disturbing similarity to some minds.[20]

More important, the Academy rapidly drifted into undignified squabbles. Dr Arbuthnot, who had originally asked Pope to devise a suitable seal and motto for the Academy, was involved in disputes on the board by October 1720, and seems to have lost interest in the project thereafter. He ceased to be director in 1721. In November 1727, Mrs Pendarves was predicting that 'operas will not survive longer than this winter, they are now at their last gasp; the subscription is expired and nobody will renew it. The directors are always squabbling, and they have so many divisions among themselves that I wonder they have not broken up before ...[21] By 1 June 1728, the demise of the Academy as an opera promotion agency was complete. Incidentally, an attack on Heidegger in that year was long attributed to Arbuthnot and reprinted in his works. Actually it was written by the young Henry Fielding: but the fact serves to show how little Arbuthnot was identified with Heidegger's activities by this time. And whether or not *The Beggar's Opera* was really a thrust at Italian opera—a point good scholars have failed to agree on—there is an earlier letter from Gay to Swift, dated 3 February 1723, making sport of the rage for eunuchs, Italian women, and the like: 'Senesino is daily voted to be the greatest man that ever lived.'[22] By the time of the first *Dunciad*, any welcome that the Scriblerians might have given the Academy's plans must have worn very thin.

In 1729 Heidegger set up a new partnership with Handel. But the venture was not particularly successful, to some extent perhaps because of an undue emphasis on revivals. Early in 1733 there arose 'a Spirit ... against the Dominion of Mr Handel.' The result was a kind of takeover (another unpleasant business overtone invading art), with Heidegger letting the Haymarket to the ambitious new Opera of the Nobility. The later developments have been summarised by Arthur H. Scouten:

> The rivalry continued for some time, with both companies [Handel's and the Nobility] laboring under severe financial strains. At the close of 1736-37 the Opera of the Nobility ended its venture. In 1737-38 Heidegger resumed his career as an impresario, with Handel as musical director but not as co-manager. Within a few years, however, Handel and the management at the King's were at odds, and in 1742-43 Handel began a series of oratorios by subscription at Covent Garden ...

It was at this approximate juncture that the revised *Dunciad* appeared. Handel had been driven into oratorio by repeated losses in opera. The history of the past two decades had been one of mismanagement, dissention, and frustration. Even the political support of the Prince of Wales and leading Opposition figures had not saved the Nobility company. Whatever else might be said of opera in 1742, it was certainly not a high road to peace and prosperity.[23]

II

So much for background. Pope's exploitation of this material ought now, I believe, to emerge with greater clarity. Of course the history was a complex one, and it is not hard to detect some 'ambivalence' in Pope's response, if one is so minded. For example, Pope expressed admiration for both Handel and Bononcini, rivals for most of the period.[24] He had links with the very companies which put on those operas most deeply implicated in the gimcrack inanity presented by *The*

Dunciad—works like *Adriano in Siria* (1736) contained as many 'chromatic tortures' as most, despite the patronage of Bathurst and Burlington. However, Pope was not the man to lose a good satiric motif for the sake of sparing individuals a modicum of diffused reproach. In any case, whatever the personal and biographic facts, the poem itself is straightforward enough. *The Dunciad* condemns Italian opera *in toto*—not just one phase or company. It shows the entire form as effete and vacuous.

The figure of Opera is introduced as early as line 45 of *The New Dunciad*:

> When lo! a Harlot form soft sliding by,
> With mincing step, small voice, and languid eye;
> Foreign her air, her robe's discordant pride
> In patch-work flutt'ring, and her head aside.
> By singing Peers up-held on either hand,
> She tripp'd and laugh'd, too pretty much to stand;
> Cast on the postrate Nine a scornful look,
> Then thus in quaint Recitativo spoke ...
>
> (B.IV,45–52)

Almost as interesting as the text are Pope's notes. 'The Attitude given to this Phantom', he writes, 'represents the nature and genius of the *Italian* Opera; its affected airs, its effeminate sounds, and the practice of patching up these Operas with favourite Songs, incoherently put together. These things were supported by the subscriptions of the Nobility.' The last remark undoubtedly points at the Nobility Opera itself, although in literal truth it applied equally to the earlier Academy venture, in which the peerage took a major share. Of the original sixty-three subscribers, listed in the Lord Chamberlain's records, very nearly half were peers who contributed almost £9000 of the £15,600 subscribed.[25] As for the musical style portrayed, it would appear to be the 'lyrical and sensuous' mode of Neapolitan writing, exemplified by composers such as Porpora and his pupil Hasse (both favourites with the Nobility company).[26]

Pope's note to line 45 ends with a significant reminder: 'This circumstance that Opera should prepare for the opening of the grand Sessions, was prophesied of in Book 3. ver. [301]. *Already Opera prepares the way, / The sure forerunner of her gentle sway.*' In this way Pope draws attention to the connections established between the 'new' poem and the predictions of Settle in Book III. Moreover, the phrase 'grand Sessions' offers a valuable clue to the structure of the final book. Sherburn derived the 'episodic' nature of this section, with 'some wavering in the transitions', from Fielding's practice as a dramatist. 'A scene with a foolish king or a mock queen or goddess enthroned makes an admirable focal point about which farcical episode may loosely revolve. These plays by Fielding were enormously popular, and they almost certainly gave form to the new Book of the *Dunciad*. Doubtless authors other than Fielding anticipated Pope in the use of this scene, but no other author at the time had prepared Pope's public for the device as had Henry Fielding.'[27] But the word *sessions* alerts us to a more basic device, one long familiar to every reader of poetry. Suckling's hugely influential *Session of the Poets* (1637) had established a formula that retained a lively currency a hundred years after its inception. Queen Dulness, in summoning her minions (as she has already done once, at the start of Book II) is one of a long line, stretching far beyond Fielding, who had convened a like assembly. Sherburn calls the opera passage 'the first abrupt episode', which is accurate. But there is an ironic edge in the fact that Opera does not even have to be 'summon'd to the Throne' (B.IV,72)—she arrives unbidden, like the upstart among the muses she (in Pope's terms) was. Her staged entrance displays the self-regarding showbiz vulgarity of contrived 'stardom.'

The next eighteen lines are taken up by Opera's famous speech, embodying a slightly back-handed compliment to Handel. This passage has been well annotated in the Twickenham edition, but certain aspects of the satire merit more detailed study. For example, Opera refers to Handel's instrumental range and power:

> To stir, to rouze, to shake the Soul he comes,
> And Jove's own Thunders follow Mars's Drums.
> Arrest him, Empress; or you sleep no more ...
>
> (B.IV,67-9)

The note remarks, 'Mr *Handel* had introduced a great number of Hands, and more variety of Instruments into the Orchestra, and employed even Drums and Cannon to make a fuller Chorus.'

The modern editor makes the literal-minded comment that 'There is no mention of Handel's use of cannon in any of his scores (not even the Fireworks Music, in spite of one biographer to the contrary) ...' This doubtless refers to the famous Royal Fireworks music of 1749, celebrating the Peace of Aix-la-Chapelle. However, in Pope's lifetime the title 'Fire Musick' was applied to the final chorus of the opera *Atalanta*, composed in 1736 for the wedding of the Prince of Wales. The orchestra was augmented at this point by trumpets and drums; the libretto mentions 'illuminations' as well as 'loud Instrumental Musick'. Elaborate sets were constructed at Covent Garden, recalling the elaborate effects of Settle and Rich satirised in Book II of *The Dunciad*. Mrs Pendarves reported a performance in November, 1736, 'with the fireworks' in a letter attacking the soporific Nobility Opera: 'They have Farinelli, Merighi, with *no sound* in her voice, but thundering action—a beauty with *no other merit*; and one Chimenti, a tolerable good woman with a pretty voice and Montagnana, who *roars as usual*! With this band of singers and dull Italian operas, such as you almost fall asleep at, *they presume* to rival Handel ...'. Again in 1741 we find the 'celebrated Fire Musik' from *Atalanta* performed in Cupers Gardens, 'the Fire-works consisting of Fire-wheels, Fountains, large Sky Rockets, with an Addition of the Fire-Pump, &c. made by the ingenious Mr Worman, who projected the same at the above-mentioned Opera [*Atalanta*], and will be play'd off from the Top of the Orchestra by Mr Worman himself'.[28] With sky rockets and all, who needed cannons to simulate fire power? It might also be recalled that another 'projector' apart from Mr Worman had a line in illuminations—for this department was allotted to Heidegger at the coronation in 1727, for which Handel wrote some noble anthems.

At the start of her speech, Opera had exclaimed, 'Joy to great Chaos! let Division reign ...' (B.IV,54). Pope's note glosses 'division' by reference to the musical application, that is the castrato's fondness for ornamental elaboration of the vocal line. But there is an obvious pun. Opera, as we have seen, was notorious as a world of dissension. Apart from the quarrels between Handel and his singers, the Handel/Nobility struggle, and the Handel/Bononcini rivalry immortalised in Byrom's famous epigram, there were particular outbursts which achieved wide notoriety. For instance, the curious decision to allot three composers an act apiece of Rolli's libretto of *Muzio Scaevola* in 1721 led to a good deal of friction. Handel's contribution was universally accepted as the best, but that did nothing to pacify matters. Pope must have known all about this affair; Gay wrote a motto for the occasion, and Anastasia Robinson took the part of Irene.[29]

An even more famous episode occurred in the summer of 1727, when the first *Dunciad* was rapidly taking shape.[30] This was the quarrel between the respective fans (the slight vulgarism is appropriate) of Cuzzoni and Faustina. It was an event which produced a whole series of pamphlets, and has its echoes in many places, notably *The Beggar's Opera*. Apart from the death of George I a week later, it was the biggest news story of 1727. Otto Erich Deutsch quotes reports in the *British Journal* and the *London Journal* each dated June 10:

> On Tuesday-night last [the 6th], a great Disturbance happened at the Opera, occasioned by the Partisans of the Two Celebrated Rival Ladies, Cuzzoni and Faustina. The Contention at first was only carried on by Hissing on one Side, and Clapping on the other; but proceeded at length to Catcalls, and other great Indecencies; And notwithstanding the Princess Caroline was present, no Regards were of Force to restrain the Rudeness of the Opponents.

> The Contention ... proceeded ... by the delightful Exercise of Catcalls, and other Decencies, which demonstrated the inimitable Zeal and Politeness of that Illustrious Assembly ... but no Regards were of Force to restrain the glorious Ardour of the fierce Opponents.[31]

Such the 'discord' of the Academy opera: Caroline, one recalls, turns up elsewhere in Book IV, at line 409. But if one wants a direct echo of this scene in *The Dunciad*, it is the second book which springs to mind. Here we actually have a braying competition ('All hail him victor in both gifts of song, / Who sings so loudly, and who sings so long', B.II,267); we have 'glorious strife' (B.II, 167), a 'clam'rous crowd' (B.II,385), competitive 'ardour' (B.II,51) and 'a gentler exercise' (B.II,366). Above all, there is an evocation of 'the wond'rous pow'r of Noise':

'Tis yours to shake the soul
With Thunder rumbling from the mustard bowl,
With horns and trumpets now to madness swell,
Now sink in sorrows with a tolling bell;
Such happy arts attention can command,
When fancy flags, and sense is at a stand.
Improve we these. Three Cat-calls be the bribe
Of him, whose chatt'ring shames the Monkey tribe:
And his this Drum, whose hoarse heroic base
Drowns the loud clarion of the braying Ass.

(B.II,225–34)

If the relevance of this to opera is in doubt, we have only to look back to the Handel passage in Book IV, where the same ideas (shaking the soul, the loss of sense, drums, thunder) appear, applied differently. Then follows a justly famous paragraph:

Now thousand tongues are heard in one loud din:
The Monkey-mimics rush discordant in;
'Twas chatt'ring, grinning, mouthing, jabb'ring all,
And Noise and Norton, Brangling and Breval,
Dennis and Dissonance, and captious Art,
And Snip-snap short, and Interruption smart,
And Demonstration thin, and Theses thick,
And Major, Minor and Conclusion quick.
'Hold (cry'd the Queen) a Cat-call each shall win;
Equal your merits! equal is your din!
But that this well-disputed game may end,
Sound forth the Brayers, and the welkin rend.

(B.II,235–46)

The 'disordant pride' of Opera is here turned directly to Dulness in action. Dissonance becomes an emblem of literary folly. Pope uses fierce and noisy contention as an image of nonsense at large. The best-known contemporary manifestation of such inane squabbling was the scene at the Haymarket, when the rival queens had come to blows and catcalls had resounded through the auditorium.[32]

Throughout *The Dunciad*, we are given indications that 'Noise and Nonsense' have common parentage. The cave of Dulness is plagued by winds, 'Emblem of Music caus'd by Emptiness'

(B.I.36). If empty stomachs go with senseless noise, so do empty
heads:

> Others the Syren Sisters warble round,
> And empty heads console with empty sound.
>
> (B.IV,541-2)

There is hissing in the poem, too (B.III,235), along with a variety
of disagreeable screeches. It is in this light that we should see the
explicit references to opera, whether the sneer at Paolo Rolli of
the Academy (B.II,204), the innuendo regarding George II's
liking for the genre (B.IV,314), or the jibing note to 'Solo'
attributed to Bentley (B.IV,324). Opera has its place in the
education of the young fribble, as it does in the retinue of Dulness
at large.[33] The 'soft Strains' of this Italianate importation play
their part in enfeebling national character.[34] Dulness operates by
drugging her votaries, as Book II makes clear; and her final
apocalyptic act is a yawn that spreads a kind of mass hypnosis.
Even the Muse is adjured in vain:

> O sing, and hush the Nations with the Song!
>
> (B.IV,626)

Dulness restores the primeval reign of Chaos, to whom the figure
of Opera had offered a paean (B.IV,54). Art after art goes out,
and in the universal darkness even the minions of
Dulness—including opera—expire.

I mentioned earlier a satire entitled *The Sessions of Musicians*,
published in May, 1724.[35] This shares with *The Dunciad* a vision
of a deep drugged sleep overtaking a whole assembly. But this
time the trumpet of Fame conquers the universal lethargy, and
Handel is crowned by Phoebus.[36] There are many other
similarities with Pope's work (*The Temple of Fame* as well as *The
Dunciad*), in phrasing, symbolism, and satiric purpose. I do not
claim, of course, that the *Session* was written by Pope. Its odd
experiments with triple rhythms, as well as its feeble use of
expletives, rule out the possibility of this. Nor would I speculate
on any connection of Dr Arbuthnot with the *Session*, though its
author was evidently close to the Academy's doings and well
attuned to Scriblerian activities. The interest of the work is

simply that it anticipates so many motifs of *The Dunciad*; it is not improbable that Pope saw the poem, while his own *Dulness* was germinating, and a number of ideas were subliminally transferred into that composition. This is still to be proved; but if it were so, it would help to explain the pervasive undercurrent of operatic allusions in *The Dunciad*.

One could indicate parallels of a casual nature, such as the common employment of a competition for the laurel; the Parnassian theme; the shared epic diction ('Dame' for the goddess, and so on); and the bawdry found in both the *Session* and *The Dunciad*. There would remain, however, a substantial area of satiric innuendo more closely connecting these poems. Most striking, perhaps, is the use in the *Session* of 'peaceful Potions' analogous to the balm of Dulness. Equally, there are many close verbal parallels, especially in the sections describing discordant sounds (B.II,221ff.; *Session*, 64ff.) or a crowd on the move (B.IV,71ff.; *Session*, 48ff.). Even more interesting is the degree of overlap between the cameo of Anastasia Robinson (*Session*, 213-14) and the portrait of opera (B.IV.45-50). One might almost suspect that Pope had Mrs Robinson in mind, despite his own friendship with the singer. However,the central point does not concern any identification of this kind. The comparison principally shows that Pope's idiom in *The Dunciad* (and occasionally elsewhere) has clear links with that used in satire of the opera in the 1720s.[37] The general fiction of 'Dulness' turns out to possess vibrant operatic overtones; the linkage of 'Noise and Nonsense' is not casual, but an echo of the fiercest *Kulturkampf* of the time—the debate over Italian opera. As elsewhere, Pope was able to turn public quarrels into the private necessities of his art.[38]

Notes

1. 'William Ayre', *Memoirs of the Life and Writings of Alexander Pope, Esq.* (London, 1745), II, 29.
2. George Sherburn, 'The *Dunciad*, Book IV,' *Texas Studies in Literature and Language*, XXIV (1944), 174-90: reprinted in *Essential Articles for the Study of Alexander Pope*, ed. Maynard Mack (Hamden, Conn., 1968), pp. 730-46. Reuben A. Brower, *Alexander Pope: The Poetry of Allusion* (Oxford, 1959), p. 321.

3. George E. Dorris, *Paolo Rolli and the Italian Circle in London, 1715-44* (The Hague, 1967), p. 79. For a convincing refutation of this view, *see* Morris R. Brownell. 'Ears of an untoward make: Pope and Handel', *The Musical Quarterly*, LXII (1976), 554-70.

4. Mary F. Klinger, 'Music and theater in Hogarth', *The Musical Quarterly*, LVII (1971), 409-26: *see* esp. p. 410.

5. For other examples of 'choreography', *see* B.IV,17ff., 45ff., 135ff., 189ff., 205-7, 275ff., 397ff., 419-20, 493ff., 655. The word *sing* and its derivatives occur six times in this single book; *voice* three times.

6. *See* pp. 43-9 above, for early opposition to Italian opera. Matter of related interest is discussed in Robert Manson Myers, *Early Moral Criticism of Handelian Oratorio* (Williamsburg, Va., 1947). On the development of Italian opera in London, see Dorris, pp. 36-49: and R.A. Streatfeild, 'Handel, Rolli, and the Italian Opera in London in the Eighteenth Century', *The Musical Quarterly*, III (1917), 428-45. Swift's observation of the new phenomenon can be traced in *Corr*, I, 121, 129, 133.

7. In general these terms are taken to be synonomous, but Mrs Pendarves made a clear distinction in writing to her sister in 1727: 'Masquerades are not to be forbid, but there is to be another entertainment *barefaced*, which are balls ... There is to be a handsome collation, and they will hire Heidegger's rooms to perform in.' Quoted by Deutsch, p. 216. This chapter is indebted both to this work and to Paul Henry Lang, *George Frideric Handel* (New York, 1966). For Heidegger's early career, see Lang,, pp. 116-17. For *Masquerades and Operas*, and Heidegger as a link between the two genres, *see* Paulson, I, 111-18, and pp. 55-60 above.

8. *The Dunciad*, ed. J. Sutherland, 3rd ed. (London, 1963), p. 444 (*TE*,V). Quotations and line numbers follow this edition. Normally the later ('B') version is cited. Pope's note at B.I,2 establishes the immediate relevance of shows at the Haymarket Theatre.

9. *The London Stage*, II, lxi. see pp. lxxi-lxxx, for an excellent account of opera management in this period.

10. See Deutsch, pp. 461, 465.

11. *See* Pat Rogers, 'Matthew Prior, Sir Henry Furnese and the Kit Cat Club', *Notes and Queries*, XVIII (1971), 46-9.

12. Cf. Pope's own note, added in 1735 at A.I,244: '*A H[eidegger]r*. A strange Bird from Switzerland, and not (as some have supposed) the name of an eminent Person, who was a man of Parts, and as was said of *Petronius, Arbiter Elegantiarum*.'

13. *See* pp. 75-6 above.

14. The section on opera finances in *The London Stage*, III, lxviii-lxxiv, is of great interest here. Suggestive, too, is the section, 'A Galaxy of Promoters', pp. lxxx-lxxxix.

15. Cited by Deutsch, p. 186. On the dramatic foreshortening inherent in opera seria, *see* Lang, pp. 148-9, and Dorrin, p. 44.

16. Alec Harman, *Late Renaissance and Baroque Music*, Man and His Music, Vol. II (London, 1969), p. 206. *See also* Lang, pp. 147-73.

17. Winton Dean, *Handel and the Opera Seria* (London, 1970), pp. 15-16. Relevant to *The Dunciad's* critique is Lang's observation that the castrato

was treated 'as a virtuoso rather than a dramatic figure, belonging to the décor rather than to the drama itself' (p. 171).

18. *See* Angus Heriot, *The Castrati in Opera* (London, 1956), pp. 53–5.

19. For the suggestion that the breaking of the Bubble would mean the fall of the Academy, *see* Rolli's letter of October 18, 1720, cited by Deutsch, p. 115: and *see* p. 45 above.

20. For Horace Walpole's caustic remarks on the constant need to subsidise the opera, *see London Stage*, III. For Heidegger's estimate of the commitment to be made by the 'undertakers', *see* Lord Hervey's letter of 2 November 1734, quoted above p. 48.

21. Dorris, pp. 78–9: Deutsch pp. 97, 115, 218. *See also* the *Old Whig*, cited by Deutsch, p. 384; and *London Stage*,III, lxx.

22. Deutsch, pp. 149, 223; Swift *Corr*, II, 447; L.P. Goggin, 'Fielding's *The Masquerade*', *Philological Quarterly*, XXXVI (1957), 475–87.

23. This paragraph draws on *London Stage*, III, lxxiii; Deutsch, pp. 303–4; Stanley Sadie, *Handel* (London, 1962), pp. 67–101; Lang, pp. 234–57. The most detailed analysis of the finances of opera at this juncture can be found in a valuable article by Judith Milhous and Robert D. Hume, 'Box office reports for five operas mounted by Handel in London, 1732–1734', *Harvard Library Bulletin*, XXVI (1978), 245–66.

24. For Pope's esteem for Bononcini, based on 'Personal Knowledge of His Character', *see* Pope *Corr*, II, 99. Bononcini set two choruses which Pope wrote for an adaptation of *Julius Caesar* by the Duke of Buckingham.

25. Public Record Office, LC 7/3/15, cited by Deutsch, p. 91. Deutsch refers to 'sixty-two' subscribers but lists sixty-three. Other subscribers well known to Pope were the Duke of Chandos, the Earl of Strafford and James Craggs. (I have not included in the count those who attained a peerage subsequently).

26. Harman, pp. 222–3. It is worth noting that the allusion to 'the warbling Polypheme' at B.III,305 refers not just to Cibber's translation of a Rolli text, but directly to an operatic version by Porpora, which the Nobility Company put on in February 1735.

27. Sherburn, in Mack, pp. 735–57. For the 'sessions' formula, *see The Works of Sir John Suckling: The Non-Dramatic Works*, ed. Thomas Clayton (Oxford, 1971), p. 268.

28. Deutsch, pp. 418, 519: Dean, p. 102. Mrs Pendarves was of course prejudiced in favour of Handel, but she was not alone in her views. For the notion of Handel, 'Professor of Harmony' to the Academy of Discord (of which Heidegger was High Priest), watching Faustina and Cuzzoni come to blows, whilst 'Cat-calls, Serpents and Cuckoos make a dreadful Din', and 'animat[ing] them with a Kettle-Drum', *see The Contre Temps; or, Rival Queens* (1727), in *The Dramatic Works of Colley Cibber, Esq.* (London, 1777), IV, 371–81. Deutsch, p. 212, and Dorrin, pp. 92–3, are sceptical of Cibber's authorship, but they do not say why.

29. Deutsch, pp. 124–7; Sadie, pp. 53–4, where it is argued that the composite opera was commissioned simply to get it ready as speedily as possible. *See also* Lang, p. 178.

30. *TE*, V, p. xv. *see also* p. 51 below.

31. Deutsch, p. 210. Caroline was a devoted supporter of Handel. For the pamphlet battles, *see* Dorrin, pp. 89-96.

32. There is also mention of catcalls (and viols) in *The Dunciad* (B.I,302). For hisses, *see* B.I,48, 260. I have discussed the symbolic use of noise as an aspect of Dulness in my *Grub Street* (London, 1972), pp. 62-4. Opera served Pope's ends because (1) it was sung in a foreign (and to most people unintelligible) tongue; and (2) because of its reputation for squabbles. The 'contending Theatres' (B.III,271) suggest the rival opera-houses as well as the 'legitimate' playhouses.

33. Note also B.IV,598.

34. The phrase occurs in a pamphlet of 1727, formerly attributed to Arbuthnot, cited by Deutsch, p. 211.

35. The title page reads: THE | SESSION | OF | MUSICIANS. | In IMITATION of the | Session of Poets. || The publisher was M. Smith. There is an edition by Friedrich Chrysander, *Handel Receiving the Laurel from Apollo* (Leipzig, 1859), but the last six lines, on p. 12 of the original, are omitted. *See* Deutsch, p. 170, for the concluding lines, further details, and identification of persons named.

36. For Pope's comments on the 'modern' Phoebus, 'married to the Princess *Galimathia*, one of the handmaidens of Dulness, and an assistant to Opera', *see* note to B.IV,61.

37. It should be remarked, however, that a passage in *The Rape of the Lock*, IV 39-46, serves to demonstrate Pope's early awareness of theatrical spectacle. One might here recall Winton Dean's point that spectacular effects were used in stage production 'not to create illusion but to excite wonder and delight' (p. 124)—which Pope might have seen as a kind of narcissistic display appropriate to Dulness.

38. Again Pope had been anticipated by *The Craftsman*. *See* issue no. 353 (7 April 1733), for a satire which 'seems to aim at Walpole by attacking Handel' (Deutsch, pp. 310-13).

5

ERMINE, GOLD AND LAWN

The Dunciad and the Coronation of George II

> The Play stands still; damn action and discourse,
> Back fly the scenes, and enter foot and horse;
> Pageants on pageants, in long order drawn,
> Peers, Heralds, Bishops, Ermin, Gold, and Lawn;
> The Champion too! and, to complete the jest,
> Old Edward's Armour beams on Cibber's breast!

> The Coronation of King Henry the Eighth and Queen Anne Boleyn,
> in which the Playhouses vied with each other to represent all the
> pomp of a Coronation. In this noble contention, the Armour of one
> of the Kings of England was borrowed from the Tower, to dress the
> Champion.
>
> Pope, *Imitations of Horace, Ep.* II.i. 314-19 and note.

I

One of the features of *The Dunciad* that has puzzled some readers
is the use made of a particular occasion, the Lord Mayor's show
in 1719. In the original version of the poem, Pope even went so far
as to particularise an individual Lord Mayor by name:

> 'Twas on the day, when Thorold, rich and grave,
> Like Cimon triumph'd, both on land and wave.
>
> (A I, 83-4)[1]

The *Dunciad Variorum* annotates, 'Sir George Thorold, Lord
Mayor of *London*, in the Year 1720'. The name was replaced by
two stars in the 1743 text, with an apparently awkward note
remarking on the change. Since Aubrey Williams' influential
account of the work, we have been able to discern a good motive
for Pope's exploitation of civic ceremonial—in order, that is, to

fill out the epic metaphor by means of a 'progress' across London from City to Court.[2] But this does not explain the decision to use a specific year, and that set as far back as 1719.

I said just now that the note provided in 1743 was 'apparently' awkward. On closer examination, it may be possible to detect greater point in what Pope does here. His note to the lines quoted (with stars now set in place of Thorold's name) reads as follows:

> Viz. a Lord Mayor's Day; his name the author had left in blanks, but most certainly could never be that which the Editor foisted in formerly, and which in no way agrees with the chronology of the poem. BENTL.

The Twickenham editor comments: 'The dropping of Thorold's name was one of numerous small changes made necessary by the change of hero and the passage of years.'[3] But Thorold had no connection with the former hero, Theobald: and as for the passage of years, 1719 was already ancient history in 1728 as far as civic politics went. To get round this difficulty, George Sherburn proposed the idea that Pope's original plan was to burlesque the choice of a Poet Laureate in 1718.[4] This in turn raises difficulties: we have no evidence that the poem had any kind of existence as early as Sherburn surmises, and then it is a counter-indication that Theobald was *not* appointed laureate on this occasion, although he was regarded as a candidate by some.

I should like to propose a different solution, which may fit the facts more neatly and which makes the changes of 1743 less lame. My suggestion is that the reference all along pointed to another George, that is the King himself; and that the later note is designed to bring this out more explicitly. Bentley's intrusive and ambiguous note serves the usual function: it appears misleading, and yet it allows the truth to squeeze out surreptitiously. Why would Thorold's name 'in no way [agree] with the chronology of the poem'? Only in one possible respect (there are no other firm indications of date in the entire work): because the crucial events must postdate Settle's death in 1724. This may seem to be taking the 'action' too literally, but Pope does not refer to such matters as chronology when he wishes us to ignore them. On that basis, it cannot be the institution of Thorold as Lord Mayor which underlies the action. Thorold himself had died in 1722, which made him a discreet camouflage when *The Dunciad* came out for the first time.[5] I suggest that in the original text he operates as a surrogate for the greater George, King George II; and that in the later version Bentley's intervention serves to make that intriguing blank a definite code-reference to the monarch.

Before I cite detailed reasons for such an identification, it is worth pointing out that nothing that is *prima facie* implausible would attach to such a reading. The most recent ceremonial 'triumph' when *The Dunciad* was published was the coronation of George and Caroline in 1727. A transference to the most obvious namesake of Thorold would be all the easier since there could be no doubt that George Augustus (and not his father George Lewis) was intended, as might have been the case up till June 1727. The word *George* (and *George's*) occurs eleven times in Pope's verse: on eight of these occasions it refers unambiguously to George II. The two stars in the 1743 text (B I, 85) could easily cover the disyllabic form 'Georgius', since we know from other evidence that Pope gave the name this metrical weight:[6] or, less likely, the form 'George Rex.' Finally, the comparison with the Athenian general Cimon makes no sense in terms of a City merchant like Thorold,[7] but applies most aptly to the commander-in-chief of the British forces—George Augustus once again. In October 1743, when the revised *Dunciad* came out, there was an obvious topical addition: for in the previous June the King had led the allied forces to victory over the French at Dettingen. He had worn the Hanoverian colours, and the event highlighted Britain's involvement in the War of the Austrian Succession, said by the opposition to have arisen in defence of Hanoverian interests. (The British fleet was active in the European theatre—as at Naples in 1742—as well as further afield; hence perhaps the sneer at triumphs 'both on land and wave'.) Familiar anti-monarchist ideas are called up by the analogy.

One more preliminary issue. Despite theories of an earlier prototype, Pope's 'Dulness' poem did not take definite shape before about 1725. And we have no firm evidence of its existence as a coherent whole until later still. The Twickenham editor considers the possibility that Swift's visit to England in 1726 was crucial to the germination of the work; and then he points out that 'the poem was rapidly taking shape in the summer of 1727', when Swift paid his second visit.[8] What needs to be emphasised is that firm references in Pope's correspondence to an achieved work—something that could be read, transmitted, construed—begin only at this stage. Pope wrote to Swift on 22 October 1727 of his inability to send 'a copy' of the new poem, owing to fears that it might be intercepted. At the same time he included the famous lines in tribute to Swift.[9] Commentators assume that this was a late insertion in a poem completed some time previously: but it would be totally in line with the facts to suppose that the work was even then in the process of composition. Four months earlier Pope had told his publisher Motte that he would 'take Time till winter to finish' the poem.[10] The original plan had been to include *The Dunciad* in the third volume of *Miscellanies*, but this of course was abandoned. All scholars agree that the poem 'had clearly grown beyond [Pope's] original conception'.[11] The juncture at which this process of inflation took place can be fixed as lying between the late summer and autumn of 1727: that is, the months surrounding the accession of George and Caroline (June) and their coronation (October). Pope displayed his keenest involvement in the act of composition at this very juncture. For example, his letter to Swift, enclosing the versified tribute, was written on 22 October, eleven days after the Coronation. It was accompanied by a message from Gay, in which the latter describes the 'settling' of the Queen's retinue—including a post in the household offered to Gay himself.[12]

What does this evidence show? *The Dunciad* as a real entity, rather than a vaguely sketched promise of things to come, is plainly a creature of 1727, not of 1726 or 1725, let alone 1719. Something happened during the latter half of the year which set Pope writing with an energy he had not displayed since turning to translation almost fifteen years before. This stimulus resulted in intensive work and in a marked expansion in the scale of the poem: it meant that *The Dunciad* could no longer be housed in the projected volume of *Miscellanies*, where the older and less topical *Peri Bathous* took its place. It is of course possible that whatever happened happened in Pope's head, and nowhere else. An alternative hypothesis, not ruled out by any of the facts so far examined, is that major public events had changed the way Pope felt about his intended poem: about its scope, themes and rhetorical trajectory. The only external events which could have possessed the imaginative resonance to effect such a shift of intent were those surrounding the accession of the new King and Queen. Swift's visits to England—a major datum in Pope's personal life—would have encouraged this awareness in the autumn of 1727, for reasons which will appear.

II

The Dunciad was once read almost exclusively in literary terms. Recent discussion has been much more willing to accommodate political meanings, especially as regards the four-book version. Two notable readings may be singled out. In *The Garden and the City*, Maynard Mack shows that the revised poem has important links with the Horatian imitations in its attack on Court figures. He instances one case where the revision makes for 'a wider range of satirical objectives', including a possible hit at both the King and his consort.[13] Similarly Howard Erskine-Hill stresses 'the connection between Caroline and Dulness in its political aspect', with an equation between 'the historical queen and the allegorical goddess'.[14] Both critics convincingly demonstrate that the political animus works not only against Walpole but also against the royal couple.

The Twickenham edition supplies several other instances of direct satire, and it would be possible to draw these references together to provide an amplified and more sustained 'political' reading than either Mack or Erskine-Hill attempts. My present intention is different. Given this thread within the total fabric of the poem, I wish to concentrate principally on one aspect of the matter—that is, the events surrounding the *accession* of George and Caroline, in particular the coronation itself. My argument will be that the original *Dunciad* already contained a body of frontal allusion to these things, and that the revised poem (especially Book IV) reinforced the political meanings and 'opened' them more daringly.

It is well known that Walpole presented a copy of the *Dunciad Variorum* to the King and Queen in March 1729:[15] Pope actually alludes to this circumstance in his note to the opening line. But even before life took its cue from art, the intent was obvious:

> Books and the Man I sing, the first who brings
> The Smithfield Muses to the Ear of Kings.

(A I, 1-2)

This couplet was slightly revised in 1743, and the opportunity taken to identify the 'son' of Dulness as Colley Cibber, 'on whom this Prince [George II] conferred the honour of the laurel'. Here is an important clue to the vexed question surrounding Theobald's substitution by Cibber in 1743. Cibbar was *inter alia* a more suitable King of the dunces, first, because he had been the recipient of royal patronage, as his predecessor had not; and, second, because he had achieved his dignity in the reign of George II, not that of George I. The most important 'updating' of the 1743 version resides in exactly this fact: the fictional design of the poem is cemented by the direct implication of the current monarch. Cibber was not a more topical choice in other respects: he was seventeen years older than Theobald, he had achieved fame two decades earlier, and he had retired from the stage some time back. The one vital difference was that he had defeated his rival for the post of laureate in 1730, when Theobald unsuccessfully 'put in for the withered laurel'.[16]

Critics sometimes write of events 'playing into' Pope's hands: I have been guilty of this myself. The truth of course is that he had an incomparable gift for seizing the opportunities which others might not have perceived. Whatever the fitness of Theobald for the role of King of the dunces, it is beyond dispute that he did not link Dulness with court patronage so effectively as did his replacement. And in terms of my overall argument, it is crucial that the elevation of Cibber allowed Pope to strike directly at the exercise of royal patronage in cultural matters: that is, to make the King's shadowy offstage role more central to the action of the poem. When Theobald occupied the role of surrogate king, Pope might have wanted us to think of George II, but there was always a risk our minds might revert to the reign of his father. (The death of Settle, for example, having occurred in 1724.) My contention is not that Pope changed his plans in this area, but that a slight ambiguity of intent was clarified when Cibber received his promotion, inside and outside the poem.

From very early in the original text, it is apparent that *The Dunciad* is to follow its model *Mac Flecknoe* as a poem concerned with the succession:

> Say from what cause, in vain decry'd and curst,
> Still Dunce the second reigns like Dunce the first?
>
> (A I, 5-6)

The couplet has been fully discussed, and an especially apposite comment is that of Erskine-Hill:

> It was an obvious response, after the recent accession of George II, to apply the last line to the Hanoverian monarchs, but those who noticed the clear echo of a line from Dryden's epistle *To Mr Congreve* would know that Pope was thus linking his poem with a fundamental cultural and political attack, by the earlier poet, upon the Revolution Settlement ... It is clear that [Pope] uses the precedent of Dryden's Epistle to make a criticism of early eighteenth-century Britain which is political as well as cultural. The great Whig aristocrats, who brought the Hanoverians to the throne, are theoretically asked to explain a consequent supremacy of dullness.[17]

This is all to the point. However, it is hard to believe that the prime thrust of the allusion is not to the Georges, who bore the precise ordinal numbers in their title which the reference demands. As the Twickenham editor remarks, 'Pope is probably glancing at George II, who had succeeded his father less than a year before the *Dunciad* was published.' Sutherland also points to an early draft which confines the reference to Settle and Theobald.[18] He deduces that it was the death of George I which prompted the change, and this seems to me a statement in miniature of what happened during the entire process of composition. A work that may have started off occupied by the literary 'succession' of Dulness, in the manner of *Mac Flecknoe*, received a fresh impetus and a new charge of implication when the second Hanoverian succeeded the first. Again the ministry is not really in question, for Walpole carried on as before. The political attack only makes sense in terms of the royal family itself: at most, in the new monarch's decision not to dismiss Walpole.

But if the poem alludes at the start to the accession of a new king and queen, then this has obvious relevance to the later action—densely packed with thrones, ceremonial, anointing, court gatherings and so on. As we have seen, at the time when Pope was most energetically at work on his poem, public attention was fixed chiefly on the coronation: at this juncture all the ideas I have just mentioned were inescapably called up. Even supposing for the moment that Pope had been led into the 'succession' theme by Dryden's treatment of the issue, it is surely implausible in the utmost degree that he could have written of such ceremony in 1727 without bringing to mind (his own, and his reader's) the particular ritual enacted at Westminster that year.

Up to now commentators have been cautious in this regard. The most direct approach to the issue I can locate is that of Aubrey Williams:

> Book IV, added in 1743, presents to us the actual fulfilment of the prophecies which forecast a reign of Dulness—the setting of the book is a royal court (presumably that of St James's), and there enthroned are Dulness and her son. This enthronement of Dulness (which is not without its suggestions that George II, as well as Theobald, is to be regarded as king of all duncery) finally brings to completion the 'removal' of the seat of empire from the City to the 'polite world.' The Smithfield Muses have then been brought to the ears of kings.[19]

This is an entirely accurate description of the action, so far as it goes: but perhaps it does not go far enough. The enthronement, in my submission, is actually a parody of that of George and Caroline.

III

Pope evidently did not attend the ceremony himself, although he might have done so despite his religious faith. At all events, this is the account given to Swift by the second Earl of Oxford, who was present on the day:

> I have seen *Pope* but once, and that was but for a few minutes; he was very much out of order, but I hope it only proceeded from being two days in town, and staying out a whole opera. He would not see the coronation, although he might have seen it with little trouble.[20]

This was written on 12 October, the day following the great occasion. It is clear that the opera Pope witnessed must have been Handel's *Admeto*, performed on 30 September, and then on 3 and 7 October. This was the year when opera had attained an unprecedented prominence in public attention as a result of the split (mentioned in the previous chapter, p. 113) between disciples of Faustina and Cuzzoni, the rival *prime donne*—Pope himself was alleged at the time to have contributed to the pamphlet war. Matters came to a head with a scuffle between the singers on stage early in June: Gay was to satirise this episode in *The Beggar's Opera*.[21] What Oxford's testimony shows is that Pope was in town around the time of the coronation, rather than hiding away in his retreat at Twickenham. The event was more than a solemn moment of national dedication: it was also a great public show, stage-managed and orchestrated for maximum effect, and with marked operatic qualities of its own. Pope had thought it admirable that Martha Blount had been as stoical as she was, when smallpox prevented her witnessing the occasion back in 1714.[22] His decision not to attend must be regarded as a deliberate act.

Oxford continues in his letter to Swift, 'I will not trouble you with an account of the ceremony; I do not doubt but you will have a full and true account from much better hands.'[23] Here the writer probably has in mind Mrs Howard, the King's mistress and a member of the Queen's household, who had taken part in the ceremony. She and Swift had been on good terms during his visit to England that summer. However no letter survives from the period (a long gap begins from 14 September, when Swift wrote to Mrs Howard apologising for not attending the Queen). He would have been able to get some inkling of the proceedings from press coverage: both London and Dublin newspapers devoted plenty of space to the event, although not quite so much as might now seem appropriate in the mass media. There was also separate published accounts:

> There are two descriptions of the ceremonial, one printed in London and reprinted in Dublin in 1727, and the other, a German one, printed in Hanover in 1728. Both are of a general character, describing Coronation proceedings, with some reference to the present one; they were probably written before the event.[24]

In the light of the last consideration, it is more useful to approach the events not directly through these contemporary accounts, which are more like souvenir programmes, but through later descriptions which incorporate a number of authorities, both public and private. A clear and connected report, derived chiefly from an English pamphlet, is found in W.H. Wilkins's life of Queen Caroline, and I shall employ this as the basis of my analysis.[25] It will be supplemented by other sources where appropriate.

Wilkins tells us that 'the day was gloriously fine, and multitudes of people lined the gaily decorated streets'. He points out that Caroline was the first queen consort to have been crowned at the Abbey for more than a century. She was determined 'not to be relegated to the background' and so 'the ceremonial at this coronation followed more closely that of William and Mary than of James the First and Anne of Denmark'. This somewhat unconstitutional prominence for the consort is reflected in the poem, where Dulness rather than the King serves as prime mover of the action. When arrayed in her sumptuous robes, she took her place by the King's side at the upper end of Westminster Hall, 'seated like him in a chair of state under a gold canopy'. After preparatory ceremonies, the Dean and Canons of Westminster arrived from the Abbey with a Bible and some of the regalia. Among these items were the crowns together with the King's sceptre 'with the dove' and the Queen's 'ivory rod with the dove'. At noon all was ready for the procession on foot to the Abbey, made on a special raised walkway.

The participants are described by Wilkins:

> The procession was headed by a military band, and began with the King's herbwoman and her maid who strewed flowers and sweet herbs. It was composed in order of precedence from the smallest officials (even the organ blower was not forgotten) up to the great officers of state. The peers and peeresses wearing their robes of state and carrying their coronets in their hands walked . . . in order mete, from the barons and baronesses up to the dukes and duchesses. The Lord Privy Seal, the Archbishop of York and the Lord High Chancellor followed.

A few paces behind came the Queen, with her crown preceding her, carried by the Duke of St Albans.

The Queen was supported on either side by the Bishops of Winchester and London, and she majestically walked alone 'in her royal robes of purple velvet, richly furred with ermine, having a circle of gold set with large jewels upon her Majesty's head, going under a canopy borne by the Barons of the Cinque Ports, forty gentlemen pensioners going on the outsides of the canopy, and the Serjeants of arms attending.' The Queen's train was borne by the Princess Royal and the Princesses Amelia and Caroline ... The princesses were followed by the four ladies of the Queen's household ... [including] Mrs Howard.

Immediately afterwards came a bishop bearing the Bible on a velvet cushion. Then his Sacred Majesty King George II, in robes of crimson velvet, adorned with jewels, and 'turned up with ermine'. The King, too, was supported on either side by bishops, with trainbearers behind, and he was followed 'by numerous and splendid company of officials'. At the west door of the Abbey the procession was met by the Archbishop of Canterbury, together with other church dignitaries. It moved up the nave to the singing of an anthem, by Handel naturally.

Once the King and Queen were seated on the chairs of state, before the altar, the ceremony began with the first part of the communion service. The Bishop of Oxford then preached a sermon, and the King took the declaration against transubstantiation and the coronation oath. He approached the altar, and knelt to be crowned. The Archbishop anointed him, and he was invested with the full regalia. When the crown was placed on his head, 'all the spectators repeated their loud shouts, the trumpets sounded, and upon a signal given the great guns in the Park and the Tower were fired'. The service then proceeded, and the bishops made their obeisances to the King. 'Then the *Te Deum* was sung, and the King was lifted upon his throne and the peers did their homage. During this ceremony medals of gold were given to the peers and peeresses, and medals of silver were thrown among the congregation.' It was now the Queen's turn, and she too was anointed prior to the crowning ceremony. After this the royal couple 'made their oblations and received the Holy Communion'.

With the protracted service over, the King and Queen made their way back to Westminster Hall on foot, accompanied by a 'long train of peers and peeresses'. Once there, they took their

seats on the dais as before, ready for the coronation banquet.
After one course had been consumed, the King's Champion
entered and proclaimed an ancient challenge, which set out the
new King's rightful title as 'son and next heir' of George I. The
Champion three down his gauntlet three times, after which the
cup-bearer brought the King a gold bowl of wine with a cover:
'his Majesty drank to the Champion and sent him the bowl by
the cup bearer'. The Champion, who had carried out his entire
performance mounted on a white charger, took the bowl and
cover with him as he left. Then the heralds proclaimed the King's
official style, and the banquet could be resumed. It was an
impressive spectacle:

> What was most admired in the hall were the chandeliers, branches
> and sconces, in which were near two thousand wax candles, which
> being lighted at once, yielded an exceeding fine prospect.

We are told that their majesties did not leave Westminster Hall
until eight o'clock that evening, when they returned to St James's
Palace 'to rest after their labours. But their loyal subjects
prolonged the rejoicings far into the night with bonfires,
illuminations, ringing of bells, and other demonstrations of joy.'
One of the liveliest accounts of the ceremony is that sent by
Lady Mary Wortley Montagu to her sister. She remarks on the
'great variety of airs' assumed by those present: 'Some languish'd
and others strutted, but a visible Satisfaction was diffused over
every countenance as soon as the Coronet was clapp'd on the
head.'[26] The splendour of the occasion continued to furnish
conversation for some time: at Drury Lane a sumptuous
production was mounted of *King Henry the Eighth*, with special
attention to the coronation of Anne Boleyn—the enormous sum
of £1,000 was spent on this one scene. As Wilkins says, 'the scene
at Drury Lane rivalled in mock splendour the ceremonial at the
Abbey'. The town flocked to see it, and the King and Queen
attended more than once.[27] Meanwhile, the City of London
showed its loyalty by putting on a Lord Mayor's Show of
unparalleled splendour at the end of the month. The royal family
attended a banquet at the Guildhall during the evening, when
279 dishes were consumed at a cost of £5,000.
It appears that the Corporation of the City set up a special

committee to organise this royal gala. One of the aldermen appointed to this body was John Barber, a friend of Pope and, incongruously, a High Tory if not a Jacobite. Five years later, when Barber was on the point of succeeding to the mayoralty, he wrote to Swift:

> Had you been here now, I am persuaded you would have put me to an additional expense, by having a raree-show (or pageant) as of old, on the lord mayor's day. Mr Pope and I were thinking of having a large machine carried through the city, with a printing-press, author, publishers, hawkers, devils, etc., and a satirical poem printed and thrown from the press to the mob, in public view . . . but your absence spoils that design.

This refers to the ancient custom of mounting allegorical pageants, 'triumphs' of London, as part of the show, a tradition that had lapsed in the early part of the eighteenth century but sems to have revived briefly around 1730. In a sense *The Dunciad* had constituted an ironic allegory of 'triumphal' Dulness enveloping the city, with authors and publishers in full prominence. Troy-Novant is reincarnated as Dultown. Barber's task in 1727 had been to help in making the Lord Mayor's celebration into a municipal extension of the coronation ceremony.

The new Lord Mayor on this occasion was Sir Edward Becher, who duly made his progress by land and water through the capital. The royal family witnessed his return to the City from a balcony near St Mary-le-Bow church; the house loaned for this purpose belonged to a linen-draper anxious to ingratiate himself with the new regime. We learn that the streets were lined from Temple Bar to witness the mayoral procession. When it was completed, Sir William Thompson gave a speech of welcome to the royal party, and everyone sat down to a 'magnificent feast' in the Guildhall. Over a thousand dishes were consumed, 279 of them at the royal table. The City spent almost five thousand pounds on this banquet, ordering 315 dozen bottles of wine, and running up a charge of £1,100 for the cooks' services alone. An orchestra of nearly fifty performed during the meal. It was in fact a full-scale rerun of the coronation banquet, stripped of its feudal panoply: the symbolic message was clear—the loyal and trusty

Hanoverian corporation would ensure that the City of London allied itself in the most open way with the new regime. The papers were full of this 'sumptuous' event, and if Pope had needed an informant he had a first-hand witness in Barber, who cannot have relished the political content of what went on. Just as City shows and City mores had invaded Westminster, so now the court was allowing itself to be feted in these municipal junketings: we are told that the royal family attended a ball and did not leave the City until eleven o'clock.[27]

To one reader of *The Dunciad* at least, it is hard to go through such descriptions without regular and forcible reminders of the poem—its design and also its verbal texture. Much of the parallelism relates to the first three books, in their unrevised state moreover. The *New Dunciad* certainly fills out the connection with court ceremonial and chimes with particular passages in the description: but the congruence begins much earlier, and surfaces in a more pervasive fashion.

At the outset Dulness claims 'her antient right' (A I, 9) to rule and seeks 'her old empire to confirm'—dynastic protestations worthy of the King's Champion. We are introduced to 'this fair idiot ... Gross as her sire, and as her mother grave' (A I, 11-12). Caroline was blonde and full in figure: all that Wilkins says of her parents is this: 'There is a picture of [them] ... which depicts her father as a full-faced, portly man with a brown wig, clasping the hand of a plump, highly-coloured young woman, with auburn hair, and large blue eyes.' It is unlikely that Pope knew of the Anspach court situation, but the Queen's personal appearance was familiar to all. The first setpiece description occurs a little later:

> 'Twas here in clouded majesty she shone;
> Four guardian Virtues, round, support her Throne.
>
> (A I, 43-4)

The allegorical personages act in an equivalent capacity to the bishops who 'supported' the Queen at her coronation, or perhaps more exactly in the role of the four ladies of the household who attended her. It is no weakening of the subtle and well-planned allegorical design at this point to see in the passage a glimpse of Caroline on her throne in the Abbey, surrounded by her retainers and gazed at by the multitude of spectators. Her role as cultural patroness and fount of intellectual honour is imaged a few lines later, but again with a hint of the showy 'forward' appearance she had made in the Abbey:

> She, tinsel'd over in robes of varying hues,
> With self-applause her wild creation views,
> Sees momentary monsters rise and fall,
> And with her own fool's colours gilds them all.
>
> (A I, 79-82)

It was said that Caroline put on everything new for the ceremony, 'even to her shift', and this despite the fact that she had to borrow jewels for the day (the old king having given away royal gems to his mistresses).[29]

At this point occurs the passage already described, in which Pope fixes the occasion as that of Thorold's investiture. The note refers to the Lord Mayor's 'Procession', which again suggests a memory jogged by the doings of 11 October—and by the specially lavish Lord Mayor's show only a matter of days later. The scene of ritualised spectacle is described as 'Pomps without guilt, of bloodless swords and maces': the Twickenham editor indicates that the first noun is used in the sense of πομπή , a procession,[30] whilst the paraphernalia of ceremonial suggest national rather than municipal occasions. The Queen of Dulness now goes over in her mind the 'sure succession' of her lineage:

> She saw with joy the line immortal run,
> Each sire imprest and glaring in his son.
>
> (A I, 97-8)

Sutherland suggests that Pope is alluding to the new coinage stamped on the accession of George II. 'Two hundred gold and eight hundred medals had been struck for the new King'—one inevitably recalls the gold and silver medals dispensed during the coronation service.[31]

Attention now switches to Theobald, and we learn of his preparations for his sudden elevation. His major act in this portion of the poem is to set fire to his 'progeny', that is, his literary works. Dulness is wakened by the glow and puts out the flames. It is just possible that there is a covert allusion to George

II's destruction of his father's will: this had been handed to him at his first Privy Council by the Archbishop of Canterbury, and was never seen again. Rumour had it that the Prince of Wales, Frederick Louis, was thus defrauded of a considerable legacy.[32] Pope could not have been unaware of such rumours, as he moved in the Prince's circle and knew several of those present at the Council meeting.

Dulness now bids Theobald to attend her at her 'sacred Dome' (perhaps Grub Street) and there invests him with his new dignity:

> The Goddess then o'er his anointed head,
> With mystic words, the sacred Opium shed;
> And lo! her Bird (a monster of a fowl!
> Something betwixt a Heidegger and Owl)
> Perch'd on his crown.
>
> (A I, 241–5)

There was no anointing at a Lord Mayor's installation, no 'mystic words': these things belong to the coronation ceremony. The real King's regalia had included a sceptre with a dove, fitly replaced here by the monstrous bird partaking of an owl (emblem of knowing stupidity) and of Heidegger. John James Heidegger was not merely an impresario of the opera-house: he was to become George II's Master of the Revels, and had actually supervised the illumination of Westminster Hall for the coronation banquet. To mention his name was thus to cement a link between court ceremonial and vacuous show-business performance, a coupling of two modes of specatacle highly convenient for Pope's satiric purpose. Like his close colleague Handel, Heidegger was a man from the world of theatrical showmanship recruited to the team responsible for the coronation. We are left with the implication that the Hanoverian dynasty needed such adventitious aids: without them, their bogus pretensions would have been exposed by the solemn ceremony and religious content of the occasion.[33]

The Queen greets her chosen instrument: 'All hail! and hail again, / My son! the promis'd land expects thy reign' (A I, 245–6). *Expects* means awaits, but there is also a sinister overtone—has nothing else to look for but, must now have in store for it, etc. Dulness sees in him 'a King who leads my chosen sons', and who will spread her empire to new regions which will 'bless (her) throne' (A I, 251-4). She is interrupted by rowdy cries of acclamation: 'God save King Tibbald!'[34] The book ends with a curious touch, the 'hoarse nation' croaking, 'God save King Log!' (A I, 260). Formally part of an extended simile, the line serves to remind us of the main action in this book: the installation of a new monarch, complete with anointing, ritual gestures, incantatory and prophetic language, acclamation and the like. It would be a very strange reader in May 1728 who never at any point recalled the events of the previous October.

We can turn now to Book II, still in the original version. The King is immediately introduced on an elevated chair of state:

> High on a gorgeous seat, that far outshone
> Henley's gilt Tub, or Fleckno's Irish Throne,
> Or that, where on her Curlls the Public pours
> All-bounteous, fragrant grains, and golden show'rs;
> Great Tibbald sate.
>
> (A II, 1-5)

The stateliness of movement and syntax would befit a description of George on his dais: the subliminal message is, 'the King belongs in the pillory, pelted by the mob, not on a throne covered in costly jewels and sprinkled with fragrant ointment'. As the people look at Theobald, 'crowds grow foolish as they gaze' (one recalls Lady Mary's account of the simpering congregation in the Abbey). Briefly, the analogy changes to that of a mock papal ceremony in the Capitol at Rome (A II, 9-12): Pope's note teases out some of the implications, and remarks on the 'solemn Festival on [Querno's] Coronation', another potentially corrosive touch. In such passages we are not merely confronted with a static picture of a monarch on his throne: again and again the verse insists on the *act* of enthronement, as though every aspect of the reign proceeds from that (propitious or baneful) deed.

Dulness now proclaims 'by herald hawkers' the heroic games which are to replace martial contests in this debased version of epic. The original setting had recalled the scene in Westminster Hall, and there are points of contact between the games and the strange episode interpolated into the coronation banquet. We have heralds, challenges, a claim laid to an august title (A II, 130–2): at stake, instead of a golden bowl, is a china jordan: and Chetwood, 'Crown'd with the Jordan, walks contented home' (A II, 182) much as the Champion departs with his allotted trophy. The parallel with real life is much less close than in Book I: nevertheless, it is possible to discern a burlesque version of the show put on by Heidegger to succeed the service proper. Similarly, the trumpets, drums and cannon-blasts booming round London figure in both 'ceremonies'. At the end of their respective festivities, the participants retire to rest: George and Caroline to St James's Palace, the peers to their mansions, and the dunces to gaols and hedge-taverns.

Meanwhile the allegorical Queen has taken her son to her cave:

> But in her Temple's last recess inclos'd,
> On Dulness lap th' Anointed head reposed.
> Him close she curtained round with vapors blue,
> And soft besprinkled with Cimerian dew.
>
> (A III, 1–4)

This ushers in Theobald's prolonged dream, which in the first version of *The Dunciad* extends to the very end of the poem. It is difficult to avoid the conclusion that Pope intends at one level an ironic picture of connubial bliss: 'th' Anointed head' in 1728 could refer to only one man, and that was neither Theobald nor Walpole. The vision of a new empire of dulness contains occasional recollections of what one might term coronation idiom—'mighty Dulness crown'd' receiving the 'homage' of her sons, her 'seat imperial' and so on. But the echoes are relatively few until we approach the end of the poem, where Pope almost risked a direct and insulting reference to the royal family (1. 299), and where he finally allows the code to crack completely:

> This, this, is He, foretold by ancient rhymes,
> Th' Augustus born to bring Saturnian times:
> Beneath his reign, shall Eusden wear the bays,
> Cibber preside Lord-Chancellor of Plays ...
>
> (A III, 317–20)

This was one of the points at which Cibber's promotion to the office of laureate made the satiric design a good deal more compact: Eusden may have served in that capacity during George II's reign, but he had been appointed whilst George I was on the throne. And Eusden was not King of the dunces, either. Nevertheless, a sharp thrust is made. Nine years before the imitation of Horace's great epistle, the name 'Augustus' inescapably points to George Augustus, the new king.[35] The reference to poor bibulous Eusden carries only subsidiary importance: it is Augustus Redivivus who occupies the centre of attention. Ministerial hacks had foretold a glorious reign, and so confirmed their dulness.[36] The true state of affairs is outlined in the following lines, with ignorant sciolists promoted to key positions and men like Gay and Swift neglected.

All this leads in the original version to the famous peroration. In some respects the three-book *Dunciad* is a more compact and organic work; and to have this concluding vision of nightmare as part of Settle's prophecy lends a special decorum to the magnificent verse—something it loses in the *New Dunciad*. From our present vantage-point the interest is that the new 'reign' is couched in terms of the future tense. This was of course the situation with regard to George II's reign in 1728. Nothing could be done about that in 1743: Pope could not restore the conditions that applied when he first conceived of the poem. Caroline was dead; Walpole had fallen from power. Both these facts made it possible to be a little more plain-spoken, but they compromised in some measure the integrity of Settle's vision. There was a risk that Book III might seem a kind of self-fulfilling prophecy: events had overtaken some of the vatic utterances. This may be one reason for Pope's revisions, and for his decision to supply a new book to conclude the poem, even though it was impossible to extend the action as such. Book III could stand, for the most part, but it could no longer be the last word.[37]

IV

Book IV reverts at several points to the coronation idiom we have observed in the early sections of the poem. That might seem surprising in view of the lapse of years, and there is in truth no obvious trigger for Pope's imagination in this instance. His

decision to present rather static court scenes may have been
made under the influence of Fielding's plays, or perhaps of
Hogarth's early allegorical designs. In any case, the effect was to
bring the poem back from Elysium into Westminster and St
James's: and in the process the lingering overtones of state
ceremony are trapped once more.

Consider the initial description of Dulness:

> She mounts the Throne: her head a Cloud conceal'd,
> In broad Effulgence all below reveal'd,
> ('Tis thus aspiring Dulness ever shines)
> Soft on her lap her Laureat son reclines.
>
> (B IV, 17–20)

The first two lines here surely carry a suggestion of indecorous
personal exposure. One of Caroline's most prominent features
was her well-developed bust: J.H. Plumb writes that 'she had
magnificent breasts, and was very proud of them, displaying
them to their maximum advantage'.[38] At the same time
biographers relate that she underwent embarrassment over the
ritual anointing of her bosom during the coronation: her
attendant was required to open her apparel so that the
Archbishop of Canterbury could perform the act. According to
Peter Quennell, she arranged that at this juncture in the service
the canopy should be dipped to protect her from view.[39] The
parenthesis seems to convey the meaning: the dull possess a
nugatory mental life, but are keen to make a vulgar display of
their bodily assets. As for the 'Laureat son', now of course Cibber,
the point is rammed home by the pedantic Scriblerus in his note:

> With great judgment it is imagined by the Poet, that such a Collegue
> as Dulness had elected, should sleep on the Throne, and have very
> little share in the Action of the Poem. Accordingly he hath done little
> or nothing since the day of his Anointing; having past the second
> book without taking part in any thing that was transacted about
> him, and thro' the third in profound Sleep. Nor ought this, well
> considered, seem strange in our days, when so many *King-consorts*
> have done the like.

The Twickenham editor comments: 'The sneer at King-consorts
was probably intended for George II, who was content in

political matters, whether he knew it or not, to follow his Queen. As a contemporary lampoon put it: "We know 'tis Queen Caroline, not you that reign".[40] Modern research would not allocate royal influence in quite the same proportions, but the thrust at George is unmistakable, much more than a 'probable' intention.

In this note, as often, Pope confronts a possible line of criticism against his poem—the lack of an active role for the titular hero. Even the new material added in Book IV does little to obviate the charge. Instead, Pope harks back to the moment of the King's installation ('from the day of his Anointing'). The apparent blunderings of Scriblerus turn out to serve a valuable artistic function: they justify the hero's passivity by comparing him to the allegedly supine monarch, George II. They reduce the possible embarrassment of a hero less potent than his 'mother' Dulness, by suggesting that the King is subservient to Queen Caroline. And, most important of all, they bridge what could have been a yawning gap between the start and end of the greater *Dunciad*. When Scriblerus reminds us of the manner in which the hero came to the throne, he cements both the fictional design—the 'action' involving Dulness and her son—and the historical infrastructure. By this last expression I mean the running commentary of allusions to England under George II. We are reminded of the high hopes instilled by sycophantic poets, led by the laureate Eusden, when George and Caroline ascended the throne. In bitter retrospect the vacuous reign is identified with the indolent non-creativity of the new laureate Cibber, appointed almost at the start of George's reign. Bentley's note to the same line concludes, 'It is from their *actions* only that Princes have their character, and Poets from their *works*: And if in *those* he *be as much asleep as any fool*, the Poet must leave him and them to *sleep to all eternity*.'[41] The antecedent of *he* is officially Cibber, but inescapably George also. The implication is clear: getting himself crowned was the last active step the King took, within the visibility of the poem and, it is suggested, of the nation.

Pope goes on to describe a new set of allegorical attendants poised beneath the footstool of Queen Dulness.[42] It could be a generalised throne-room scene: but once more there are marked lines of contact with the coronation ceremony. The arms of Logic are borne by Sophistry, the robes of Rhetoric have been purloined to adorn Billingsgate; and we witness

> *Morality*, by her false Guardians drawn,
> *Chicane* in Furs, and *Casuistry* in Lawn.
>
> (B IV, 27–8)

Dignitaries of the law and of the church only came together in full dress at a limited range of state occasions: as when the Archbishop of York and the Lord Chancellor walked in procession, directly in front of the Queen, at the coronation service. (It may be significant that Caroline herself had been 'supported' by two bishops, one of them Edmund Gibson—Walpole's ecclesiastical fixer,who was an expert on canon law known as 'Codex'.) The allegorical arrangement belongs to a moment of high ritual such as the coronation: it was replicated at court only on very special occasions, such as a royal birthday, and imperfectly then.

The first intruder into this stylised tableau is the 'Harlot form' of opera. It was noted earlier that Pope attended an opera, unquestionably Handel's *Admeto*, on the eve of the coronation. Until the late 1730s Handel was of course known chiefly as a composer of opera, rather than oratorio: his most famous piece of church music for many years was the set of four Coronation Anthems composed in 1727 (ten years later Handel was to produce a funeral anthem for Caroline). Considerable public interest was shown in the music for the service and it was even found necessary to keep the time of rehearsals secret 'lest the Crowd of People should be an Obstruction to the Performers'. There was a choir of at least forty, and an orchestra of something like 160, with violins, trumpets, hautboys, and kettle-drums.[43] The orchestral side has its echo in *The Dunciad*:

> Strong in new Arms, lo! Giant Handel stands,
> Like bold Briareus, with a hundred hands;
> To stir, to rouze, to shake the Soul he comes,
> And Jove's own Thunders follow Mars's Drums.
>
> (B IV, 65–8)

'A hundred hands' refers specifically to the augmented orchestra, used not at Haymarket Opera-House, but in the Abbey. The vocal side had already found a place in the text: for the nucleus of the choir in the Abbey had been formed by boys and men of the Chapel Royal. In the revised version of 1743, the acclamation of newly crowned Cibber is described thus:

> Then swells the Chapel-royal throat:
> 'God save king Cibber!' mounts in ev'ry note.
>
> (B I, 319–20)

The note remarks that the Chapel Royal forces were also 'employed in the performance of the Birth-day and New-year Odes': that underlines the Cibber connection, but again the most public expression of Chapel Royal hosannas had been on the occasion of the coronation.

A blast from 'Fame's posterior Trumpet' now sounds, to summon the throng of duces to make obeisance to the Queen. 'Nor absent they, no members of her state, / Who pay her homage in her sons, the Great' (B IV, 91–2): it is a burlesque replay of the latter stages of the service in 1727. The duces kneel before Baal, bestow livings ('vest dull Flatt'ry in the sacred Gown'), and 'give from fool to fool the laurel crown' (B IV, 93–8). The disposal of patronage is a central theme of Book IV, and it was in this very area that criticism of Caroline, in particular, often centred. Walpole took particular care with the allocation of rewards when the new king came to the throne,[44] and Swift was not alone in the curiosity with which he watched the exercise of the prerogative in July, August and September 1727. It was the Lord Chamberlain who made one crucial appointment, that of the laureate: but the passage embraces a much wider range of court patronage. Only when the monarch acceded could a major change in the system of rewards be hoped for, and the expectations of Pope's friends were at their highest in the first few weeks of George's reign.[45] Very quickly these optimistic calculations were dashed, and cynicism set in again. On Swift, particularly, the impact was lasting. This is yet one more reason for locating the epicentre of dulness in 1727: the poem constantly insists on this critical juncture immediately following the accession.

The duces march past, 'the bard and blockhead, side by side' (B IV, 101), much as the heterogeneous procession had filed into the Abbey. They crowd in upon Dulness, eager to present her with 'the first' loyal address, as so many had done at the start of the reign, the City of London included. A series of applicants present themselves, and for a time the proceedings can be directly identified with the distribution of honours on a royal birthday. George's fell on 30 October; Lord Mayor's Day (now 9 November) was fixed on the very same day before the change in the calendar of 1752. A central fact about the poem, concealed by this apparent shift in dates, has been overlooked. The basic reason for locating the duncely junketings on Lord Mayor's Day was that it happened also to be the birthday of the monarch. Largesse and ceremony were the order at court on this day above all others in the year. Consequently there is a real propriety in the design of the greater *Dunciad*: coronation in the morning, with sports in the evening (parodying the banquet, perhaps), and then the following day birthday ceremonial.

Among those who present themselves at the levee is a botanist who has produced a carnation to which he gives the title 'Caroline' (B IV, 403-18). The flower is decked out with a ruff together with a 'gilded button'; it is 'throned in glass.' The bloom has now been nibbled away by a rival virtuoso's butterfly; 'this gay daughter of the Spring' now lies in dust. Pope's note explains that a gardener actually painted a choice variety on his sign, with the inscription '*This is* My *Queen Caroline*'. The equation of carnation and queen makes one wonder if the lines do not at some level constitute a grisly allusion to Caroline's painful death in 1737. She had suffered for many years from what was described at the time as a 'ruptured navel' but may have been a prolapsed womb, since it became apparent after her last confinement. The 'mortification' which set in towards the end suggests that the ultimate cause of death may have been cancer. In the passage we surely have what Erskine-Hill calls an 'oblique elegy' for this 'crucially powerful woman whom [Pope's] satire had often accused'. It is one of the moments where, beneath the surface of the text, we can discern a recognition that things had changed since 1728. The episode is finely described by Erskine-Hill as 'a strangely beautiful emblem of court-corruption'; he adds that 'the final irony is that Dulness passes judgement on her own fate and survives her own death'.[46]

The passages satirising freethinkers and deistic metaphysicians have sometimes been found inorganic. It should therefore be noted that Caroline's patronage of men like Samuel Clarke is often at the root of the matter (as at B IV, 506). The blasphemous parody of transubstantiation at B IV, 549-62, may receive added force when we remember that communion was actually taken during the coronation service: the King before taking his oath had to make a declaration against the 'papist' doctrine of transubstantiation of the eucharistic elements into the body and blood of Christ. As a serious, if not enthusiastically devout, Catholic Pope would have accepted this doctrine and deplored its blank protestant rejection: hence, it may be, the savagely reductive use of language in this passage.

We have now arrived almost at the climax of the action. This begins with a blessing (there was one in the Abbey service), and then Dulness lists the anticipated glories of the new monarch. She is interrupted by her vast yawn, which spreads across London and then the whole nation:

> Churches and Chapels instantly it reach'd;
> (St James's first, for leaden Gilbert preach'd)
> Then catch'd the Schools; the Hall scarce kept awake;
> The Convocation gap'd, but could not speak:
> Lost was the Nation's Sense, nor could be found,
> While the long solemn Unison went round:
> Wide, and more wide, it spread o'er all the realm,
> Ev'n Palinurus nodded at the Helm:
> The Vapour mild o'er each Committee crept;
> Unfinish's Treaties in each Office slept;
> And chiefless Armies doz'd out the Campaign;
> And Navies yawn'd for Orders on the Main.
>
> (B IV, 607-18)

The imaginative geography of the poem is sometimes a little ambiguous; but it is absolutely plain that the effects of Dulness begin in Westminster. Despite line 613, all the events prior to the final couplet belong to this part of the capital—St James's, Westminster School (remembering an earlier passage), Westminster Hall, Convocation, the Commons (the 'Nation's Sense'), Walpole, offices in and around Whitehall. National torpor starts from St James's Chapel and adjoining churches:[47] the Abbey, which had seen the installation of the monarch, is

among the very first places to catch the infection. So we pass to
the peroration, now transferred from Book III, where the
grandeur of generality makes topical and political satire for once
otiose.

V

The body of allusion I have been seeking to explore does not turn
the poem upside down: *The Dunciad* plainly works at a level of
high literary achievement without it. However, this does not
mean that the attempt is supererogatory. As a great and timeless
work, *The Dunciad* contains multitudes, and to miss one of its
component parts will seldom impair our enjoyment to any
marked degree. On the other hand, to overlook meanings which
would have forced themselves on the attention of a contemporary
is to abstract ourselves unduly from a full response.

It might be retorted that contemporaries kept surprisingly
quiet about the theme I have discussed, if it was indeed forced
upon their attention. To this there are two answers. The first is
that Pope commits *lèse-majesté* with such finesse that
commentators risk a charge of sedition if they tease out the full
implications. It is noteworthy that hostile reactions to works such
as the *Epistle to Augustus* stop cautiously short of paraphrasing the
sharpest anti-court thrusts. The second answer is less lame than it
may initially appear. Some of the overtones we can now recover
only with considerable effort would have seemed too obvious to
mention at the time. The death of George I and the accession of
George II and Caroline were the biggest 'events' of 1727: even
the general election was a quiet affair by comparison, involving
as it did only a minority of the nation. The coronation was the
largest 'happening' in the public arena: lavishly mounted,
elaborately stage-managed, energetically promoted to bolster a
still fragile dynasty. It is understandable that modern historians
find more substance in the intrigues at court, the brief power-
struggle between Walpole and Spencer Compton, and so on. But
politics is drama as well as ideology, and the public awareness of
major issues is rarely as minutely attentive as their observation of
impressive spectacle.[48] The scene in the Abbey caught the
imagination of Lady Mary Wortley Montagu, who was far from

incompetent in the analysis of ideas and beliefs. It is surely plausible to catch echoes of the occasion in a great poem, full of spectacle and crowd-effects,which was even then in the process of composition.

The discovery of such a motif enriches *The Dunciad* in several respects. First, it gives a direct occasion for the action of the very first book. Second, it permits a more cohesive relation to operate between the *New Dunciad* and the earlier books. Third, it provides a justification for the use of the Lord Mayor's Day setting, over and beyond any factors we have known about previously. By allusion to the events of 30 October, it enriches the satire on a Court-City misalliance. Fourth, it makes the choice of Thorold's mayoralty less arbitrary than it has seemed. This element, latent in the original text, becomes more explicit when the poem is revised. Fifth, it underlies a sustain body of allusion to the royal family, and makes the politics more integral to the action. Sixth, it supports the important role given to Caroline in both versions, especially through her association with the Queen of Dulness. Seventh, it focusses the reader's attention on the moment of accession, which was particularly crucial in terms of Scriblerian hopes and ambitions—1727 was the time when Walpole came to see immovable. Eighth, it helps to sustain the dynastic theme, of Hanoverians following one another in duncely succession. Ninth, it gives another charge to the satire against Cibber in the revised poem. The laureate's promotion under George II made him that much more suitable a choice for King Dunce; conversely, his elevation within the poem reflects back on to the theme of accession to power. Lastly, it links with some of the other major components in Pope's satire, particularly the criticism of elaborate theatrical spectacle. The coronation itself, and even more its recreation in a Drury Lane pageant, support an extensive body of material satirising garish display and loudly nonsensical 'shows'.[49]

These latter concerns are focussed in a letter which Pope wrote just a month after the Coronation, during the run of Cibber's theatrical re-enactment:

> Here the most unhappy gay people are reduced to mere child's play, and childish sights, to divert them. They go every day to stare at a mock coronation on a stage, which is to be succeeded by a more

ridiculous one of the Harlequins (almost as ridiculous a farce as the real state one of a coronation itself). After that, they hope for it again in a puppet-show, which is to recommend itself by another qualification, of having the exact portraits of the most conspicuous faces of our nobility in wax-work, so as to be known at sight, without Punch's help, or the master's pointing to each with his wand as they pass. So much for news! 'Tis what passes most material in this metropolis . . .[50]

So 'sights' have become an explicit emblem of the farce of state, and the puppet-master is seen as directing the immaterial antics of a debased metropolis.

Once we read the theme back into the text, then, we have many deft topical jokes reanimated, but we have a great deal more as well. We have recovered a leading agent of the comedy, and a significant element in the satiric structure of *The Dunciad*.

Notes

Epigraph: *TE* IV, 223

1. All quotations and references follow *TE*. For the queston, 'Why 1719?' see *TE*, V, xiv.
2. Williams, pp. 29–41.
3. *TE*, V, 275.
4. *See TE*, V, xiv.
5. *See* A.J. Henderson, *London and the National Government, 1721–1742* (Chapel Hill, 1945), p. 81. Another George, George Merttins, was elected Lord Mayor in 1724; but unlike Thorold he was a Tory.
6. *See Hor. Ep.* II ii, 184.
7. He was a member of the Ironmongers' Company.
8. *TE*, V, xiii–xiv. Pope himself originally stated that the poem 'was writ in 1727': in 1735 he altered this to '1726' (*TE*, V, 60). No real weight can be placed on this testimony, although I think 1727 is the single year in which most writing was performed.
9. Pope, *Corr*, II, 455–6.
10. Pope, *Corr*, II, 438.
11. *TE*, V, xv.
12. Pope, *Corr*, II, 454–6.
13. Maynard Mack, *The Garden and the City* (Toronto, 1969), esp. pp. 150–5.
14. Howard Erskine-Hill, *Pope: The Dunciad* (London, 1972), pp. 48–60.
15. *TE*, V, xxxviii. Arbuthnot told Swift that the King 'declared (Pope) was a very honest man' after reading the Variorum edition: *see* Swift, *Corr*, III, 326. This could be obtuseness or a calculated deceit. The King's curiosity

regarding the poem had first been whetted on the appearance of the original edition in 1728 (*Corr*, II, 502).

16. *TE*, V, 456.
17. Erskine-Hill, p. 49.
18. *TE*, V, 61.
19. Williams, p. 26.
20. Swift, *Corr* III, 243-4. Oxford may mean only that Pope could have witnessed the procession, but he seems to refer to attendance at the service itself.
21. Deutsch, pp. 206-13.
22. Pope, *Corr*, I, 268.
23. Swift, *Corr*, III, 244.
24. Deutsch, p. 214. The English pamphlet was published in 1727 by James Roberts; the Dublin edition is by S. Powell. It sets out the ceremony in detail, allotting several paragraphs to the successive phases of the ceremony, including the communion service. There is a French translation, probably done from the German text.
25. W.H. Wilkins, *Caroline the Illustrious* (London, 1904), pp. 344-51. Wilkins's main source is *A Particular Account of the Solemnities used at the Coronation of his Sacred Majesty King George II and of his Royal Consort Queen Carolina* (W. Bristow, 1760; 2nd edn, 1761), obviously stimulated by the coronation of George III. Wilkins follows this pamphlet closely for most of his account. It is less detailed as regards the service in the Abbey than Roberts's description, but it supplies useful additional material concerning the Lord Mayor's Day proceedings. I have collated all these sources.
26. *The Complete Letters of Lady Mary Wortley Montagu*, ed. Robert Halsband (Oxford, 1965-67), II, 85. Also quoted by Wilkins, p. 350. Lady Mary speaks of being 'very well diverted' by the procession and service.
27. Wilkins, pp. 350-1. For a possible reference to the Drury Lane performances on 26 October, *see* Sutherland's Note to A III, 310 (*TE*, V, 185). *See also* R.H. Barker, *Mr. Cibber of Drury Lane* (New York, 1939), p. 140. Clear proof that Pope was aware of the spectacle in some detail is provided by the lines used in the epigraph to this chapter. *See also* Pope, *Corr*, II, 462-3 for his account of mock-coronations on the stage, written in November 1727: and *see TE*, IV, 222 for the success of the pageant scene. At the time of the next coronation, in 1761, Garrick attempted unsuccessfully to rival John Rich with a pageant at Drury Lane, involving bonfires and parades: for an amusing description, *see* Thomas Davies, *Memoirs of the Life of David Garrick*, esq. (London, 1780), I, 328-30.
28. Most of the information is derived from Bristow's pamphlet, mentioned in note 25 above. For the detail concerning the linen-draper, *see* Robert Withington, *English Pageantry: An Historical Outline* (Cambridge, Mass., 1920), II, 88-9. Withington supplies the fullest account of the tradition of pageant, allegory and 'triumph': *see* esp. II, 71-85. Settle's contribution whilst City Poet is described at II, 65-6. These naively patriotic, strongly protestant and crudely emblematic pageants must have been in Pope's mind when he wrote of the shows contrived by Settle (*see* AI, 88 note). He even remarks that the verse-part of these shows had been abolished 'by the

frugality of some Lord Mayors', which is surely a dig at the lavishness and waste of the City in 1727, when the Corporation sought to propitiate the new monarch. For Barber's letter to Swift, *see* Swift, *Corr*, IV, 62. On its implications for *The Dunciad, see* my *Grub Street* (1972), pp. 111-12.

For Mrs Pendarves's account, *see Mrs Delany at Court and among the Wits*, ed. R. Brimley Johnson (London, 1925), pp. 38-42. Note that according to her report the King and Queen remained at the Guildhall until midnight on 30 October.

See also the evocative description by Derek Jarrett of 'the store cupboards of the various City companies ... piled high with masks and costumes intended to depict ... members of the Greek and Roman pantheon', together with other 'colourful images of popular pageantry' used in the Lord Mayor's shows: *The Ingenious Mr Hogarth* (London, 1976), pp. 32-3. Giants and dragons (A III, 231-2) were amongst the very commonest properties used.

29. Wilkins, pp. 7, 343-4.
30. *TE*, VI, 69.
31. *TE*, VI. 71: cf. the coin-collector Annius at B IV, 347. Both Pope and Swift took some interest in numismatics: Swift was a friend of Sir Andrew Fountaine, a leading expert in the field.
32. Wilkins, pp. 337-9.
33. It was reported in the press that singers from the opera were to take part in the coronation music (Deutsch, p. 214). Other contemporary observers tend to look at matters another way, deploring the fact that Westminster Abbey choirmen were permitted to sing in the opera-house.
34. One of the 1735 revisions is noted by Mack, p. 150: '"God save King Tibald!"—the roar of Grubstreet alleys in 1729—becomes ... "God save the king!" acknowledgement of a less specific but therefore actually more libellous allusion.'
35. This is recognised by Williams, p. 51, in a somewhat oblique fashion: none of the other commentators remark on the allusion to George Augustus. For the concealed reference at 1. 299, and a manuscript variant, *see TE*, VI. 184.
36. For a 'typical specimen' from Eusden, see Williams, pp. 50-1.
37. An important revision at A I, 251-4, made in 1735, is discussed by Mack, p. 151. It depicts George and Caroline respectively as 'a Monarch proud my race to own' and 'A Nursing-mother, born to rock the throne'.
38. J.H. Plumb, *Sir Robert Walpole: The King's Minister* (London, 1960), p. 159. *See also* Peter Quennell, *Caroline of England* (London, 1939), p. 15: 'a bosom so smooth and so expansive that even in advanced middle age it could still command from her husband an almost doting admiration'. And further Lewis Melville, *Lady Suffolk and her Circle* (London, 1924), p. 20, on Hanoverian bosoms.
39. Quennell, p. 124. Vanity and modesty concerning one's own most attractive feature may coexist more often than one supposes.
40. *TE*, VI. 341.
41. *TE*, VI, 342.
42. *See* Mack, p. 153, for the 'gain in significance' achieved by the new

material.

43. Deutsch, pp. 214–15. *See also* Chapter 4 above. King George was addicted to opera, alone among the arts, and a loyal patron of Handel. Trumpets and drums also figured in the Lord Mayor's banquet on 30 October.

44. Plumb, pp. 175–6.

45. *See* James Woolley, 'Friends and Enemies in *Verses on the Death of Dr. Swift*', *Studies in Eighteenth-Century Culture*, vol. VIII, ed. Roseann Runte (Madison, Wisconsin, 1979), pp. 205–32. Woolley argues that for Swift 'the decisive event of these years [the late 1720s] was the failure of Walpole's government to fall when George II came to the throne in June 1727' (p. 210) and he reads the *Verses* as, in part, a rebuke to the Queen and Mrs Howard for their treachery.

46. Erskine-Hill, pp. 57–9, provides by far the most apt commentary on the passage. He suggests that the butterfly may represent Lord Hervey, only to retract the suggestion: the identification may however be valid. Erskine-Hill discusses the theme of corruption without reference to the bodily corruption that ravaged Caroline at the end: I think this contributed to the strange, horrified tone which informs the verse.

47. I assume that Gilbert is preaching before the royal family at St James's Palace, not at nearby St James's, Piccadilly.

48. For the development of politics in this direction in the middle of the eighteenth century, *see* John Brewer, *Party Ideology and Popular Politics at the Accession of George III* (Cambridge, 1976). *The Dunciad*, it could be said, treats of party ideology and popular politics at the accession of George II.

49. *See* Chapter 3 above. It was the joint involvement of Handel *and* Heidegger in the coronation ceremonies which made them so apt to Pope's purposes.

50. Pope, *Corr*, II, 462–3.

6

GRUB STREET BIOGRAPHY

Defoe and Others on Jonathan Wild

Our selves, like the Great, to secure a retreat,
When matters require it, must give up our gang:
    And good reason why,
    Or, instead of the fry,
    Ev'n *Peachum* and I,
Like poor petty rascals, might hang, hang,
Like poor petty rascals, might hang.

               Air LVI, *The Beggar's Opera*

With Defoe, we reach an author who characteristically exploits popular forms directly, rather than parodying them. Nevertheless, his relationship with the modes he employs (biography, conduct-book, tourist guide) is by no means a simple one. Despite his relatively disadvantaged background, he had become by the reign of George I a literary craftsman of unparalleled range and experience. His way with the stock genres is not that of the hacks at large, and one can see in his works of the seven-teens and twenties a kind of scholarly application of the demotic. It is a common exercise to compare Defoe with Swift and other figures of high literature. For a change, it may be worth considering him in a different frame of reference, that is to say alongside popular compilers performing their daily Grub Street activity.

I

Jonathan Wild was perhaps the greatest folk-villain in the English-speaking world during the eighteenth century. Not even George III, Lord North or Benedict Arnold achieved so widespread a notoriety. Eighteen years after he went to his death

151

at Tyburn, Wild was still familiar enough to the popular imagination for Henry Fielding to use him as an emblem of crime and corruption. He had already served as the basis for Peachum, the character who really controls events (as opposed to striking sexy attitudes, like Macheath) in John Gay's music-drama *The Beggar's Opera* (1728). But before this, his death in 1725 had released a broad current of criminal literature—more or less straight biographies, effigies and cartoons, ballads, jest-books and assorted ephemera. There had been a trickle of such material in Wild's lifteime; none the less, it was his fall which opened the floodgate. The thief-catcher was not allotted a theatrical narrative of his own; but he turns up in the Jack Sheppard chronicles, such as Thurmond's *Harlequin Sheppard* (1724) and the anonymous *Prison-Breaker* (1725), the retort mounted by John Rich at Lincoln's Inn Fields. (William Wood and his 'brass' occur in the former, another confirmation of the interchangeability of these Augustan villains.)

The implicit appeal of many works which came out at this time was—truthfully or otherwise—'now, at last, it can be told'. Some of this material has been described by W.R. Irwin, though his main concern lay in the making of Fielding's highly individual and patently 'inauthentic' account of Wild.[1] I shall address myself to the more orthodox stream of popular literature. The 'availability' of Wild to every class of writer makes him an especially revealing test-case: people had been in the habit of refering to him in the same breath as Walpole, or Wood, or Peter Walter, or Colonel Charteris. But here was one powerful individual, with a strong hold on the contemporary imagination, who actually went to Tyburn—the destination to which Swift and Pope would have liked to consign Walpole and the rest. (See the introduction, pp. 29–30, above.) Again we find the archetypal Augustan 'villain' as a key figure in popular cultural modes of the day, apposite to the stock imagery of public debate and the preferred literary forms.

One acknowledged literary master made his contribution to this first mass of Wildiana. Daniel Defoe, who had filled in the last few years with the fictional doings of Crusoe, Moll, Colonel Jack, the pirate Singleton and the courtesan Roxana, now had a subject he possibly considered worthier of his pen. Since he was an experienced journalist on all subjects related to crime, a student of the London underworld, and the biographer of Jack Sheppard during the previous year, it is not surprising that Defoe should have joined in the fray. Indeed, it now seems likely that he wrote two separate accounts, for different publishers and perhaps slightly different markets. The work I wish to discuss was published by John Applebee (the leading exponent in the trade of criminal lives) under the title of *The True and Genuine Account of the Life and Actions of the late Jonathan Wild*, Howson 2. But it would be misleading to treat this short narrative in isolation. It was, after all, deliberately issued to rival existing entrants in a competition already known to be tough. Besides, it is in many respects the standard Grub Street job: though, as we shall see, not in all.[2]

The *Memoirs* issued under the *nom de plume* 'Capt. Alexander Smith' represent something like the norm. Wild comes first in a collection of about thirty criminals, some of them belonging to the previous century and ending with Jack Sheppard and the Burnworth gang (about both of whom Defoe wrote his own narratives).[3] Smith comments, 'As *Jonathan Wild*, exceeded all Mankind hitherto Born in all Manner of Villany, we give him the Preference of all other Vallains [sic], in permitting him to lead the Van of 'em.' A brisk and straightforward account follows, uncritical in its use of popular stories, and culminating in three sets of verse. The first is a 'Hymn to *Tybourn*, that was compos'd by some prime Wits, a little after the fatal *Catastrophe* which sent him [Wild] out of the Land of the Living'. This poem is loosely related to Defoe's *Hymn to the Pillory* (1703), although it is written in rugged heroic couplets instead of Defoe's ode-like structure. Second come an elegy, probably printed separately in addition (though I have not located it); and third a ten-line epitaph, recalling the chapbook efforts to encapsulate Moll Flanders's career.[4] Smith's narrative is certainly derivative, probably unreliable, and structurally incoherent. In the first two respects Defoe might be accused of similar flaws when he composed his life of Wild; but his literary skills are immensely greater. It might even be argued that his distinction as a writer shows up more plainly in this context of hack compilation than anywhere else.

II

It happens that a clearcut relation exists between Defoe's *Account* and another biography which, in one guise or another, cropped up for decades. This was the variant used by 'Captain Charles Johnson' in his *General History of the Highwaymen* (1734), Howson no. 81, it also figures in *The Lives of the most Remarkable Criminals*, a collection published in 1735 and reprinted most lately in 1927 (Howson no. 83). It is the 1735 text of this 'Life of the famous Jonathan Wild, Thief-Taker', which I shall use as a control here.[5] A cut-down version of this can be found in *Select and Impartial Accounts . . . of the most Remarkable Convicts* (1745), issued by Applebee and including some of Defoe's criminal lives (Howson no. 86). Could the *Life*, then, be yet a third essay on Wild's career by Defoe?[6] I think not; but the exact state of indebtedness remains uncertain. It is possible (1) that Defoe's *Account* derived from the earliest version of the *Life*; (2) that the *Life* is based on the *Account*; or (3) that they both derive from a third source. They are certainly not independent. My view is that (2) is the likeliest of these, and (3) the least likely. But for our present purposes it is enough to note that the *Account* and the *Life* contain a very large proportion of overlapping material.

Allowing for this close similarity in content and phrasing, there still emerges a broad and substantive difference between Defoe and his rival. (I will call the latter 'Johnson', a convenient rather than an accurate identification.) In outline, Johnson gives us a straight narrative, factual, 'historic', undistracted. Defoe *shapes* the material much more: he fills in more of the background, provides a wider range of comparison and conjecture, and points up his conclusions much more sharply. Johnson's is essentially a life-story: Defoe's, a moral dramatisation of Wild and his career. This can be illustrated by a number of detailed contrasts between the two works.

First, Defoe takes much longer to get into his narrative. Both lives start with an introductory puff, in the manner of the time, warning the reader against 'Fabulous Relations' (*Lives*, 14) put out by rivals—a staple ingredient of Grub Street biography. But Johnson gets his over in a sentence, and needs only one short paragraph by way of preliminaries. By contrast Defoe begins, *Tale of a Tub*-like, with a Preface and an introduction, running to seventeen paragraphs in all. Even then Johnson is quicker into his stride. He has Wild suffering his first reverse (admission to the debtor's gaol) within little more than a page—inside 300 words. The same is true of Captain Smith in his *Memoirs*. It takes Defoe eight paragraphs, amounting to some 750 words, to reach the same point. Incidentally, Defoe is far more liberal with paragraph divisions: that is one of the ways in which he orders his mterial and signals rhetorical intent to the reader.

In this opening section everything Johnson supplies is also present in Defoe. But additionally Defoe gives much fuller information on Wild's family, especially two brothers who experienced their own troubles—thus giving Defoe an opportunity for characteristic sententiousness: 'so that it seems, all the three Brothers have had some Acquaintance with the inside of a Gaol, tho' on different Accounts' (275). Even at the local verbal level Defoe tends to be more copious with details: Johnson has Wild's mother selling fruit in the market at Wolverhampton, Defoe says '*Herbs* and *Fruit*'. (Captain Smith, who is consistently weak on background, passes rapidly on without touching such matters.) Defoe consistently names names: where Johnson speaks of 'a Gentleman of the long Robe' (15) in whose service Wild came up to London, Defoe identifies him as 'one Counsellor *Daniel* of *Staffordshire*' (276). The explanation for this perhaps lies in Johnson's abridgment of Defoe's earlier text. Conceivably it is Defoe elaborating and burnishing a copy-text as we know him to have done on other occasions.[7] But either way, the artistic consequence is plain. Defoe sets the events in a richer world of human relationships and precise social circumstances.

Second, Defoe is more informative on the mechanics of thieving and the technique of fencing. Again he separates off in a paragraph by itself the crucial statement: 'Thus without being a Thief or a Receiver, he brought a Gain to himself, and his Business went on Prosperously' (278). Though both writers are a little coy about the relations of Wild with his moll, known as Mary Milliner, and about her own 'trade', Defoe reveals more of their way of life together (*Account*, 278-9: *Lives*, 18-19). In this section again Defoe provides fuller illustration, with more specific cases cited (as those of Jack Sheppard and Blueskin Blake), and in a very idiosyncratic manner he itemises certain categories of criminal (285). Both writers use dramatic speech at one point in this section, but where Johnson serves the cause of the narrative (24), Defoe presents a kind of self-revelatory soliloquy (283–4).

Third, Defoe is readier to disturb the flow of the ongoing narrative to make a particular point. He quotes (299–300) the anti- Wild clauses of the Transportation Act when the measure is passed by Parliament, whereas other accounts postpone this to the time of the trial, when they were invoked. Actually such checks do occur in Johnson's account in one or two places but it would seem accidentally. Defoe is more willing to acknowledge what he is doing, with phrases such as 'But to return to the History it self . . .' (286). One good example of this procedure can be found in the treatment of Wild's wives and mistresses. Johnson saves these up for a juicy morsel at the end: 'Before I part with Mr. *Wild*, 'tis requisite that I inform you in Respect of his Wives, or those who were called his Wives' (64). Defoe had supplied much of this material as he went along, notably on the earlier mention of Wild's third paramour (as he calculates it), Elizabeth Mann (288–90). Even in this section Defoe cannot resist slipping in a little supplementary information concerning a highwayman named Skull Dean, whose widow Jonathan had married. Once more we get a sense of a whole criminal environment—a denser portrait than Johnson can supply with his narrow concentration on Wild. It might be added that rival biographers perform even worse than Johnson; for example, Captain Alexander Smith omits Elizabeth Mann altogether and seemingly invents a wife called Mary Read.[8]

As hinted just now, a fourth difference lies in Defoe's lifelong habit of itemising and tabulating (285, 286, 287). Even where Johnson uses the same formula, he suppressed the enumerators, simply listing the two factors in turn which Defoe had carefully dubbed (1.) and (2.)—see *Lives*, 24–5. In general Johnson allows his points to emerge as they will: Defoe hammers them home with a variety of syntactical and typographical devices. The trick of capitalising (as well as indenting) the first word of each paragraph reinforces that strong stress which Defoe normally lays at that point: 'IN this Time . . . HE had two Wives . . . BESIDE those five . . . THE said *Skull Dean* . . . THIS Mrs. Dean, (288–9). Often the same juncture is marked by a short linking phrase, suggesting the temporal or modal relation of the new paragraph to its predecessor: 'AT your second coming ... THE next time ... BUT then it remains to be asked ... IT must be confess'd that in all thise ... HOWEVER ... UPON this ... / NOR, on the other hand ... BUT ... / SO that in a Word ...' (292-3). The effect is to set out a much clearer train of argument than Johnson's headlong progression allows. Defoe is particularly good at switching the point of attack: 'BUT to return to the History it self... BUT be that as it will... / IT must be allow'd ...' (286-7). By contrast Alexander Smith often makes an abruptly fresh start: 'Two old Women once came to *Jonathan Wild's* house ...' (*Memoirs*, p. 7).

Fifth, Defoe lays more emphasis on first-person involvement. One anecdote begins, 'I remember I had Occasion, in a Case of this Kind ...' (294). Elswhere we have, 'This Trade I found by his own Discourse ...' (281). Johnson on the whole is more impersonal, further from events, as befits the objective chronicler. Defoe is an active, meddlesome narrator by camparison. He is freer with allusions to other contemporary crimes and criminals, for example, Moll King—the likely origin for Moll Flanders (295-8)—and the celebrated Arundel Coke case (299).[9]

Sixth, although both writers use direct speech to describe exchanges between Wild and his victim, only Defoe sets out a formal snatch of dramatic dialogue (295-8), much as he does in the *Complete English Tradesman*. The effect of the speech prefixes '*Wild*' and '*Lady*' is, in the context, almost Brechtian. We have a strong sense of a ritual contest, organised and tidied up by the narrator. Johnson's naive he-said-and-she-said comes out, paradoxically, far more 'straight'. Captain Smith does not employ dialogue at all; neither does the best known *Newgate Calendar* version, other than its citation of a court deposition.

Seventh, Defoe is notably fond of the phrase 'for example' and its variants. His account of Wild's office methods employs a vague past tense: 'When you first came to him ... perhaps the very Thing you came to enquire after... At your second coming' (291-2). Note the unspecified 'you'. This goes along with a liking for conditionals ('If the Number of his Instruments was very great', 290). Defoe merely offers a summary rather than a definitive survey: 'this may serve for a Sketch of *Practice*, as I call it

... It would be endless to give a particular of the many Tricks and Cheats of this kind that he has manag'd, during a continued Life of Wickedness, for about 16 Years, among which it would be very Instructing, to give an account' (298–9). This is very far from the orthodox historicity of Johnson. Part rhetorical pretence ('I have many more examples I could give') the passage also serves to remove Wild from bare 'facts' and push him towards an archetypal status. We are to study repeated or representative doings, rather than precise events which took place on a localisable, once-for-all occasion.

There are relatively few differences of any moment in the section dealing with Wild's trial and execution. Johnson includes a long letter from a divine, sent to Wild in the condemned cell: Defoe omits it, with more restraint than he often shows in these matters. However, the respective endings are strongly indicative of the two authors' methods. Defoe comes to a brisk, functional close; like Mozart, when he has said his say he does not linger:

> Thus ended the Tragedy, and thus was a Life of horrid and inimitable Wickedness finish'd at the Gallows, the very same Place where, according to some, above 120 miserable Creatures had been hang'd, whose Blood in great measure may be said to lye at his Door, either in their being first brought into the thieving Trade, or led on in it by his Encouragement and Assistant; and many of them at last betray'd and brought to Justice by his Means; upon which worst sort of Murther he valued himself, and would have had it prais'd for Merit, even with the Government itself,
>
> (307–8)

On the other hand, Johnson tags on to the death of Wild two crowded paragraphs, the first listing the thief-catcher's wives, the second describing his person and naming many obscure criminals supposed to have been his victims. This is a piece of supreme literary incompetence, and its flat banality caused even the unfastidious compiler of *Select and Impartial Accounts* to indulge in some cutting.[10] Johnson, of course, is reduced to these shifts partly by his earlier reluctance to stray from the narrow confines of the life-history.

One reason that Defoe can afford to be more curt at this stage is that he has earlier on established a strong sense of impending doom. A characteristic passage has the narrator remarking, 'It must be confess'd, *Jonathan* play'd a sure Game in all this; and therefore it is not to be wonder'd at that he went on for so many Years without any Disaster' (284). It is a commonplace among students of Defoe that *fear*, especially the fear of sudden reversals of fortune, plays a large part in his imaginative workings. *Disaster* may have been connected in his mind with his early financial troubles; after 1720, it came to be associated with the traumatic effects of the South Sea Bubble. One branch of narrative in which he has no superior is the relation of prosperity suddenly brought low. So it is with Wild: we are gradually made ready for the turn of events ('in the prosperous part of his Business'; 'In this time of his Prosperity', 288), and then comes the laconic conclusion.

III

What emerges from this comparison is principally a discrepancy in manner, rather than in matter. The picture of Wild offered by Defoe is broadly akin to that provided by Johnson. Both writers show their subject as an odious monster, though in less extreme colours than do some of the chroniclers. But while Johnson performs not too badly by the accepted standards in this genre, Defoe is able to go further: the greater freedom and range he commands allow him to depict Wild as a cultural threat and not just a villainous individual. Yet, on a cursory reading, the two books follow a closely allied pattern. Defoe, in fact, adheres to most of the conventions of popular biography. His departures are not radical, because fundamentally Defoe was at home in the non-elite forms of his day. As I have suggested elsewhere, he was a Grub Street writer of genius.[11] When he came to write the life of Wild, he was equipped by his experience as a novelist to evoke a world as well as tell a story. He does many of the same things as the hack Johnson—but he shapes and stage-manages the narrative far more intricately. A considerable writer like Defoe, it is evident, can turn popular vehicles to purposes more finely expressive than their general currency seems to promise.[12] Fielding made a satiric masterpiece out of Wild's career, but for this he needed the high literary resources of mock-heroic, and he moved a long way from the ordinary recital of fact. For *his* deeply interesting version, Defoe barely stretched the norms of Grub Street aesthetics.

Notes

1. *See* W.R. Irwin, *The Making of Jonathan Wild* (New York, 1941) esp. pp. 80–95; as well as the useful list of works on Wild in Gerald Howson, *Thief-Taker General* (London, 1970), pp. 317–21. ('Howson' numbers refer to items in this list.) For graphic satires, *see* Stephens, II, 610–14.

2. Quotations and references in the text follow the convenient reprint in Michael F. Shugrue (ed.), *Selected Poetry and Prose of Daniel Defoe* (New York, 1968), pp. 270–308. Where the context does not make it clear, the page reference is preceded by the word *Account*. The other putative life by Defoe is Howson no. 18, and forms no. 471 in J.R. Moore, *A Checklist of the Writings of Daniel Defoe* (Bloomington, Ind., 1960).

3. The Burnworth gang is treated *A Brief Historical Account of the Lives of the Six Notorious Street-Robbers*, published in April 1726. This is Moore no. 478, and it is undoubtedly the same item as Howson no. 62, despite Howson's statement that this last entry is not in Moore.

4. 'Capt. Alexander Smith', *Memoirs of the Life and Times of Jonathan Wild, Together with the History and Lives of Modern Rogues* (London, 1726; rptd New York, 1973), pp. 1, 19–25. This is Howson no. 26. For Moll in the Chapbooks, *see* Chapter 8 below.

5. *The Lives of the most Remarkable Criminals* (London, 1735, II, 14–69. References in the text are preceded where necessary by the word *Life*. Howson states (p. 325) that the life of Wild in this collection is identical to that in the *General History*, which collection was in turn 'mostly taken from Smith', that is, 'Capt. Alexander Smith', *A Complete History of the Lives of the most Notorious Highwaymen* (London, 5th edn 1719; rptd London 1926), which is Howson no. 74. But Wild came on the scene too late to figure in this compilation by Smith. The *Memoirs* cited in note 4 above occupy a separate volume from the better-known *Complete History*. It might be added that one or two contemporary references appear to point to an identification of 'Captain Smith' with the journalist Richard Burridge; but the evidence is scanty. For 'Burridge the Blasphemer', *see* James Sutherland, *Background for Queen Anne* (London, 1939), pp. 3–32, where there is however no mention of the Smith story.

6. Or, more accurately in that instance, a precis by Defoe of his own *Account*—improbable but not impossible.

7. *See* my article, 'Defoe as Plagiarist', *Philological Querterly*, LVII (1973), 771–4, for this process at work in the *Tour thro' the Whole Island of Great Britain*.

8. *Memoirs of the Life and Times of Jonathan Wild*, pp. 4–5. For some possible sources of this confusion, *see* Howson, pp. 129–30. In the section on Wild supplied by George Theodore Wilkinson, *The Newgate Calendar* (London, 1962), 73–97, the wives are similarly reserved for a paragraph at the end.

9. For Moll King, *see* Howson, pp. 156–70, and the same author's article, 'Who was Moll Flanders?', *Times Literary Supplement* 18 January 1968, pp. 63–4. The Coke affair occasioned a large body of comment in pamphlets and newspapers in 1722; Defoe (who elsewhere refers more than once to the episode) may easily have been responsible for some of the accounts.

10. *Select and Impartial Accounts of the Lives ... of the most Remarkable Convicts* (London, 2nd edn, 1745), II, 80.
11. *See* my *Grub Street: Studies in a Subculture* (London, 1972, pp. 311-27.
12. For an interesting discussion of some widely practised modes of crime literature, *see* the section on 'Rogues and whores' in John J. Richetti, *Popular Fiction before Richardson* (Oxford, 1969), pp. 23-59.

7

CLASSICS AND CHAPBOOKS

I

We know a little more these days about the reading matter available to the bulk of the population 200 years ago. Students of the subject, notably Victor Neuburg, have alerted us to the range and popularity of 'penny histories' for children and adults; we have come to be aware of the continuing tradition of chapbook publishing which went on alongside the conventional 'literary' production of eighteenth-century England. However, there have been few attempts to explore the connections which occasionally emerge between the high forms and their popular equivalents. In this essay I shall try to investigate one mode of contact, namely the treatment of some classic works of literature in popular abridgments and adaptations.

There are not many candidates for such an inquiry. Neuburg mentions a few authors whose work from time to time appeared in the guise of a chapbook: Bunyan, Deloney, Defoe, Burns, Allan Ramsay and Pierce Egan. (He further observes that few known, that is to say identifiable, authors were responsible for 'original' chapbook texts: Hannah More is the most striking exception to this rule.)[1] Among this group, Deloney should perhaps be excluded in that popular tradition was only reclaiming materials which derive from its own province. *Jack of Newbury* and *Thomas of Reading* are the authentic stuff of orthodox chapbooks; whilst Deloney's ballads and broadsides can be designated 'literary' (if they can be so designated) only on account of some anachronistic distinctions. Egan, in a different way, seems scarcely to be representative of mainstream high literature. In fact, the only authors on Neuburg's list who provided texts that survived both as ordinary classics and as stock items in the chapbook repertoire were Bunyan and Defoe. For much of the eighteenth century, even *Gulliver's Travels* remained

162

impervious to the abridgments. This fact may appear surprising, and some explanation would be in order.

Most of the standard fare of Augustan literature was simply beyond the reach of a chapbook audience. Poetry such as *The Rape of the Lock*, *The Seasons*, the *Elegy in a Country Churchyard*, *The Task*—such work was too dense, too allusive, too verbally sophisticated, too independent of 'plot', to be converted easily into popular expression. Drama was seldom the basis of chapbook publications, and the subject matter and style of *The Beggar's Opera* or *The School for Scandal* made each play an unsuitable case for treatment. One might have anticipated that prose fiction would prove a more promising field. In fact, most of the major novelists were equally recalcitrant. Richardson's works, above all *Pamela*, did generate a series of sequels, retorts, dramatisations and parodies. But these were designed for more or less the same audience as had read the original book. There is nothing more remote from the self-consciousness and knowing manipulation of literary technique found in parody than a chapbook. Similarly, Smollett rarely was published in any adulterated form, though the length of *Roderick Random* led to its occasional abridgment. One curious transmigration in 1784 appeared as *The Theatre of Fun, or Roderick Random in High Life*. The same novel was published along with *Robinson Crusoe* as *The Adventurers* early in the nineteenth century. Meanwhile Smollett produced his own bowdlerised version of *Peregrine Pickle*, and *Humphry Clinker* yielded a farce in sequel to the original work.

A more interesting case is *Tom Jones*. Cleary the hero attained within a few years the kind of independent, quasi-mythical status that might have permitted him to become a regular chapbook subject. The evidence for this statement lies in critical comments, but also more concretely in a variety of musical and theatrical derivatives. By the early 1760s Antoine-Alexandre-Henry Poinsinet (1735–69) had compiled a *comédie lyrique* based on the novel. In 1765 J.H. Steffers produced *Thomas Jones: ein Lustspiel nach der Grundlage des Herrn Fielding*. There was another French comedy, *Tom Jones à Londres*, in 1783: this time the author was P.-J.-B. Cloudard-Desforges. Meanwhile the first comic opera treatment had appeared in 1769; this version, by Joseph Reed (1723–87), enjoyed moderate success at Covent Garden, though it had the assistance of the expert comedian Ned Shuter in the rôle of Squire Western. Certainly its popularity fell a long way short of that attained by a later comic opera, the treatment by Edward German in 1907, a melodious but not especially faithful version. It should be added that the composer and chess-master Philidor was responsible for an opera produced at the *Comédie Italienne* in Paris (1765), but I have not seen this item.

In addition to these varied ministrations, Tom Jones attained enough celebrity to have a race-horse named after him, and to follow in Pamela's footsteps with the appearance of a sequel detailing his later career in the married state. But the length, or the technical elaboration, of the novel deterred British abridgers.[2] Beauties of Sterne and gleanings from *Tristram Shandy* were features of the publishing world in the second half of the eighteenth century, but Fielding escaped. The time had not yet arrived when he required to be 'edited for the use of modern readers' (a Victorian sub-title), and the unquestionably demotic side of his appeal counted for little in the face of his formal weight, one might almost say the inviolability of his narrative. The British Library contains only one true chapbook version of the book, conjecturally dated 1820, and entitled *The Remarkable History of Tom Jones*. It is a typical production, an undistinguished 32mo crudely laid out; the treatment is without life and energy, and nobody seems to have wished to repeat the experiment.

So much by way of a process of elimination. The texts which did over time enjoy real currency at the lower end of the market are *The Pilgrim's Progress, Robinson Crusoe, Moll Flanders*, and (later and more fitfully) *Gulliver's Travels*. Bunyan's great work was abridged almost from the date of the appearance of the first part in 1678. The first rendition into verse was that of Francis Hoffman, who worked around the world of newspapers and Tyburn ballads: this dates from 1706. Almost a century later George Burder (1752–1832), theologian, engraver and miscellaneous writer, also attempted to versify the work. Burder had been a travelling preacher, and this serves as a reminder that no less a figure than John Wesley had concocted his own abridgment of *Pilgrim's Progress* (1743). Hundreds of editions of Bunyan testify to his enduring renown among all classes of society. If further confirmation of his standing were required, then his enlistment by Mary Godolphin for one of her famous series in 1869 ought to make the point. *The Pilgrim's Progress in Words of One Syllable* followed two years after a similar volume consecrated to *Robinson Crusoe*.

Unquestionably, then, Bunyan survived among the common people, and his masterpiece may properly be regarded as one of the chapbook classics. Only one other book of the period has comparable claims. The staple element continues to be folklore and legend, exemplified by stories such as those of Jack the Giant Killer, Robin Hood, or Tom Thumb. Boswell's allusion to these productions in his *London Journal* (to July 1763) is well known:

> Some days ago I went to the old printing-office in Bow Church-yard kept by Dicey, whose family have kept it fourscore years. There are ushered into the world of literature *Jack and the Giants*, *The Seven Wise Men of Gotham*, and other story-books which in my dawning years amused me as much as *Rasselas* does now. I saw the whole scheme with a kind of pleasing romantic feeling to find myself really where all my old darlings were printed. I bought two dozen of the story-books and had them bound up with this title, *Curious Productions*.[3]

It is worth reflecting that the devotee of such 'curious productions' had recently sat with his friends discoursing of Helvétius, Voltaire, Rousseau and Hume. The literary slumming at Bow Churchyard bespeaks a genuine affection and an unmistakable familiarity, but there is no sign that Boswell's liking for the popular forms in any way affected his judgment of what constituted literature, or how the high forms should be assessed.

Yet, as we have seen, *Pilgrim's Progress* managed to bridge this yawning divide to a remarkable extent. And the case of *Robinson Crusoe* shows that a secular work could invade the world of the Diceys and establish itself as a modern legend. In some respects *Crusoe* is the more striking instance. It was spoken of by literary people in rather less disparaging terms than was *Pilgrim's Progress*. Unlike *Moll Flanders*, whose chapbook career I shall take up in the next chapter, it possessed an authentic currency among the devotees of polite letters. This was more marked after the book had received the suffrage of Rousseau in *Emile* (1762). Though the popular versions sometimes attempt to lay particular emphasis on the religious message of *Crusoe* (in their final paragraph, if not before), the popularity of the book among uneducated people seems to have had comparatively little to do with religion—a statement one could not make, without severe qualifications, in the case of *Pilgrim's Progress*. Long before the Victorians turned Crusoe into a hero of self-sufficiency and the work ethic, generations of readers had responded to the book as a story of survival, as an epic of mastery over the hostile environment, as a parable of conquest over fear, isolation and despair. These messages seem to have come through, however the book was truncated or travestied. It was above all the shipwreck and the early part of Crusoe's sojourn on the island that drew attention to these aspects of the myth, and this is a part of the narrative that is never sacrificed, however abbreviated the text. *Crusoe*'s 'readability' for a mass audience was variously negotiable, but the *sine qua non* can be firmly located in this crucial episode.

Another significant piece of evidence here lies in the iconography of the 'basic' Crusoe illustration. Virtually all the abbreviated versions have one initial cut, often as a frontispiece or on the title page itself. This corresponds to the illustration in the first edition (1719), and the crucial factors in the design are carried over from one picture to another. First of all, the wrecked ship is always visible, sometimes in the background, sometimes virtually as the most prominent feature in the cut. This ship could of course be the Spanish wreck which Crusoe finds years later: his goatskin dress would, strictly speaking, preclude the possibility that this is the original vessel on which Crusoe was cast adrift. But symbolically one does read the illustration in the latter way, and the cut does have the simultaneous effect of much popular art: the design lays out different portions of the story, almost as a biblical narrative is shown in stained-glass windows or illuminated manuscripts. Secondly, Crusoe is invariably shown *alone*, without Friday, pirates, shipmates, or cannibals. He is heavily armed, against no visible predator. The sea and the land normally conjoin in the design. Crusoe himself is bearded, unkempt and more heavily accoutred than we expect for a desert island castaway in a near-equatorial region. All these elements combine to reinforce our sense of Crusoe as a man alone against the elements, threatened by unseen terrors. Above all, we are reminded of the fact of his condition as a castaway.

How the various abridgments handle such a *mythos* will be touched on in the next section. By way of background, let me add that there were perhaps 12 or 15 separate recensions of the narrative between 1720 and 1830. An exact count is hard to make, because a number of the texts overlap in some parts, and then strike out independently in others. Until a comprehensive bibliography is attempted, it will not be possible to specify every discrepant feature in successive editions. My discussion will cover a sample of ten texts, representing rather fewer independent attempts to abridge the text. Some of these are what would normally be described as 'chapbooks', that is they are short, simplified texts, crudely produced for a very low price. Others are not: they are, rather, popularisations and piracies, which evidently assume a level of education and literary sophistication not much inferior to that required by the original work. Others fall in between these categories, and might be regarded as fringe-chapbooks. For the present, it is more useful to compare examples of each category than to refine theoretical distinctions.

II

The immediate success of the first part of *Robinson Crusoe* can be gauged from several pointers. These include the alacrity with which Defoe produced a sequel; the speed with which piracies appeared; the publication of the work in triweekly newspaper parts; the steady run of authentic editions over following years; the buzz of comment in books, pamphlets and periodicals; the considerable sum left by William Taylor, the bookseller who had bought the copyright (for what sum we do not know), when he died in 1724, and the high price these rights brought at auction in 1726. Of these, the last indicator is perhaps the most cogent. The book trade defines a bestseller by the simplest of criteria, and no one would have paid hard cash for a worthless title.

It is in this context that there began the flood of translations, adaptations, imitations and *Robinsonades*. *Crusoe* was first of all a trade success, and then the myth could spread and evolve. By 1723 the proprietor of Don Saltero's famous coffee-house and popular museum in Chelsea was to advertise in Mist's *Weekly Journal*:

> Monsters of all sorts here are seen,
>   Strange things in nature as they grew so;
> Some relics of the Sheba Queen,
>   And fragments of the famed Bob Crusoe.[4]

Such waxworks and collections may have ensured that the name of Crusoe became familiar to wide sections of the public, even those who were totally illiterate. The name 'Crusoe' began to escape from the literal confines of a single printed text.

Within a few weeks of the appearance of the first part of *Robinson Crusoe* in 1719, the bookseller Thomas Cox issued an edition in which the text was said to be 'abridg'd' and made 'more portable'. The identity of the abridger is not known, but it is a fairly competent piece of work, and one candidate who has been suggested is the experienced miscellaneous writer Charles Gildon. Taylor began a suit in Chancery against Cox, the outcome of which I have been unable to discover. Around the same time the *Farther Adventures* appeared: from the outset, this sequel was overshadowed by its predecessor, but there was enough interest in the book to justify new editions every few years during the first half of the century. A year later, in August 1720, Taylor issued the *Serious Reflections* which constitute the third part of the work. This item was never remotely as popular as the original novel. Its later life was confined to its presence in the abridgments. One notable fact is the emphasis that abridgers put on Crusoe's 'Vision of the Angelick World'. Even where they draw on the earlier sections of *Serious Reflections*, they habitually use the phrase just quoted as a sub-title for the section.[5]

The first attempt to reduce all three parts into the compass of a single volume was the most successful. It first came out in 1722 in the form of a duodecimo of 376 pages. The booksellers were all figures of substance in the trade: Bettesworth, Brotherton, Meadows and Midwinter were none of them fly-by-night operators or fringe publishers. This suggests that they considered themselves to possess a defensible right in law to issue abridged editions, though strictly interpreted the Copyright Act of 1709 would not seem to open up this loophole. As we shall see, a similar claim was made in connection with a piracy of *Gulliver's Travels* a few years later. It has been suspected that this particular version was the abridged version of *Crusoe* which Thomas Gent confessed to having made: Gent was apprenticed to Edward Midwinter, printer of the volume, and so the theory is plausible—although another account is that Gent made the woodcuts. It would be safest to say that the abridger is, as usual, an anonymous figure—something pretty well inherent in his rôle.

This abridgment continued to be issued at regular intervals for some decades. It was usually reset, and minor compressions effected to squeeze the text into a still smaller volume. By the fifth edition (c. 1735) the length had been reduced to 336 pages. This was largely a matter of resetting, although the preface was cut: otherwise the proportions remain the same—the first part occupying about 55 per cent of the whole, with the 'Vision of the Angelick World' occupying about a tenth of the text at the end. As usual, the latter subtitle is a misnomer, in that other parts of the *Serious Reflections* are used. The preface is a significant item in the presentation of the work: it confronts the objection 'that there never was such a Man as *Robinson Crusoe*, and that it is impossible such incredible Things should be accomplished in a distant and uninhabited Island'. The answer is to see the entire relation as allegorical. Stress is laid on 'divine Reflections to comfort the afflicted Mind', and on 'such an heavenly Prospect of the Wonderful Providence of God'. Evidently the preface in Taylor's original edition, claiming the work to be 'a just History of Fact', was no longer felt to be a tenable line to defend: Defoe's own preface to the *Serious Reflections* had in any case undermined the editor's ground here. There is naturally some puffing of the 'faithful Abridgment' and a reminder of the popularity which the work had instantly achieved: '*Robinson Crusoe* was in every Body's Mouth, as much as in the Mouth of *Pretty Poll*!'[6]

This version is probably closer to the original than any of the other abridgments, both in its handling of the narrative and in its stylistic character. However, it resembles the others in its habit of shifting words around to no obvious purpose. Particularly noteworthy is the apparent inability of any abridger to leave the opening sentences alone, even though the same information is to be conveyed. One suspects that this may have something to do with legal precautions: the publisher might be able to claim he was not infringing the Copyright Act, since his text was not a literal reprint of the Taylor text. The point can be made simply by comparing the opening lines.

TAYLOR (1719): I was born in the Year 1632, in the City of *York*, of a good Family, tho' not of that Country, my Father being a Foreigner of *Bremen*, who settled first at *Hull*: He got a good Estate by Merchandise, and leaving off his Trade, lived afterward at *York* . . .

ABRIDGMENT (1772): In the Year 1632, I was born at *York*, of a reputable Family. My Father was a Native of *Bremen*, who Merchandizing at *Hull* for some time gain'd a very plentiful Fortune . . .

The abbreviated versions nearly all consider it essential to provide all these details, but they display ingenuity in their ways of avoiding the basic text. 'Merchandise' generally defeats them, and in some shape or other this word turns up in most versions.

The present abridger begins his cutting operations from the start, allowing no more than a page to Crusoe's father in his efforts to set his son on the right course. Nevertheless, each considerable section of the plot is covered, however briefly, and this particular version is a paraphrase rather than a précis. In this respect the famous episode of the footprint is representative of the methods employed. That historic paragraph, running to some 250 words in the Taylor edition, is presented in this form:

> But one Day it happen'd that going to my Boat, I saw the Print of a Man's naked Foot on the Shore, very evident on the Sand, as the Toes, Heels, and every Part of it. Had I seen an Apparition, in the most frightful manner, I could not have been more confounded . . .[7]

There is some slight attempt to make the syntax simpler, but the vocabulary is not conspicuously different. Most of the abridger's efforts seem to have gone into reducing the compass of his text, and his paraphrase involves few obvious aids to greater intelligibility. One might summarise the position by saying that this first, and frequently reprinted, abridgment serves some of the purposes of a nineteenth-century pocket edition or a modern paperback text. Compression is achieved not by leaving out whole blocks of the work, but by a steady attrition of the word-count, by removing detail and qualification. The reader gets more for his money in that the significant *events* arrive more promptly, with a consequent diminution of reflection and conjecture. There is thus a literary processing at work, but one rather different from that seen in the chapbooks proper. Here, in the 1722 abridgment, the audinece is presumed to have a measure of reading skill, but to be bored by excessive elaboration. In the chapbooks much more is done to alter the basic legibility of the text for a barely literate public.

One of the most striking contrasts to the Bettesworth edition of 1722 is a little book entitled *Voyages and Travels: Being the Life and Adventures of Robinson Crusoe of York, Mariner*, which has been tentatively dated c. 1750. It is found in the British Library in a volume of ballads and broadsides, and resembles such works in its physical dimensions. The formula 'Written by Himself' is retained on the title-page, in black letter: this had been dropped in the Bettesworth edition, no doubt as it contributed to the pseudo-realistic claims that this edition found too embarrassing to sustain. *Voyages and Travels* is a thoroughly naive production, and quite willing to promote such claims of 'authenticity'. The unsophisticated woodcut on the title-page simply conveys the message of Crusoe with his guns and the wreck behind him. Printing is best described as primitive with blunders such as '*Soh*' for '*Son*' and '*doy*' for '*dog*'. All this is understandable when one adds the central fact: this version extends to no more than eight pages. The abridgment in these circumstances cannot be much more than a digest. However, it starts off as though there were all the time in the world; indeed, the opening paragraph survives almost intact. After that, things speed up, but it still takes half the available space to reach the shipwreck. The reluctance of abridgers to cut the pre-island sections is a curious fact which deserves attention.

Despite the narrow confines in which he works, this abridger devotes some space to Crusoe's reactions on finding himself alone on the island. Equally, his efforts to retrieve objects from the wreck are given detailed coverage. After this, an abbreviated rendition of Crusoe's journal (half a dozen extracts) takes us to within two pages of the end of the minute volume. There is just time to mention the pirates: Friday enters the text in the very last paragraph, and the value of Crusoe's property when he regains it at the end is duly recorded. There is obviously no room for the coda recording Crusoe's adventures in the Pyrenees—it might be added that abridgers display far less reverence towards the postlude than to the prolegomena to Crusoe's island adventures.

What is much more surprising, both historically and aesthetically, is the total omission of the footprint episode. One might have supposed that this graphic emblem would survive in any popular version, since it appears to us the most imaginative stroke in the entire narrative. It is difficult to be sure whether this absence is a matter of conscious policy: the fierce abridgment on the concluding pages would seem to suggest nothing less than high incompetence. If so, we should be rash to impute the crazy proportions of this chapbook to any sort of planned ordonnance. Nevertheless, it is quite evident that the shipwreck and its aftermath are the heart of the book for this compiler. In that judgment he was backed by the title-page woodcut. All the signs are that early readers were captivated by Crusoe's initial trauma, possibly because they were familiar with stories of disaster and delivery in popular theological manuals.

Some twenty years later, a chapbook version allowing itself the luxury of twenty-four duodecimo pages found room for ten woodcuts. Most of these seem to concentrate on scenes of fighting, not very expertly handled by the artist. At the end we see Crusoe in his new prosperity, dressed in a laced tricorn, a full-bottomed wig and a brocaded jacket; he carries a cane almost worthy of Sir Plume. The text is not so badly mangled as in the previous example. The journal section is presented at greater length, the Pyrenean episode is included (Friday kills the wolves and bear 'with a great deal of Sport'). As in all the chapbooks proper, the material is confined to the first part of *Crusoe*. And as in other cases, a sententious peroration is provided: 'And indeed the many miracles of this man's life is very strange and surprising. The events by a serious application, may be as examples to others, and the wisdom of Divine Providence, in all our circumstances, may be justified and honoured, let them occur when they will.' In terms that are genuinely faithful to the original, the compiler refers to the 'very remarkable chain of Providence' evident in the story of Crusoe, and recommends the work's perusal to those who would learn the 'art of patience, in submission to the divine will'. These phrases appear in a new version of the 1770 text, issued by C. Randall at Stirling in 1801.[8] The text has been cut to sixteen pages, and three chapters inserted, dealing respectively with Crusoe's early years, the ill-fated voyage and the aftermath of the wreck, and finally the story from the sprouting of the corn. In other respects this version is very close to the 1770 edition, as regards letter-press. It comes off worse in the matter of illustration, since only a title-page woodcut of a ship is provided. Where cuts are present, they tend to be better executed over time: but by no means all chapbooks contain illustration within the body of the text.

Around 1770 (perhaps even a little earlier) J. Sketchley of Birmingham produced a so-called 'ninth edition' of the full three parts. This amounts to 408 pages, though it lacks a preface. It is based on the original editions, possibly with some reference to the Bettesworth paraphrase, but as usual some variants are present throughout: the opening sentence runs, 'I was born at York, in 1632, of a reputable family . . .'. As far as the first two parts are concerned, such a text is not very much shorter than Defoe's original, and one wonders whether the labour of extensive paraphrase would repay the effort. But verbal detail aside, the reader of Sketchley's does get the whole of the book, with a customary snatch of the *Serious Reflections*. It is simply hard to detect a literary purpose in what has been done.

Another item deriving from the West Midlands is a version issued by F. Houlston of Wellington and Ironbridge. No date is given; one supposes that the work must postdate the rise of Ironbridge in the late 1770s and 1780s: an advertisement at the end includes *The Vicar of Wakefield*, another novel which was less frequently made into a chapbook than one might have anticipated. The volume contains 189 pages, but in some respects its procedures recall the chapbook tradition. Unusually, the original preface from Taylor's edition is included. Defoe's text is treated without reverence, but also without any great freedom or invention: the degree of alteration may be judged from the following comparison:

TAYLOR: It was not till almost a Year after this that I broke loose, tho' in the mean time I continued obstinately deaf to all Proposals of settling to Business, and frequently expostulating with my Father and Mother, about their being so positively determin'd against what they knew my Inclination prompted me to. But being one Day at *Hull*, where I went casually, and without any Purpose of making an Elopement that time; but I say, being there, and one of my Companions being going by Sea to *London*, in his Father's Ship, and prompting me to go with them . . .

HOULSTON: It was almost a Year after this, being one day at Hull, where I went casually, and without any design of making an elopement, I met one of my companions who was going by sea to London . . .[9]

This time the alternative does seem an improvement. It has got rid of the straggling detail, and eliminated a few, if not all, of the awkward participles that clog Defoe's style. (Sketchley, incidentally, had 'I was then, I think, nineteen years old, when one time being at Hull . . .').[10]

The cuts in this edition, mentioned on the title-page as a major adornment, are distinctly more sophisticated than those in the chapbooks. A notable variant appears in the frontispiece, which for once does not concern the wreck. Robinson is seen as a boy—he looks no more than eleven or twelve—with his parents expostulating to him on the errors of his ways. His father has a crutch and his foot is lifted on to a gout-stool: a nice individuating touch, at long last. Other cuts involve the raft, the rescue of Friday, and Friday dancing with the bear. The wreck is one incident among many, rather than the focus of total attention.

Roughly contemporary is a Dublin version, published in 1799, which covers all three parts in 180 pages. This is one of the more defensive productions, with an anxious preface: 'In this new Epitome . . . all possible care has been taken to preserve the History entire.' The epitomiser asks, 'What if the whole was, as is suggested, a mere fiction?' His answer is predictable:

> Yet the design is so justly carried on, and so interspersed with curious Observations and moral reflections, that all Persons, who have any taste of the metaphorical way of writing, must allow this to be a Masterpiece.

Even at the start of the narrative, this same note is apparent:

> He that pretends to publish to the world an Account of his own Life and Actions, is doubtless under the strongest Obligations, to Confine himself within the strictest Rules of Modesty and Truth, and this I can assure the Public, I most solemnly determine in the following Narration.
>   I was born at *York*, in the Year 1632, of a reputable Family. My Father was a Merchant, born at *Bremen* . . .[11]

It is noticeable that 'reputable' seems to have become a standard replacement for 'good' in popular versions. Otherwise this edition calls for little comment. It naturally omits more than the Houlston text, which had confined itself to the first part of *Crusoe*, and had made only light excisions. The section from the third part in the Dublin 'epitome' ends with verses. There are woodcuts of moderate quality.

Another publication of around 1800 is the volume entitled *The Exploits of Robinson Crusoe*, put out by 'the booksellers': here a new formula, 'written originally by himself', is adopted. The two first parts are covered in 128 pages, with the ratio slightly more in favour of the *Strange Surprizing Adventures* than was customary (roughly eight to five). The frontispiece reverts to the traditional subject, and the cuts are quite good, in contrast to some indifferent printing. It looks as if the compositor was following some earlier printed text, which I have not identified: at all events, on the last leaf of sig. F, the type-face suddenly gets smaller, apparently in order to accommodate the material, whilst on pp. 49–50 an entire page of copy appears to have been omitted. The missing material happens to include the footprint episode, which does not suggest great care was taken with the presswork.

It was not until 1813 that the first identifiable bowdlerised text appeared. This was published by Cradock, Joy and others in London, and is basically devoted to the first part (though hints of the sequel are present at the end). The book is said to have been 'originally written by Daniel Defoe', a fact which only achieved general notice following George Chalmers' edition in 1790. The book has been 'revised for the use of Young Persons', and the text 'corrected and improved'. However, the Podsnappery of the title-page is not really maintained in the bulk of the succeeding volume, once the editor has got a few pious sentiments out of his system:

> Notwithstanding the acknowledged merits of DEFOE'S interesting narrative of the Adventures of *Robinson Crusoe*, it will be admitted, that, as he did not address it expressly to Young Persons, it must contain many things which are not well adapted to an early age, and which, when read by them, it were better should be omitted.[12]

It is true that this version passes quickly over the opening scene with Crusoe's parents, and the hero's rebelliousness is muted: but the volume does include the Xury section, Friday, renegade English sailors, and the rest: only tiny adjustments seem to have been attempted. The frontispiece has a suitably young-looking Crusoe returning on his raft laden with provisions from the wreck.

The last item to warrant individual discussion is an Edinburgh publication, *The Wonderful Adventures of Robinson Crusoe* (c. 1815). 'Embellished with Elegant Cuts', this volume manages to cover both the first two parts of *Crusoe* inside 93 pages. In fact, no more than 15 pages at the end are devoted to the *Farther Adventures*, which are reduced to a breathless summary that carries us across continents in a few sentences. An unusual feature is the provision of a caption from the text for each of the cuts. The journal is omitted, and slightly less emphasis is attached to the wreck than in some earlier versions. The degree of paraphrase may be gauged by examining a passage already cited in the original (see p. 36), describing Crusoe's departure from his home:

> As if bent on my own destruction, I hardened myself against the prudent and kind advice of the most indulgent parents; and being one day at Hull, where I met with one of my companions, who was going to sea in his father's ship, he easily persuaded me to go with him.[13]

By contrast, the footprint is presented almost in Defoe's own words, suggesting that by this date the episode had achieved a classic status which discouraged editors from tampering too much with the description.

The 1813 edition for young persons shows that we have reached the eve of Victorianism. It would take us into different aspects of the history of taste if we were to pursue the story further into the nineteenth century. By this date, the novel was beginning to grow in critical esteem; it was firmly associated with Defoe, whose career was better known to the educated public, thanks to Chalmers' biography (1785) and the Ballantyne edition of the works. By 1830 editions had appeared in a diverse range of cities and towns, including Gainsborough, Warrington, Derby, Dunbar, Braintree, Bewdley, Wotton-under-Edge and other provincial localities. There was an edition in Worcester,

Massachusetts, in 1795. Some of the chapbooks proper continued to appear in more or less identical guise. The work entered Park's Juvenile Library; there is a version of 32 pages, 'with a Fragment called Begging Sailors'.

The examples taken are, I hope, representative of the publishing history over a century. They range from chapbooks in the strictest sense to popular abridgments aimed at a moderately sophisticated readership. Certain of the books examined may be described as intermediary cases. The Dublin version of 1799 is such an example: it allows itself more room than the highly abbreviated versions, but it simplifies and condenses much more than the full-length editions. Much the same may be said of the *Wonderful Adventures* in 1815, though this incorporates some direct transcript from the original text. It would be possible to assert, by way of general summary, that the book was cut down and stripped to the space available, the limits of vocabulary applicable to a presumed audience, and the individual skills (or lack of them) possessed by the abridger. The shipwreck and its aftermath in the days, weeks and months immediately following clearly constitute the major point of interest for most compilers. Yet they never feel free to omit the opening sections entirely, and commonly devote more of their space to the pre-island episodes than seems easily justifiable from a literary standpoint. Friday is allowed to wander into the story casually, his education is usually given little emphasis, and the second half of the *Strange Surprizing Adventures* is reduced to a rapid series of events with bloodshed blandly reported. Attempts to cover the *Farther Adventures* are generally made only by those with a good deal of space at their disposal: shorter abridgments can find no effective way of incorporating the sequel. The *Serious Reflections* are usually presented as straightforward didactic material, without any link with what has gone before. A sententious coda is a feature of the chapbooks proper and the intermediate category, rather than the full-scale versions.

III

Crusoe was not the only novel by Defoe to encounter popularisation by the trade. *Moll Flanders*, first published in

1721, indeed survived only in truncated forms: unlike *Crusoe*, it lost almost all its currency in its full and authentic form.[14] In the next chapter I shall discuss the fortunes and misfortunes of *Moll* in the chapbooks. Here it is worth noting that the radical adaptations of *Roxana* date from the last quarter of the eighteenth century, and totally supplant the original in general consciousness.

The final work to be considered is *Gulliver's Travels*. This does not belong to the world of the chapbook proper, but it did increasingly receive the attention of abridgers and editors. Two particularly noteworthy examples from the eighteenth century may be singled out. The first dates from 1727, only one year after Gulliver had come before the world. Two London booksellers were responsible for a shortened version which was published in two duodecimo volumes, generally found bound together. These men, J. Stone and R. King, were not exactly pillars of the book trade, but they were freed members of the Stationers' Company, with a certain amount of reputation to lose. Their decision to produce what was obviously a pirate edition in the guise of an abridgment has interesting implications for the legal and commercial side of publishing. Fortunately, they provided an elaborate justification for what they had done, and this enables us to get some idea of the issues at stake.

The rights in the work were held by Benjamin Motte, a shrewd, even sharp, member of the trade who had paid Swift the £200 he requested. According to John Gay, Motte had contrived to get rid of the whole of the first edition within a week;[15] and it would not be excessive if we were to estimate the total sales within a few months as numbering up to 10,000 copies. However, the pirates who were anxious to gain a foothold in this lucrative market had one possible line of attack: they could argue that Motte had kept the price artificially high. This is the basis of the claims made in the prefatory note by the publisher in the Stone/King edition. However, they concede that an objection may be made:

> It must be confessed, that Undertakings of this Nature are liable to Exceptions, and are frequently charg'd with depriving the Original of those Ornaments which recommend it to the Judicious; because many of them, through ill Management, have neither answered the

Intention of the Author, or the Satisfaction of the Reader: But we hope this under Consideration, will answer the Ends of Both. It is true, that some Passages in the Original, which the Generality of Mankind have thought immodest and indecent, are entirely omitted, and many triviall Circumstances contracted into a very narrow Compass: But at the same Time, we may truly say, that Care hath been taken to make the History as uniform, and the Connection as just and smooth, as the Nature of the Performance would allow.

This unconvincing review of the aesthetics of abridgment is followed by a still more strained bout of argument, when the publishers turn to the efforts made by the proprietors of the original work to put a stop to the abridged edition, 'upon a wild Supposition it was the very Copy, and not an Abridgment'. In order to defend their right, they cite a number of titles where such activity has gone on unchallenged, notably the *Philosophical Transactions* [of the Royal Society], 'for 20 Years, *abridg'd* by Mr. B. *Motte*.[16] Other titles cited are Locke's *Essay*, Camden's *Britannia*, the *State Trials*, Burnet's *History of His Own Time*, and '*Robinson Crusoe's Adventures*'. None of these, apart from the last, appears to have much relevance to the case in question: and after all Taylor had taken Cox to court over the matter. Whatever the legal position over abridgment of a literary work, it could hardly be adequately decided in terms of such imperfect analogies as *State Trials* or the *Philosophical Transactions*. Stone and King, in their anxiety to get one over on Motte, have surely displayed the weakness of their position.

The volumes which follow are something of an anti-climax. At the outset, one observes the absence of the letter to Sympson and the message from the publishers to the reader, which contribute so much to the rhetoric of mystification surrounding the opening.[17] The entire text is steadily reduced line by line: as with *Robinson Crusoe*, abridgment takes the form of gradual attrition rather than wholesale excision. In the second chapter of Lilliput, Gulliver's phrase about 'the Necessities of Nature' is left out: but in the fifth chapter, perhaps for plot reasons, the voiding of wine is retained. In Brobdingnag, the abridger likewise leaves in the potentially offensive section on the maids of honour in chapter 5. There is some minor bowdlerisation in chapter 8 of the voyage to Houyhnhnmland, but excrement still gets thrown around in this book. One is forced to the conclusion that the point of mentioning 'immodest' material in the preface is to remind readers of its existence, in the hope they may buy the book. Very little by way of genuine censorship is apparent in this abridgment. It simply leaves out a lot of small details, and impoverishes the text not by radical surgery so much as by steady dimunition of local point and wit.

In the nineteenth century, immodesty was excised more brutally. The commonest means, of course, was simply to exclude whole chunks of the text, starting with the last voyage. The earliest attempt I have seen to produce a universally acceptable *Gulliver* was that of Francis Newbery, son and successor to John, in 1776. His sixpenny compilation consists of 128 tiny pages, and includes some pleasant engravings to scale. The frontispiece, showing a young lady in dress of the period, has no discernible relevance to *Gulliver*—but that is by the way. One of the illustrations shows Gulliver tied up by the Lilliputians, a motif almost as central to the imaginative trajectory of this work as the wreck is to *Crusoe*.

The most notable feature of this children's version is the decision to put the story into the third person. Only the first two voyages are present, and they are censored with some discretion. The maids of honour are toned down, but Gulliver puts out the fire in his accustomed manner, and the sillier manifestations of bowdlerisation are avoided. For some reason, though, Gulliver's amusingly disordered behaviour on his return from Brobdingnag is suppressed almost to nothing.

It was another century before the heyday of censorship, with *Gulliver's Travels* 'revised for family reading' (a representative title from 1873). By that date, the work had become a classic in every sense, and in every corner of our culture. Henry J. Byron produced his 'comic operatic spectacular extravaganza, in five acts and twelve tableaux' at the Gaiety Theatre, London, c. 1880. The action moves from Plymouth to Lilliput, Brobdingnag and then (accountably) the Palace of Comic Song. The Flying Island is followed by an allegorical tableau of the Golden Age. Characters include King Teenyweeny and Queen Petsywetsy. It has certain links with the pantomime versions of *Crusoe* then becoming popular. Gulliver is a *travestie* rôle. In that respect there is a difference from W.M. Ackhurst's *Gulliver on his Travels*, presented at Sanger's National Amphitheatre in 1876, where Crusoe is played by a girl but Gulliver, straying into the same action, is a male rôle. One might add that the same era witnessed the performance of Offenbach's opera (1876) in which the curtain opens to disclose Sir William Crusoe telling the story of the Prodigal Son to his assembled womenfolk—Robinson, as usual, is late.

Such extreme perversions were a thing of the future when the chapbook still dominated popular reading. What this brief survey shows is that popularisation could take many forms, and abridgment could be undertaken for a variety of motives. At its crudest, popular adaptation involved formulaic and hasty writing, the mere degutting of a text. At its best, sustained paraphrase could be employed to reproduce a work in simplified but not distorted terms. For a long time, bowdlerisation was rather a threat, or a dishonest publisher's claim, than a reality. Only a very few books proved equal to the dual function of literary classic and popular favourite. Leaving aside *The Pilgrim's Progress*, whose appeal was primarily that of a devotional work, we are left with two or three works which regularly survive adaptation: and of these it is *Robinson Crusoe* whose elemental design and stark outlines best fit it to bridge a yawning gap in public taste.[18]

Notes

1. V.E. Neuburg, *Chapbooks: A Guide to Reference Material on English, Scottish and American Chapbook Literature of the Eighteenth and Nineteenth Centuries* (2nd edn, 1972), 5-6. Neuburg has supplied the only serious modern treatment of the subject that takes proper account of the eighteenth century. See also his *Popular Education in Eighteenth Century England* (1971), esp. chapter 5, 'Chapbooks: origins and distribution', pp. 115-25; and *The Penny Histories: A Study of Chapbooks for Young Readers over Two Centuries* (1968).
2. In America it was different: the book was 'most often published' in the last quarter of the eighteenth century in an abridged edition. *See* Jay Fliegelman, *Prodigals and Pilgrims* (Cambridge, 1982), p. 118.
3. F.A Pottle (ed.), *Boswell's London Journal 1762-1763* (1950), p. 299.
4. Quoted by Altick, p. 17.
5. For early editions and abridgments, see P. Rogers, *Robinson Crusoe* (1979), pp. 4-10.

6. *The Life and Most Surprizing Adventures of Robinson Crusoe* (2nd edn, 1724), sig. A3r; *The Life and Most Surprizing Adventures of Robinson Crusoe* (5th edn, n.d.), sig. A2v.

7. *The Life and Strange Surprizing Adventures of Robinson Crusoe* (1719), pp. 181-2.

8. *The Life of Robinson Crusoe* (Stirling, 1801), pp. 15-16: compare *The Surprising Life, and Most Strange Adventures of Robinson Crusoe* (n.d.) p. 24.

9. *The Life and Strange Surprizing Adventures of Robinson Crusoe* (1719), p. 7; *The Life and Surprizing Adventures of Robinson Crusoe* (Wellington and Ironbridge, n.d.), p. 7.

10. *The Life and Most Surprising Adventures of Robinson Crusoe* (9th edn, Birmingham, n.d.), p. 3.

11. *The Life and Most Surprising Adventures of Robinson Crusoe* (Dublin, 1799), pp. 5-6.

12. *The Life and Adventures of Robinson Crusoe* (1813), iii.

13. *The Wonderful Adventures of Robinson Crusoe* (Edinburgh, n.d.), p. 3.

14. It has recently emerged that chapbook publishers south of the Thames put out a single volume of Defoe's *Tour* in the 1740s: see my article, 'Defoe's *Tour* and the Chapbook Trade', *The Library*, (1984), pp. 275-9.

15. Swift, *Corr*, III, 182.

16. *Travels into Several Remote Nations of the World, by Capt.Lemuel Gulliver* (1727), sigs. A2r-A3r.

17. See A. Ross, *Swift: Gulliver's Travels* (1968), p. 19.

18. Since this chapter was written I have learnt of the existence of a German monograph dealing with abridged editions of *Crusoe*, namely E. Dahl, *Die Kürzungen des 'Robinson Crusoe' in England zwischen 1719 und 1819* (Frankfurt, 1977). Unfortunately I have so far been unable to locate a copy of this work. For the career of *Crusoe* as an avowedly pedagogic work, heavily abridged and garnished with additions, *see* Fliegelman, *Prodigals and Pilgrims*, pp. 69-83. The same source reveals that no less than 125 editions of *Crusoe* were published in America between 1774 and 1825, 'virtually none reprinting the full text of the original' (p. 81). For abridgments of *Clarissa, see* pp. 87-8.

8

MOLL IN THE CHAPBOOKS

[This] *History* will astonish! and is not compos'd of Fiction, Fable, or
Stories plac'd at *York, Rome,* or *Jamaica,* but *Facts* done at your Doors,
Facts unheard of, altogether new, Incredible, and yet Uncontestable.
Dnaiel Defoe, *The History of the Remarkable Life of John Sheppard*

I

Alluding to the kind of material discussed in Chapter 7, Victor
Neuburg has claimed that chapbooks represent a 'unique source'
for any exploration of the 'mental universe of the poor in the
eighteenth century'. He suggests that they 'made a considerable
contribution to the development of mass literacy' in the period,
and contends that they reveal to us a public 'which in its
attitudes, tastes and values was very different from the more
sophisticated one, and is at least as worthy of detailed
investigation'.[1] There are theoretical obstacles here: can a study
of literary texts ever tell us anything directly about the audience
who read them, unless we know a good deal about the producers
as well as the consumers, and can make proper allowance for the
conventions of genre and style? Nevertheless, Neuburg is surely
right to fix our attention on what is still a surprisingly neglected
area of literary expression. Chapbooks have an interest over and
above any dubious sociological messages we can derive from
them. Some of them, for example, might appear to represent in
their clumsy way a kind of literary editing.

As we have seen, Neuburg refers to a small group of chapbooks
comprising 'unauthorised adaptations and abridgements of
books which enjoyed a considerable popularity'. He also
mentions 'a few' printers or 'unknown hacks' who took works
such as *Robinson Crusoe* or *Moll Flanders* and reduced them to

twenty-four pages.[2] Such abridgments were always in a minority; the majority of chapbooks take traditional themes, folk-tales or well-known legends such as Robin Hood. In the limited number of cases where publishers attempted a potted version of literary classics, we can detect some of the rhetorical and stylistic marks of the chapbook more sharply than by any other means. It would be rash to interpret this evidence as a reliable guide to critical history: to see a chapbook *Crusoe* as indicating how the popular audience regarded Defoe's novels is invalid on at least two counts—the text which the readers received was not really *Crusoe* in any true sense, and they had never heard of Daniel Defoe. Still, the evidence of chapbooks may supply a kind of marginal gloss to the critical heritage on some occasions.

One might have expected that it would be one of the anonymous abridgments which had so impressed George Borrow's old fruit-woman. The narrator of *Lavengro* encounters her on London Bridge, as he explores the city, and she shows him the prized copy of her favourite story, that of 'blessed Mary Flanders'. But the book is described as 'a short, thick volume, at least a century old, bound with greasy black leather'. No twenty-four page pamphlet could be so described: the presumed date of this meeting is around 1820 or shortly afterwards: and so the copy must be one of the early editions of the complete novel. It could perhaps be one of the early piratical abridgments, which prune the text only to a limited extent and add excrescences of their own: thus T. Read's version (?1723) is as much as 280 pages. *Fortune's Fickle Distribution* (1730) contains 130 pages, but some of these are devoted to the stories of Moll's governess and her Lancashire husband. In fact, *Fortune's Fickle Distribution* might be regarded as halfway to a chapbook, despite its uncharacteristic length. Any of these unauthorised texts would help to explain the moralistic reading of the book offered both by the fruit-woman and by Lavengro himself. Eventually the book (having been lost and stolen) turns up again, and is sold as a 'first edition' for five guineas—the bookseller remarking during this transaction that 'there have been nearly fifty editions to my knowledge'. This episode sets off a number of resonances within *Lavengro*: the old woman has had a son transported, the hero is contemplating writing criminal tales for a living, and is engaged at one time in compiling Newgate trials. The immediate point is that Moll survived in a ramshackle way, though never with the popularity of *Crusoe*. Throughout the chapbook era there continued to be the occasional 'authentic' edition of the full novel, and even the humblest reader, possessing few other books, might chance to possess such a version, as did the old apple-woman. She had, significantly, read no other literature, and had scarcely heard of the Bible.[3]

If we disregard for the moment the longer abridgments to which I have referred, there are in substance only two basic chapbook texts, though they appeared in a variety of forms. The pamphlets generally contain 24 pages, but 16 and even 8 page versions are found. The main line of descent is represented by the editions put out by the major chapbook firm, with the imprint, 'Printed and sold in Aldermary Church Yard, London'. (The proprietors were the Dicey family, William and his son Cluer, later in partnership with William Marshall.)[4] The basic form can be found in the British Library copies listed below, here designated A1-4. A4 is the same text in all fundamental respects, squeezed into sixteen pages by the omission of cuts and by the employment of a smaller type-size from p. 12 onwards. A slight variant of what is in essence the same abridgment is found in copies listed as B1-2. However, C is a brief precis of the novel, only some 2000 words in length. The pattern of chapbook editions represented in the British Library can be set out along these lines:

A1   *The Fortunes and Misfortunes of Moll Flanders*. London [c. 1750]. 12mo. 24pp. B.L. 1079.i.13 (21).

A2   *Fortunes and Misfortunes* London [c. 1768] 12mo. 24pp. B.L. T 18555 (22).

A3   *Fortunes and Misfortunes* London [c. 1770]. 12mo. 24pp. B.L. 12315.aaa.7.

A4   *The History and Misfortunes of Moll Flanders*. Manchester [c. 1805]. 12mo. 16pp. B.L.12331.de.5(9)[5]

B1   *The History of Moll Flanders* Newcastle [c. 1790]. 12mo. 24pp. B.L. 1076.1.24.(12).

B2   *History.* Stirling 1823. 12mo. 24pp. B.L. 1078.k.5(29).[6]

C   *The History of the Famous Moll Flanders.* Newcastle [c. 1820]. 8vo. 8pp. B.L. 1076.1.2(6)[7]

The conjectural dates are those supplied in the B.L. catalogue.[8]

It should be noted that the Aldermary Church Yard editions are reset, and contain different wood-cuts: that is, each fresh edition has some cuts not in its predecessor. A new cut on an old design (for example, a ship when Moll is crossing the Atlantic) may be supplied, doubtless because the old block was worn out. Alternatively a completely new subject may be illustrated. The general ratio is about six or seven cuts in a twenty-four page chapbook. However the A4 text has only a *memento mori* cut on the title-page, and the C text has none. The C version specifies the price, one penny, which was normal and almost certainly applied in the other cases.

Crude as these versions are in typography and design, some minimal attention was given to the letter-press. Thus a misprint at the bottom of p. 15 in A1 (where the last line of a previous paragraph was wrongly inserted) was corrected in A3. Outright nonsense otherwise seems to be absent from the A text, though it is found in B2, p. 16. The title-page is regularly revised throughout, and I shall turn to this aspect presently. In other respects the changes in content over time are small. Once the basic abridgment represented by A and B had become established, variations were confined to minor additions, new cuts, and presentational devices. No notice seems to have been taken of the appearance of *Laetitia Atkins*, for example: the chapbook text had its own integral status, and was unaffected by the publishing history of fuller versions. There is of course no attempt to mimic Defoe's style: the chapbook is not an alternative rendition of *Moll*, as are the longer abridgments, but a hasty précis of certain events in her career. To this extent chapbooks cease to maintain any organic relationship with the classic text they feed upon: they treat their subject as a legend, an object of common property, and ignore the precise literary mechanics of whatever book it is that lies behind their production. Any subsequent lack of freedom in invention has nothing to do with the authentic version. It results simply from a well-justified inertia: the barely literate public addressed would not value (and might not even recognise) novelty. The aim seems to have been to deliver the expected message to a pre-selected public.

The stock version of *Moll* which emerges does preserve the proportions of Defoe's narrative in a rough way; that is, the first half gives us marital escapades, the second criminal living. Beyond that there is very little sense of a human existence, merely a rush of anecdotes and a moralising conclusion. Names are occasionally supplied: thus at Bath we have 'Sir Walter Cleave', variously spelt Clare, Clave, Clove, and so on.[9] The style is only just literate, with errors such as the use of 'personal' for 'personable' in B2, when Moll disguises herself as a man.

One of the most striking features of each edition is the title-page. Here, clearly, a good deal of care was expended in an effort to make the book saleable when produced from a pedlar's bag: presumably the hawker would read out the appetising contents to potential buyers. The standard form of the *Fortunes and Misfortunes* put out by the firm of Dicey was loosely based on the original Chetwood title-page of 1722, but considerable variation went on in the details of their editions, as of others. The original statement that Moll was 'Twelve Year a *Whore*' becomes 'twelve times' in A1; in A2 and A3 this is 'seventeen times', possibly a mistranscription by origin. The practice begins of specifying Moll's places of incarceration: the general Aldermary tally is eleven times in Bridewell, nine in the New Prison [Clerkenwell], eleven in Wood Street, fourteen in the Gatehouse, twenty-five in Newgate, plus fifteen times whipped at the cart's arse, four times burnt on the hand and eight years in Virginia. Other editions delicately substitute 'tail' for 'arse'; the number of sojourns in Bridewell generally becomes eighteen; and later publishers weakly resort to the phrase 'forty times in other prisons' after giving the Bridewell score. The B title-page sticks closer to the original, bating its tendency to insert capitals and exclamation marks to emphasise the scandalous nature of its contents. The A4 version ends up, 'And after having led a wicked life, and passed thro' the various scenes described in the course of this History, at length grew rich, lived honest, and died penitent', a nice compromise with the original. Together with the woodcuts prepared for the title-page, these changes constituted the sole effort to attract new readers for the work. A2 has a fancy tailpiece, possibly representing Juno or Flora, with little obvious relevance to the preceding text.

One feature of the A editions does demand attention. This is the provision, along with a frontispiece of Moll in the woods of Virginia, of this quatrain:

> Reader, observe the sudden turn of fate,
> And from her Fortune, thy true Omen date.
> Thro' all degrees of life you plainly see:
> Man's fate is ordered by God's just decree.

This moralistic doggerel is altogether characteristic of chapbook literature. It is a simpler version of what Read offered in his abridgment, which I shall describe shortly. The verses were taken over into version A4, where they were shifted to the title-page itself. In no respects is the truncated *Moll* more typical than in this pious set of preliminary verses. One could see how a reader with little education could accept the story as a four-square penitential fable, and how the work could even be accommodated to hagiography—'blessed Mary Flanders' joining the Seven Champions of Christendom as an exemplar of timely conversion.

It is remarkable that the chapbooks do little to sensationalise the story, outside their title-page at least. There is no special emphasis on lubricity, and indeed the element of explicit sexuality is no more pronounced than in Defoe. The moralism of the doggerel is certainly a crude adjunct to the story, rather than a natural outcome of the narrative: but again the split between moral and story is, arguably, just as wide in the original novel.

The most interesting feature of all, from a literary standpoint, is the epitaph found in the A version, and supposed to have been written after Moll's death in Virginia. The pervasive clumsiness of expression is less damaging here, for there is a curious fidelity to the inner feeling of Defoe's work: something of the heorine's desperate search for security comes through the splayfooted lines:

> Newgate thy dwelling was, thy beauty made thee
> A goddess seem, and that alone betray'd thee.
> Twelve years a whore, a wife unto thy brother,

And such a thief there scarce could be another.
Unweary'd traveller, whither dost thou roam?
Lo! in this place remote to find a tomb
Transported hence, to heaven, 'tis hoped thou'rt sent,
Who wicked liv'd, but dy'd a penitent.

The final verse includes a strange use of chiasmus, that favourite device of high Augustan rhetoric. What is even more extraordinary is the splendid Yeatsian line, 'Unweary'd traveller, whither does thou roam?' It is highly suggestive that the best touch in any of the chapbook versions comes in one of the most stylised and seemingly intrusive areas of the text, a verse elegy for a woman who doesn't even die in the novel proper.[10]

II

Thus far we have confined ourselves to the 'authentic' chapbooks. Their nature can be defined further by looking at three main abridgments on an ampler scale. The first is the early piratical version published by T. Read within about a year of the first appearance of *Moll Flanders*. Second, there is a three-part compilation entitled *Fortune's Fickle Distribution* (1730), imparting an Irish connection to the novel. Third, the *History of Laetitia Atkins* (1776), which claims that Defoe doctored the text of Moll's memoirs and offers to print new materials from her own manuscript. These are better known to literary scholars than the true chapbooks, mainly on account of the new ending to Moll's career they provide. Fresh details emerge in the second and third of these books, especially *Laetitia Atkins*, but Read is their *fons et origo*. I shall therefore give a fuller account of this abridgment, which was highly influential in the first century of Moll's existence.[11]

Read's version supplies not just the usual title-page abstract of events, but something more like a summary of all her transactions:

THE LIFE AND ACTIONS OF *Moll Flanders* CONTAINING Her Birth and Education in Newgate; her Ambition to be a Gentlewoman; her being taken into a Gentleman's Family; her being debauch'd by her Master's Eldest Son, and married to her own Brother; her going over with him to, and settling in, *Virginia*; her Return to *England*; her Marriage to an Highwayman, who pass'd for a Person of Quality; her being reduc'd, and turning Thief; her taking some Plate from an House on Fire; her turning Informer; her robbing in Man's Clothes; A singular Adventure that happen'd to her at *Bartholomew-Fair*; her being apprehended, committed to *Newgate*, try'd, and cast for her Life; her obtaining Transportation; her meeting with her Quality-Husband in the same Condition; her being transported with him; her secret Settlement, and happy Success in *Virginia*, and Settlement in *Ireland*, her Estate, Penitence, Age, Death, Burial, Elegy, and Epitaph.

Naturally, the text is 'adorned with Cuts suitable to each Chapter'. The price is one shilling, slightly less than one would have expected to pay for a duodecimo of almost 200 pages.[12]

Even on a cursory reading, this title-page shows that the pirate was taking deliberate pains to make sense of the story: more pains, some might say, than Defoe himself took. The pirate (whom I will call Read for simplicity) singles out each phase of the narrative, omitting inessential details and concentrating on the most striking events. The inordinate number of marriages, which usually figure in the preliminary build-up, are given less emphasis here. Instead Read stresses the role of the 'quality' husband. Equally there is little account taken of the *duration* of the various phases, something that does not come across very strongly in the reader's experience of the novel, no matter how many times Defoe alludes to such things. The seriatim list of happenings has been turned into a connected story, with the suspicion of an underlying chain of causality.

Many of these procedures are those which modern readers adopt to bring in some sense of pattern to a life-history which can seem a mere recital of events. This is particularly clear in the case of Read's most radical departure from the original, which lies in his provision of chapters. This is obviously a step with far-reaching literary consequences, and one need not approve of the results to assert that it is a distinctively literary act. It is the editing of a reviser or adapter, rather than that of a publisher. The principal aim is not just to squeeze a narrative into less space, but to give the story a more expressive form. All this, let it be noted, long before we come to the most noteworthy feature of the adaptation, that is the inclusion of a new ending describing Moll's last days. Read is concerned to make the moral outlines of the narrative more clearcut.

The text is divided into nine chapters of markedly unequal length (Chapter 8 is misnumbered '7'). Most of the chapters are only a few pages long, but Chapter 2 extends to sixty pages and Chapter 3 to thirty-five. This could be a subtle formal arrangement or naive inelegance: the latter is the more likely explanation. At the head of each chapter three cuts are provided on a single page: they are executed with a good deal more sophistication in technique than those of the chapbooks. In short, the piracy is quite different in its whole feel: standards of physical presentation are as high as in some of Defoe's own authentic publications.

Chapter 1 begins with a short summary to place the narrative, and then takes the Colchester episode as far as Moll's loss of virginity (p. 29 in the Oxford English Novels edition). The long chapter which follows perhaps attempts to cover too much ground: it includes the first voyage to Virginia and the return (up to p. 105, OEN edition). Chapter 3 again includes a large stretch of the narrative, and proceeds as far as the death of banker husband (p. 189, OEN edition). There follows a succession of short chapters. The contents of Chapter 4 take up only four pages in Read's edition (pp. 189-99, OEN), describing the start of Moll's career as a thief. Those of Chapter 5 (pp. 199-206, OEN), and Chapter 6 (pp. 207-24) cover further episodes in her criminal life, including events mentioned in the title-page summary. Chapter 7 extends as far as p. 265 in the OEN edition, that is the end of the Harwich trip. Chapter 8 occupies forty pages in Read's text, and crowds in many of the climactic scenes, up to the end of Defoe's narrative: that is, we witness Moll's arrest, trial, transportation and fortunes in America. Chapter 9 provides an epilogue in which the heroine describes her return to Ireland and the sale of her Virginia property. We learn of the death of Moll's husband, two years later, and are given her will dated 30 March 1722, signed 'Eliz. Atkins'. Suddenly a third-person narrator breaks in to describe Moll's final illness and death. An elegy composed by the 'prime wits' of Trinity College, Dublin, is appended. We are told of her charitable gifts, her funeral, and the epitaph cut on her 'fine white Marble

Tombstone'. By comparison with the chapbook epitaph, it is a conventional and unsurprising piece of work, which ends:

> When People all, in after Times,
> Shall read the Story of her Crimes,
> They'll stand amaz'd, but more admire
> That one so bad should e'er desire
> To live a godly, righteous Life,
> And be a loving, faithful Wife.
> Of all her Sins she did repent,
> And really dy'd a Penitent.

Read's effort to impose a firmer design on the fiction was not well executed, but that does not invalidate the whole attempt. What he did was to introduce greater economy into the writing, abbreviate the reflections, and (on the level of intention at least) to provide a more intelligible narrative structure. It would be a small-minded critic of Defoe who could assert that no such changes are conceivably for the benefit of the novel. Read's abridgment loses some of the human richness of the original, but it very nearly compensates by means of greater pace and lucidity. No doubt the venture was inspired by commercial rather than artistic motives: the decision to allow Moll to die in 1722 could be seen as pre-empting any plans for a comeback by the old woman. The familiar moralising gloss is placed on the story in some verses at the start:

> From *Tyburn* freed by her indulgent Fate,
> Sh' attained a wealthy and a worthy State;
> So just is what's proverbially said,
> *None truly know their Fortune till they're dead.*

The opportunity is taken to stress Moll's exemplary last hours, and so the cunning pirate seems to have outdone even Defoe, habitually as tricky a writer as could be found. No sequel was possible, and no part of the book now seemed more central than the account of Moll's death—the very thing Defoe had neglected to describe, and which was missing in the 'authentic' edition.

Fortune's Fickle Distribution announces three stories for the price of one. The first is the life and death of Moll Flanders ('twelve years a Common Whore', but no mention of her various spells in prison); following Read, the title-page summary promises her return to Ireland, penitence, age, last will and testament, death, burial and epitaph. The second part is the life of Jane Hackabout, Moll's 'governess'. The use of this surname anticipates its application to the heroine of *The Harlot's Progress* two years later. Part 3 consists of the life of 'James Mac-Faul', Moll's Lancashire husband. It is a characteristic of all adaptations of the novel (whether literary or cinematic) that this figure, the most attractive male in the book, should be given a fuller identification than Moll chooses to provide. A composite frontispiece has Moll in the centre surrounded by four scenes from the tale, rather crudely executed.

The business of the book starts with a moralistic preface along customary lines: 'In all the Variety of this Book, there is not a superlative Villain mentioned, but either he is brought to an unhappy End, or made a Penitent.' The work 'encourages Virtue and generous Principles.' In a more sophisticated context one might suspect the existence of a political message, but nothing of that sort emerges. Then on to Moll's story. For this edition she provides a fuller account of her parentage, a feature culpably absent from Defoe's original. We learn that her grandfather came from Carrickfergus in Northern Ireland. Her father, James Fitzpatrick, was a rogue who was finally hanged at Tyburn for his exploits on the highway. Her mother, Mary Flanders, was a prostitute in the notorious Whetstone Park district of London; after Fitzpatrick's death she was pressed into gaol by his creditors. Tempted by a fellow-prisoner in the Marshalsea, she took to stealing in Cheapside on her release, and duly found herself in Newgate. Moll's own story proceeds much as in the original, with a few supernumerary touches. The compiler selects different passages from those of the Read abridger, and prunes the text more severely. Her career takes up only about ninety pages in this volume: the concluding sections of her life are all based on Read, though the verses from the Trinity College 'wits' are omitted.

As for Jane or Jenny Hackabout, a name bestowed on her in the text, she commands only about twenty pages. One of her distinctions is to have employed Jonathan Wild as 'Head Clerk, or Chief Manager' of her receiving business. However, Moll was to her favourite *protégée*. Her repentance comes in time for her to endow six almshouses for 'ancient widows' in her native Yorkshire: predictably, she dies lamented by all. James Mac-Faul reeives even shorter shrift. He was born in Carrickfergus, at the time of the Irish massacre; it should be noted that the pirate versions ignore Defoe's supposed timescale and give Moll a life-span not of *c.*1614–*c.*1684, but one of *c.*1645–1722. A brief account of his liaison with Moll leads up to his capture on Hounslow Heath. The detail is exiguous, and obviously the compiler was stretched to invent a career fit for Moll's paramour.

The last eighteenth-century adaptation, *The History of Laetitia Atkins*, displays greater inventive power. In the introduction 'which the reader may or may not peruse', there is a weary complaint that the world is now taken up with 'Novels and Romances', issuing from the brains of needy authors. Against this, the story of Laetitia Atkins, beautiful but incapable of expressing herself on paper, is literally true: the editor has simply given it a better rendering, as he has already done with *Roxana*. This evidently refers to a recent edition of *The Fortune Mistress*, in which the same claims had been with regard to tampering on Defoe's part.[13] The writer goes on to assert that his father was an 'intimate' acquaintance of Defoe, and that he was able to compare manuscripts as a result. All this bogus appeal to veracity has the full authority of Defoe's own practice behind it, and it makes the forgery in one sense all the more plausible.[14]

In the narrative proper, Moll's story is largely rewritten. We are told that the heroine, 'vulgarly called Moll Flanders', was really Laetitia, daughter of a glazier and painter named Theophilus Atkins. After her father's death (the heroine having been legitimised in this version), her mother is arrested for stealing a lady's gold watch at the Opera House: another touch inconsistent with the seventeenth-century setting Defoe had purported to employ. The Colchester episode is paraphrased at length, with a considerable degree of freedom: unlike most of the adapters, this writer is not afraid of inventing fresh dialogue. The Lancashire husband turns up with yet another identity, this time James Carrol. Moll's criminal side is reduced almost to nothing: on a visit to Jemmy in Newgate, a woman prisoner claims to recognise her, but this proves to be a case of mistaken identity: 'Upon enquiry I found there had been a woman in Newgate, who was extremely like me in her person; but she was not only known to be a woman of the town, but she was as notorious as a thief; and for the latter, she was at this present time abroad under her sentence of transportation.' The heroine then accompanies Jemmy to Virginia voluntarily. Her return to Ireland and last days are taken essentially from Read: the main text is signed 'Daniel Defoe' but the editor claims to have information from a figure mentioned by Read, that is Mr Price, master of the Free School at Galway. The Reverend John Price (d.1729) was a real individual, but the claim is obviously bogus.[15] *Laetitia Atkins* is the work of a literary fabricator almost as cunning as Defoe himself.

This is by far the most radical adaptation, although it derives a good deal of material from Read. *Laetitia Atkins* is in some respects a cleaned up version of *Moll Flanders*: the second half of the novel, dealing with Moll's life as a criminal, is severely curtailed, and we are left with a more or less respectable, if not blameless, woman. The unhappy confusion with a true Newgate gaolbird explains some of the bad reputation she has acquired. Artistically, the narrative is skewed by a heavy concentration on the earlier phases of Moll's career. The writer's willingness to produce bogus pieces of evidence recalls the practice of Defoe himself; the more transparent the fraud, the more we are reminded of Defoe's procedures. The chapbooks are mere huddled exercises in precis; *Fortune's Fickle Distribution* is an opportunist hack work, relying on unconvincing 'background' material to eke out the story; and even the Read abridgment is no more than a competent transposition, a sort of para-*Moll* for a wider audience. *Laetitia Atkins* is an alternative version of the novel: the data have been reprocessed, the meaning thought out afresh. Not many people will actually prefer the compiler's adaptation, but it is within its limits a critical interpretation of the text, like the modern recensions which have Friday educating Crusoe.

III

Abridgment and adaptation by a competent editor could produce fairly interesting results. Read attempts to provide a more intelligible narrative, with only moderate success in the event. The author of *Laetitia Atkins* seeks to rewrite Moll's story in more acceptable terms: he displays some literary skill in the process. All three of the longer adaptations were commercial ventures, aimed at an unsophisticated audience, but in most respects one not very different it would seem from Defoe's own. By contrast the chapbooks are hasty, formulaic, with no sense of tempo or climax, and no relation beyond plot outline to the original text. The worst offender in these respects is version C, which allots about a sentence per episode, and pares everything down to the bone. The English is not particularly simple, in vocabulary or syntax: the simplification lies in plot summary, and very little else.[16] But the other short versions enjoy only relative superiority. On this evidence, such abridgments of the classics belong to the main corpus of chapbook texts: unlike the longer adapted versions, they have virtually no relation of a literary kind to the parent work.

Notes

1. Victor Neuburg, *Chapbooks* (London, 2nd edn, 1972), pp. x, 7.
2. Neuburg, *Popular Education in Eighteenth Century England* (London, 1971), p. 121. Chapter 5 of Neuburg's work, 'Chapbooks: Origins and Distribution', provides a valuable conspectus of the subject.
3. George Borrow, *Lavengro* (London, 1906), pp. 189-91, 226-9, 242-5, 281-2. For Borrow's earlier discovery of *Robinson Crusoe*, see *Defoe: The Critical Heritage*, ed. Pat Rogers (London, 1972), pp. 123-5.
4. For the Diceys, *see* Neuburg, *Chapbooks*, pp. 48-9, 78-9, and 'The Diceys and the Chapbook Trade,' *The Library*, 5th ser. XXIV (1969), 219-31.
5. For the publisher of this version, A. Swindells, *see* Neuburg, *Chapbooks* p. 58. The older pattern had been for chapbooks to appear as octavo pamphlets of 16 pages, but the 24-page duodecimo was more usual in the later part of the eighteenth century.
6. For the publisher of this version, W. Macnie, *see* Neuburg, *Chapbooks*, p. 69.
7. For the publisher of this version, J. Marshall, *see* Neuburg, *Chapbooks* p. 60.
8. The order affixed to the chapbooks in the catalogue corresponds with my own observations: thus, the cuts in A3 are visibly more worn than those in A1 or A2, in cases where the same cut is used.
9. The original has 'Cleave': *see Moll Flanders*, ed. G.A. Starr (London, Oxford English Novels, 1971), p. 117. In addition, there are minor discrepancies in the details of the narrative, *e.g.* disagreement as to whether the pickpocket mentioned by Moll's mother should be 'Major——' (as in the original, OEN edn, p. 87),or 'Mayor D——', as the B version christens him. 'Busby's hole' is the A text variant of *'Bugsbys Hole'* (OEN ed, p. 306):

in the B text this becomes 'Busty Hole', which might almost suggest corruption from oral transmission.

10. The snatch of versified '*Newgate* wit' quoted in the original (OEN ed, p. 275) finds its way into A and B versions.

11. Short extracts from the conclusion of Read's abridgment are printed in *Moll Flanders*, ed. Edward Kelly (New York, Norton Critical Edition, 1973), pp. 306–10. 'T. Read' may well have been a *nom de guerre*, based upon the bookseller James Read, who often issued Defoe's work. Such perversions of names were a common device of the pirates: Tonson is converted into 'Thompson', and so on.

12. Anything up to 3*s*.6*d*. might be charged for a book of this length, unbound: in octavo, current prices were about 1*s*. for 64 pages of text, and *pro rata*. Duodecimos were slightly cheaper.

13. *The History of Mademoiselle de Beleau, or the New Roxana* was issued by the same publishers in the previous year, 1775.

14. The introduction is signed 'Daniel Defoe', from Islington, on 20 December 1730. This argues some rough acquaintance with the facts of Defoe's life, but of course by no stretch of imagination does it establish real familiarity with the novelist. In the chapbooks proper, any mention of a named author would have destroyed the legendary quality of the work: its sales appeal rested on its status as a kind of folk-tale like Bevis of Hampton.

15. *See Moll Flanders*, ed. Kelly, p. 307n.

16. *See* for example the concluding remarks: 'Thus far has Moll Flanders related her own life history in letters to her friends; accounts from Virginia, several years afterwards announced her death, and informed that she departed this life a true penitent, after bequeathing much money for charitable purposes' (p. 8). It will be noted that the Read ending is ignored, for once. This prose would seem appropriate to an audience capable of reading more than an eight-page plot synopsis. It might possibly be geared to the needs of a public used to newspapers and political pamphlets, fully literate in a technical sense, but wholly unused to the sustained act of reading *literature*.

EPILOGUE

Let such raise Palaces, and Manors buy,
Collect a Tax, or farm a Lottery,
With warbling Eunuchs fill a licens'd Stage,
And lull to Servitude a thoughtless Age.

Samuel Johnson, *London*, 11. 57–60

There is a great quantity of eating and drinking, making love and jilting, laughing and the contrary, smoking, cheating, fighting, dancing, and fiddling; there are bullies pushing about, bucks ogling the women, knaves picking pockets, policemen on the look-out, quacks (*other* quacks, plague take them!) bawling in front of their booths, and yokels looking up at the tinselled dancers and poor old rouged tumblers, while light-fingered folk are operating upon their pockets behind. Yes, this VANITY FAIR: not a moral place certainly; nor a merry one, though very noisy. Look at the faces of the actors and buffoons when they come off from their business; and Tom Fool washing the paint off his cheeks before he sits down to dinner with his wife and the little Jack Puddings behind the canvas.

W.M. Thackeray, *Vanity Fair*

I

In April 1711 Addison devoted *Spectator* no. 31 to an extended satire on London entertainments of the day, and particularly on the operatic scene. The paper is organised around the schemes of a shabby individual holding forth in a coffee-house near the Haymarket Theatre. Mr Spectator easily identifies him as one 'of that Species who are generally distinguished by the Title of Projectors'. The fertile brain of this gentleman ('for I found he was treated as such by his Audience') has devised a new plan to save time and effort among the paying public. Previously great

198

inconvenience had been caused by the wide geographical dispersal of 'the several Shows':

> The dancing Monkies are in one Place; the Puppet Show in another; the Opera in a third; not to mention the Lions, that are almost a whole Day's Journey from the Politer Part of the Town.

To remedy this situation, the projector has arrived at a composite form, in the shape of an opera to be called *The Expedition of Alexander the Great*. The idea was taken, he explains, from several stage-performances he had witnessed, 'in one of which there was a Rary-Show; in another, a Ladder-dance; and in others a Posture-man, a moving Picture, with many Curiosities of the like nature'. It is thus apparent that a target of the satire will be the incursion of a kind of multi-media theatrical entertainment into the West End theatre.[1]

In his edition of the *Spectator*, Donald F. Bond supplies a number of true-life parallels and referents: the burlesque version of *The Rival Queens* at Drury Lane in 1710 (with Cibber as Alexander), the ladder-dancers in Lincoln's Inn Fields productions mounted by Christopher Rich (father of John), 'the Surprizing Mr Higgins, Posture-Master', who had appeared at the Haymarket, the moving picture shows in Fleet Street and elsewhere. Significantly, Bond draws much of his evidence from press advertisements. The booths and sideshows of the capital were clearly meant to attract part of their audience, at least, from the literate sections of society.[2]

The projector now goes on to give an account of his opera, which turns out to feature a large proportion of the most celebrated 'acts' of the day. These include 'the dumb conjuror', that is Duncan Campbell: another habitual advertiser, who was to form the subject of a biography in 1720—usually, but not certainly, attributed to Defoe. The eccentric vocal impressionist Clench of Barnet is to perform, whilst 'the Tent of *Darius* is to be Peopled by the Ingenious Mrs *Salmon*, where *Alexander* is to fall in Love with a Piece of Wax-Work, that represents the beautiful *Statira*'. Another scene will be set in Hockley in the Hole, 'in which is to be represented by all the Diversions of that Place'. The Asian setting through which the hero travels will provide the opportunity to 'give the Audience a Sight of Monkies dancing

upon Ropes'. Any other 'strange Animals' available will be let
loose in the forests at the same time. But there will be human
interest too: 'In the last great Battel, *Pinkethman* is to personate
King *Porus* upon an Elephant, and is to be encounter'd by
Powell, representing *Alexander* the Great upon a Dromedary,
which nevertheless Mr. *Powell* is desired to call by the Name of
Bucephalus.' Bond's note establishes from press advertisements
that Penkethman did indeed speak an epilogue to *The Silent
Woman* riding on an ass: and that in his production of *The Rival
Queens* George Powell had taken the part of Alexander.[3]

The two combatants, reconciled with surprising ease, will
thereupon go together to the puppet show, in which 'the
ingenious Mr. [Martin] *Powell, Junior*, may have an Opportunity
of displaying his whole Art of Machinery'. The projector further
suggests that the two kings might entertain one another with
turns such as 'the *German* Artist' (Bond suggests this is a posture-
master advertised in the *Flying Post* in 1698, but there may be a
more recent performer in Addison's mind). Or they could savour
instead 'Mr. *Pinkethman's* Heathen Gods': this was a moving
picture show Penkethman had put on in 1711, under the title of
'The Pantheon, Or, the Temple of the Heathen-gods'. He
advertised it in subsequent numbers of the *Spectator*:

> At the Duke of Marlborough's Head in Fleetstreet, is now to be seen
> a new Invented Machine, composed of five curious Pictures, with
> moving Pictures, representing the History of the Heathen Gods,
> which move as Artificially as if Living: the like not seen before in
> Europe. The whole contains near an hundred Figures, besides Ships,
> Beasts, Fish, Fowl and other Embellishments, some near a Foot in
> height; all of which have their respective and peculiar Motions, their
> very Heads, Legs and Arms, Hands and Fingers, Artificially moving
> to what they perform, and setting one Foot before another like
> Living Creatures, in such a manner that nothing but Nature it self
> can excel it. It will continue to be seen every Day from 10 in the
> Morning 'till 10 at Night. The Prices 1s. 6d. 1s. and the lowest 6d.

This was exactly the kind of show, if not the show itself, which
Swift described to Stella in such glowing terms (see p. 2 above).
One notices that the shift in meaning has given a new irony to the
adverb *artificially*, then conveying 'artistically'; and that the
cheapest seats in the house were a considerable outlay for the

poor, when labourers earned only about ten shillings per week. More centrally to my purposes, the fantastic scenes on display approximate to the 'visions' shown to Gulliver in Glubbdubdrib (where, it may be recalled, the first hero called up from the past, at the visitor's request, is Alexander the Great).[4]

Finding his scheme to be generally acceptable, the projector goes to supply further refinements which he has in store. The opera is to be couched in Greek, or more specifically in Ionic dialect, which would make it even more unintelligible—and thus pleasing—than it would have been in Italian. After explaining how performers are to be recruited, the 'undertaker' addresses himself to Mr Spectator, having apparently mistaken the latter's rapt attention for fascinated admiration. He tells the Spectator that he has heard of 'a very extraordinary Genius for 'Musick that lives in *Switzerland*, who has so strong a Spring in his Fingers, that he can make the Board of an Organ sound like a Drum'. Plainly this is none other than Heidegger, who at this date was attaining greater prominence in operatic circles. The projector will undertake to fetch this remarkable man to London, 'if I could but procure a Subscription of about Ten Thousand Pound every Winter'. Mr Spectator resists the blandishments and contrives to make his escape.[5]

Here are many of the targets of Swift, Pope and Hogarth, already clearly identified and sharply focussed. It might seem surprising at first sight that such matters as the projecting spirit, or the tendency to finance ventures by subscription, should appear this early; and even more surprising that the arch-Whig Addison, apostle of progress and trade, should resent the incursion of money into artistic enterprises. But Addison did not survive to witness the great Bubble in 1720, and it was this event above all (permitting at the same time as it did, the rise of Walpole to power) which polarised attitudes. In 1711 emergent cultural tendencies could be blamed on the Tory ministry, if the commentators chose to see it that way. Harley was still attempting to woo the City of London; the embryonic South Sea Company was nurtured by the Lord Treasurer; and it was only after great seismic shifts—the death of Anne, the fall of Harley and Bolingbroke, the settling of the Hanoverian regime, the South Sea collapse, the emergence of Walpole—that it became at all plausible to link showmen with Whig statesmen, or to see the entertainment impresarios as symptomatic of a new social and economic order.

There is a different point here. Modern criticism has tended hugely to underrate the importance of Addison and Steele in laying down the ground-rules of satire for a generation to come. Along with Dryden—and more than Butler or Rochester—it was the *Tatler* and *Spectator* which helped to forge the idiom of eighteenth-century satire. The influence was often direct and particular. Thus Swift's famous lines on fleas and smaller fleas, in his poem *On Poetry: A Rhapsody*, derive directly from a *Tatler* paper by Addison (No. 229), although no editor has remarked on it. Similarly Pope learnt some of his craft by writing *Guardian* papers for his friend Steele: the techniques he developed in such an essay as 'The Club of Little Men' (*Guardian*, nos. 91–2) bore fruit in later Scriblerian farces—the vainglory of Lilliputian pygmies, or the childish squabbles of the Dunces. The essay on pastoral poetry and the 'Receit to make an Epick Poem' look forward to the strategies of burlesque in *Peri Bathous*; whilst in the revived *Spectator* (no. 457), Pope's 'project' for 'An Account of the Works of the Unlearned' looks forward to *The Dunciad* itself.[6] *Tatler* no., 257, on a waxworks, foreshadows a common Scriblerian image. Our sense of the differences in political and social outlook between the Addison circle and the Scriblerus group can easily blind us to an important area of congenial feeling, and to longlasting debts as regards both the topics and the procedures of satire. Addison's current reputation for priggish aloofness is not without some foundation, but taken by itself it travesties the man, particularly insofar as it neglects his great fund of humour. As we have seen throughout the book, the periodical essayists were regularly the first to exploit a vulnerable spot in the armoury of Handel, Heidegger, Penkethman and their like. Of course, *Gulliver's Travels* and *The Dunciad* create a richer imaginative world than any individual *Spectator* number; they employ a more elaborate fictional framework, and they contain more impassioned writing: their intensity is raised by two or three pitches. But the more relaxed and short-winded mode practised by Addison and Steele has its own comic invention, and its own vivid realisation of social and cultural trends. Certainly it is striking to observe how many concerns of major Augustan satire are adumbrated in *Spectator* papers such as no. 31.

There is a curious aftermath to this story. About nine months following the publication of this number of the *Spectator*, a real-life project was brought to Swift's attention. Swift reports it to Stella on 8 February 1712:

> This morning a scoundrel dog, one of the queen's musick, a German, whom I had never seen, got access to me in my chamber by [the servant] Patrick's folly, and gravely desired me to get an employment in the customs for a friend of his, who would be very grateful; and likewise to forward a project of his own, for raising ten thousand pounds a year upon Operas: I used him civiller than he deserved; but it vexed me to the pluck. He was told, I had a mighty interest with the lord treasurer, and one word of mine, &c.[7]

The mysterious Grman has never been identified: but a strong suspicion must arise that Heidegger was the intruder. He was not a member of the Queen's musical establishment, and indeed seems to have had no executant skills. However, he was by now at the head of the Queen's Theatre (that is Haymarket), and Swift's deafness, already well marked, could easily have produced a confusion. It would be wholly characteristic of Heidegger to seek support in this barefaced manner; few would have made it so obvious that they regarded Swift as a mere intermediary to Harley. It may also be worth mentioning that Heidegger knew Swift's friend Sir John Stanley, a Commissioner of the Customs; indeed Mrs Delany reports an occasion in 1710 when Heidegger introduced Handel to Sir John.[8] The cumulative evidence, though not wholly conclusive, would indicate Heidegger (rather than, say, Pepusch—or even Handel himself) as the most plausible candidate. In any case the episode makes its own point. Nothing would have irritated Swift more than this confident effort to use him in the flotation of a costly venture.

It is, however, to Addison that we must return for the next incisive treatment of a theme drawn from popular culture. This occurred in the periodical which Addison set up at the time of the Jacobite Rising, the *Freeholder*. Late in the series, in no. 44 (21 May 1716), Addison brought out of temporary retirement a figure he had developed earlier that year, that is a foxhunter from the shires with distinct family resemblance to Sir Roger de Coverley. The foxhunter reluctantly comes up to London in order to speak in court on behalf of a captured rebel. On arrival at Charing Cross, he encounters to his surprise a curious assortment of characters: a footman in a chair, followed by a waterman and a chimney-sweep similarly borne along the street. In the Strand, he is astonished to find 'that Persons of Quality were up so early . . . and to see many Lawyers in their Bar-Gowns, when he knew by his Almanack the Term was ended'. Other figures in strange attire pass by, and the foxhunter concludes that they must be foreigners The illusion is dispelled by the sound of 'a Shepherdess quarrelling with her Coach-man and threatening to break his Bones in very intelligible *English*, though with a masculine Tone'. The countryman's amazement grows as he witnesses 'a continued Procession of Harlequins, Scaramouches, Punchinello's and a thousand other merry Dresses, by which People of Quality distinguish their Wit from that of the Vulgar'.

The centre of all this activity turns out to be Somerset House. From its doors emerge a venerable matron, who proves to be a 'smock faced young Fellow', and a grotesquely painted countenance which the observer finds to be the actual face of an aged coquette. A female quaker and half a dozen nuns are in close attendance. The foxhunter imagines these to be sectaries of some unorthodox religion, but on enquiry he finds them to be of no religion at all—it is just a masquerade. Offended by the sight of a profane judge, a drunken bishop, and a seeming milkmaid who is really a duchess in disguise, the foxhunter quits the scene—but not before his pocket has been picked by a cardinal. Addison seems to be using the paper to discountenance fears and alarms, and to show that the new 'foreign' regime is not as sinister as it might appear. Other political implications which could easily have emerged (for example, the rebuke of frivolous antics at a time of national crisis) are tactfully silenced. Again the technique recalls that found in the *Spectator's* pioneering satires on popular entertainment.[9]

II

Neither the Scriblerian party nor Hogarth had any real heirs: only Fielding could be said to sustain their critique of fashionable entertainment, and this to a decreasing extent as his career went on. In the second half of the eighteenth century the social reality showed little propensity for change: Mrs Cornelys stepped easily enough into Heidegger's shoes, and pantomimes survived at Drury Lane, with Sheridan burlesquing *Robinson Crusoe* where Theophilus Cibber had travestied Hogarth. But the satiric response was comparatively feeble, with little attempt made to connect modish forms of leisure with deeper social or political developments. It is perhaps only with the Regency that it becomes possible again to think in such terms. A contrast might be drawn between the visit of the four Indian kings in 1710 and the sojourn of the Tahitian Omai in the 1770s. In both cases the round of sightseeing went on, there were balls and masquerades to attend, metropolitan nightlife flowered suddenly in order to try to capitalise on the opportunities for publicity. The difference is that in 1710 the sights are reported as eagerly as the visitors, so that newspaper readers are exposed to a double stream of exoticism.[10] IIn 1774 to 1776, it was the noble savage Omai who stood at the centre of attention: he sat to Sir Joshua Reynolds and dined with Mrs Thrale. The events he attended fade into the background, as thought the literary imagination can no longer gain any purchase on such well-entrenched pursuits as oratorios and assemblies. Familiarity is a mortal foe of the satirist.

There is, however, one significant after-event in literature. I am thinking of the passage in Book VII of *The Prelude*, in which Wordsworth renders with extraordinary energy the tumult of Bartholomew Fair.[11] Throughout the London section Wordsworth has shown himself alive to the elaborate sign-language of the capital, its posters and banners, its shops 'with symbols, blazoned names' (VII, 174), and

> fronts of houses, like a title-page
> With letters huge inscribed from top to toe (VII, 176-7).

The allegorical tradesmen's signs turn the whole of the city into a kind of gigantic billboard. The metropolis has become a living advertisement, where 'dazzling wares' confront the gaze of every passer-by, and 'tradesman's honours' have replaced the old badges of civic life. Hogarth's vivid show-cloths, Pope's instructive 'tapestries', now seem to loom everywhere. The satirists had accepted commerce in its place, though not in the areas they reserved for high art: a part of Wordsworth seems even to resent it when shops devote their energy to selling. It is the very fact of urban existence, not its perversions and excesses, which affronts his soul.

Wordsworth's vision of London is of a 'concourse of mankind / Where Pleasure whirls about incessantly', with his own role described as 'an idler's place'. His sense of the city is strongly tinged at the outset by the accounts he heard at school of the sights and shows:

> Vauxhall and Ranelagh! I then had heard
> Of your green groves, and wilderness of lamps
> Dimming the stars, and fireworks magical,
> And gorgeous ladies, under splendid domes,
> Floating in dance, or warbling high in air
> The song of spirits!
>
> (VII, 121-7)

And there are other wonders—the bridges; the Whispering Gallery at St Paul's; the tombs in the Abbey; 'the Giants at Guildhall' (see p. 31); Bedlam, with its 'carved maniacs'; the Monument, and

> that Chamber of the Tower
> Where England's sovereigns sit in long array,
> Their steeds bestriding,—every mimic shape
> Cased in the gleaming mail the monarch wore,
> Whether for gorgeous tournament addressed,
> Or life or death upon the battle-field.
>
> (VII, 136-41)

The response to this pageantry of 'mimic shapes' is matched by youthful expectation of civic splendour: dreams of 'mitred Prelates, Lords in ermine clad,' fed by the Dick Whittington legend.[12]

When the young Wordsworth actually arrived in the capital, his attention was caught both by waxworks and exhibitions ('those sights that ape / The absolute presence of reality'), and by theatrical entertainments

> where living men,
> Music, and shifting pantomimic scenes,
> Diversified the allurement.

(VII, 261-3)

At Sadler's Wells he witnessed a motley display of

> giants and dwarfs,
> Clowns and conjurors, posture-masters, harlequines,
> Amid the uproar of the rabblement.

(VII, 271-3)

But it is above all in the evocation of Bartholomew Fair that the poet's mingled excitement and revulsion emerge most clearly. Here Wordsworth registers his confused reaction to what he sees as a 'true epitome' of city life in its directionless energy.

The passage contains all the data used by the Augustan satirists, but where Pope and Hogarth see the monstrous as an aberration, Wordsworth perceives it as the general condition of urban humanity:

> What a shock
> For eyes and ears! what anarchy and din,
> Barbarian and infernal,—a phantasma,
> Monstrous in colour, motion, shape, sight, sound!
> Below, the open space, through every nook
> Of the wide area, twinkles, is alive
> With heads; the midway region, and above,
> Is thronged with staring pictures and huge scrolls,
> Dumb proclamations of the Prodigies;
> With chattering monkies dangling from their poles,
> And children whirling in their roundabouts;
> With those that stretch the neck and strain the eyes,
> And crack the voice in rivalship, the crowd
> Inviting; with buffoons against buffoons
> Grimacing, writhing, screaming,—him who grinds
> The hurdy-gurdy, at the fiddle weaves,
> Rattles the salt-box, thumps the kettle-drum,
> And him who at the trumpet puffs his cheeks,
> The silver-collared Negro with his timbrel,
> Equestrians, tumblers, women, girls, and boys,
> Blue-breeched, pink-vested, with high-towering plumes.—

All moveables of wonder, from all parts,
Are here—Albinos, painted Indians, Dwarfs,
The horse of knowledge, and the learned Pig,
The Stone-eater, the man that wallows fire,
Giants, Ventriloquists, the Invisible Girl,
The Bust that speaks and moves its goggling eyes,
The Wax-work, Clock-work, all the marvellous craft
Of modern Merlins, Wild Beasts, Puppet-shows,
All out-o'-the-way, far-fetched, perverted things,
All freaks of nature, all Promethean thoughts
Of man, his dulness, madness and their feats
All jumbled up together, to compose
A Parliament of Monsters. Tents and Booths
Meanwhile, as if the whole were one vast mill,
Are vomiting, receiving, on all sides,
Men, Women, three-years' Children, Babes in arms.

(VII, 685–721)[13]

In this superb passage, the reader's gaze is drawn haphazardly around a crowded yet meaningless scene. We move from the particular to the general, from sight to sound, from authorial judgment to hucksters' claims (taken, apparently, at their own valuation). Despite Wordsworth's rather archaic appeal in the lines immediately preceding, where he asks the Muse to provide him with a vantage-point above the teeming spectacle, there is in fact no clear perspective on the data. The poet is unable to discern a pattern in the objective, phenomenological material; the poetry is about that inability, and depends for its effect upon our sense of the perceiver rather than the perceived. (Contrast the schematic organisation of Hogarth's *Southwark Fair*, or the sharp precision of Pope's lines on monstrous theatrical spectacle in *The Dunciad*, A III 237–44.)

Another singular disparity in outlook might be expressed in this way—that the satirists are often comic without being funny, whereas Wordsworth here writes in a style that is funny without being comic. The verse expresses outrage at urban disorder, but it no longer embodies any surprise. There is a peculiar confidence in the freakish performers, who have inherited the new world of raucous activity. The pained observer has lost all 'urbane' perspective on events, and can only retire (as the following book of *The Prelude* does) to Helvellyn, where the proportions of man and environment are reversed. Where the Augustan satirists had been able to borrow some of the barbarous energy of London street-life, Wordsworth is depleted by his contact with the fairground. He has no concern for the management or financing of the shows: there is little sense that the public is being exploited, little awareness of a producer-consumer relationship, no more than a perfunctory glance at the posters ('dumb' proclamations, because they are felt to be inexpressive as well as mute). The hucksters are treated almost as innocents; it is the gawping spectators who blur the picture as they throng every nook in the place, who contribute much of the din, and who—at the end—are milling from one booth to another like some half-chewed vomit. The poet's disgust invades the entire scene he has called into being. We lose any sense of manipulator and manipulated. It is an art, not of moral placing (as with the Augustans), but of nervous reaction: Wordsworth explores bruised feelings, rather than cultural cause and effect.

The shows of London, as Richard Altick has demonstrated were to attain their fullest expression in the first half of the nineteenth century.[14] By this time they were unmistakably 'popular' culture, not merely in the sense of attracting a wide audience, but also in the sense that they were cut off from the serious artistic endeavour of Victorian England. Elite and popular culture had been diverging, indeed, for a hundred years and more, with the diversions of Ranelagh an ineffectual effort to check the process. Hogarth, Swift and Pope had devised their fictions when it was still feasible to apply some of the criteria of high art to the lower-class cousin. Defoe had written when Grub Street still utilised some of the themes, if not the techniques, exploited by the literary aristocracy. This situation made for a degree of mutual commerce; an interaction of 'levels' highly congenial to the Augustan mind, which seems to have preserved an attachment to the 'kinds' precisely to facilitate cross-generic play (mock-heroic, ballad opera, urban pastoral, opera-ballet, and so on). The satirists may not have approved of the rising entertainment industry, but they were sufficiently entertainers themselves to borrow some of its gusto and glamour for their own purposes.[15] They do not parody the world of Rich and Heidegger so much as digest it. In their vivid comic treatment of popular diversions, they ensured that the hucksters did not have all the best shows.

Notes

1. *Spectator*, I, 127-8. Three days before, Addison had devoted a paper to the plans of another projector, to set up an office which would oversee the contents of London Street signs.
2. *Spectator*, I, 128-9.
3. *Spectator*, I, 129-30.
4. *Spectator*, I, 130-1: Swift, *Prose*, XI, 195. For Penkethman and his Pantheon, see Altick, pp. 59-60: Ashton, p. 216. For the word 'artificial' see Altick, p. 8.
5. *Spectator*, I, 131-2.
6. *The Prose Works of Alexander Pope*, ed. Norman Ault (Oxford, 1936), pp. 59-62, 97-106, 115-29. Note also the essays in which Pope sets up bogus newspapers (pp. 56-8) and poses as a quack doctor (pp. 83-7). Not all these attributions by Ault are quite certain, but as a group they are dependable. Their place in Pope's development as a satirist seems to me to have been seriously underestimated.
7. *Journal to Stella*, II, 482.
8. Deutsch, p. 31.
9. *The Freeholder*, ed. J. Leheny (Oxford, 1979), pp. 232-4. The editor notes a masquerade in Somerset House on 17 May 1716, attended by the King, Prince and Princess.
10. See Richmond P. Bond, *Queen Anne's American Kings* (Oxford, 1952), esp. pp. 1-15. Among the places of resort mounting a special performance in honour of the four kings were Haymarket Theatre, the concert rooms at York Buildings, Powell's puppet theatre and the bear-garden at Hockley in the Hole. See also Atlick, p. 46, 48.
11. *The Prelude* is quoted from the 1850 text in the parallel-text edition by J.C. Maxwell (Harmondsworth, 1971). For Wordsworth's references to museums and galleries in Book III, see Altick, p. 33.
12. Although there was as yet no 'pantomime' in the modern sense, the Dick Whittington story was kept alive both by chapbooks and by fairground representations. For Mrs Mynn's droll on the subject, see Ashton, p. 193.
13. For a good discussion of this episode, see Max Byrd, *London Transformed* (New Haven, 1978), pp. 150-2. For the 'learned pig' mentioned in 1.708, see Altick, pp. 40-2.
14. See Altick, esp. pp. 221 ff.
15. It might be remarked that *The Dunciad*, in blending a myth of fecundity with fairground diversions and a carnival, unites elements of *The Rite of Spring*, *Petrushka* and *The Firebird* in a single work. The comparison is not arbitrary: Stravinsky, like Pope, treats popular themes in a sophisticated manner—as well as sophisticated subjects in a *faux-naif* manner.

INDEX

(a) Persons

Addison, Joseph (1672-1719) 2, 25, 44, 198-9, 200-4

Altick, R.D. x-xi, 209

Anne, Queen of England (1665-1714) 81, 201

Applebee, John (d. 1750 ?) 19-20, 153-4

Arbuthnot, John (1667-1735) 45, 79, 103, 107-8, 115

Barber, John (1675-1741) 2, 132-3

Bathurst, Allen, Earl (1684-1775) 107, 110

Bentley, Richard (1662-1742) 115, 121-2, 140

Blunt, Sir John (1667-1733) 11-12, 29, 63-4

Bononcini, Giovanni (1670-1747) 46, 103, 109, 112

Boswell, James (1740-95) ix, 1, 21, 61, 165

Brewer, John 19, 22

Bullitt, John M. 78-9

Bunyan, John (1628-88) 162, 164-6, 181

Burlington, Dorothy Boyle, Countess of (1699-1758) 53, 92

Burlington, Richard Boyle, Earl of (1695-1753) 41-2, 53-4, 65, 107, 110

Burnet, Gilbert (1643-1715) 27, 179

Carey, Henry (1687?-1754) 17, 46

Caroline of Anspach, Queen of England (1683-1737) 29, 113, 122-4, 127-31, 133-4, 137-46

Chalmers, George (1742-1825) 175-6

Charteris, Francis (1675-1732) 11-12, 29, 152

Cibber, Colley (1671-1757) x, 11-12, 20, 23, 26, 29, 57, 64, 90, 95, 97, 99, 105-06, 120, 125, 137, 139-42, 146, 199

Cibber, Theophilus (1703-58) 29, 90

Clayton, Thomas (1675?-1725) 43-5

Cornelys, Teresa (1723-97) 62, 205

Curll, Edmund (1683-1747) 11-12, 18, 26-8, 30, 64, 93, 136

Cuzzoni, Francesca (1700?-1770?) 45-6, 48-51, 53, 106-7, 113, 128

Defoe, Daniel (1660?-1731) *general* 18-19, 33, 56, 58, 60-1, 71, 73, 151-60, 178, 193, 194, 199, 209

Moll Flanders 73, 152-3, 157, 164, 178-9, 183-96

211

(b) Places

(c) Topics